infoGreece

The complete travel guide

ATHENS

Tourist Publications

1-3 Mavrokordatou St.
Tel: 3646105
106 78 Athens, Greece
Historical Chart: J.A. Blish, 1986

Managing Editor: Y. Scordilis
Authors: B. Biggins & J.A. Lawrence
Historical Chart: J.A. Lawrence
Design and Layout: T.P. Studio
Charts: V. Gikapepas
Phototype-setting: K. Deligianis
Colour Separations: Alfa-Scan Ltd.
Montage: E. Paizakis
Printed in Greece by Tsakiris Ltd.

Cover photograph: Y. Yiannelos
Inside photographs by Y. Yiannelos, John Tanner, David John, G. Papathanasiadis.

Acknowledgements
We would like to thank the following people for their help: Dr. J. Camp. Director of the American school of Archeology for correcting the Acropolis section; L. Mesthenaios for information, proof-reading and support, Don Sebastian for generous help with information on shopping, S. Kingdom for last minute up-dates; the G.N.T.O. for their information and support; the O.A for their flights charts; the Network Directory.

ISBN 960 - 7587 - 00 - 6

Due to the wealth of treasures this small area has to offer it has been necessary to be selective. Sufficient detail is given to allow the visitor to make choices depending on personal taste, and the information has been carefully checked. However errors creep in and changes will occur. We hope you will forgive us our errors and omissions and find this book a helpful companion.

ABOUT THIS GUIDE

Whether you come to Athens for a sunny holiday or to travel in living history this guide offers you what you need. Part I offers general information about Greece and Athens, history and culture, Greeks and Greek customs and language. Part II offers conveniently described sightseeing both in and out of the city, arranged for both a casual tour and a more detailed inspection - you pick out what you want. Part III consists of a hotel listing with much useful additional detail. Part IV is full of practical information, starting before you arrive, and taking you through shopping and eating, getting around, tipping and a page or two for "Help!". Part V is a special section for business visitors.

Maps of central Athens, Piraeus and Attica are included.

A special feature is INFOTIPS - those little things that took some of us years to find out.

We hope you have a wonderful trip to Athens and that you will love our city as we do, honouring her virtues and forgiving her faults. She's unique, special and full of surprises.

A note on spelling:

There is no generally accepted system for the transliteration of Greek into the Latin alphabet. There are signs for the port, reading "Pireefs", "Pireas", "Pireus" and the more familiar "Piraeus", because those signs were written at different times under different circumstances.

Recently the Greek National Tourist Organization has adopted a system of transliteration of place names and proper names in a form approximating to their pronunciation. Wherever possible we have adopted this system, as there are obvious advantages to being able to pronounce a name correctly when asking your way. This has led to some inconsistencies as we have not changed names that are already familiar, but have given the alternatives, except where the change consists of simply changing 'C', to 'K' or 'PH' to 'F'.

See also GREEK LANGUAGE, Page 14.

Table of Contents

Alphabetical Index: Sightseeing, Part II

GREECE AND HER PEOPLE

A JOURNEY THROUGH TIME

Greece and her islands emerge in a wide curve from Asia to the European peninsula, caressed by sapphire seas and burnished by the Aegean sun. Mountains climb from the sea, sweep through the Balkans from the jagged coastline of the peninsula. Mountains are a defence, a challenge, a mystery. In them are hidden timeless villages.

For thousands of years people have sought the clear Greek light and warmth. The very sand on the beaches is white with marble, perhaps from ancient statues buried in the sea, or from lost Atlantis. When the captain of the ferryboat is called Jason, and your chambermaid Aphrodite is (only) eighty years old, and the sun is burning a scarlet path across the harbour against the blue evening, time shimmers into the sea. Today is blurred into yesterday, and into millennia past. Greece is here, and now, and then, all at once.

Nothing much has changed through Greece's stormy history. The mountain men who go to sea still come back, like Odysseus, with a touch of foreign ways and a great longing for home - the village in the valley, the island. In the village, in the hills, or even in a far away land, long-familiar customs are preserved, religious observances are honoured, families know where everybody is and what they are doing. The village is isolated, with only the slowest effects from the outside world, but today's Greek youngster studying computers has cousins in Australia, New York, Canada, who come home when they can - to the changeless village. Of course young people go to the city where everything is *Allagi* (Change).

Mainland and islands alike are embedded in the sea, which has brought the land its history. Trade, war, innovation and invasion have come most often by water: Scythians, Persians, Turks from the East, Slavs, Goths and Vandals from the Black Sea, Romans, Sicilians and Venetians from the West. And each invader has left his traces. Turkish words linger in the names of such foods as Imam (for short: fully entitled "The Imam Bayaldi Fainted with Delight When He Tasted of This Dish", a pleasant eggplant casserole in red sauce. One feels that the Imam's life must have been just a bit dull, though.) The picturesque Sunday uniform of the Evzone is a version of the mountain soldiers' wear during the War of Independence.

The coastal plains have been invaded again and again, but the defeated have risen again, absorbed the enemy and... rebuilt the village. In the process, there may be a few new words, or a different shape to a house ... or to the family nose.

Nothing much has changed, and everything. The recent gallop of the provinces into sudden industrialization is bringing physical and social changes to the village, even while the goat still strips the countryside of foliage where cows can't be pastured and the donkey still hauls the cart up the winding road.

But the family still pitches in to pick the olives in season, even if they have to leave their jobs for a week. And they watch "Dynasty" in the same spirit as they listened to the story of Zeus visiting Danae as a shower of gold.

It's not difficult to believe that the Greek's love of his native soil, however rocky, has driven him to many hardships rather than surrender his village, his island, his tiny hard-won stony field.

The Village is where the heart is, wherever the body may find itself, even into many generations. In exile, the Greek still works, disputes, dances, feasts and lives life to the fullest, always with one aim in mind: whatever happens, he will get back to The Village some day, like Antaeus who had to touch the earth to renew his strength. The economic pressure of postwar years has scattered many Greeks further than ever before from their villages, but no matter how comfortably settled in America or Australia, The Village is where home really is.

Geology and Geography

Greece is part of the folded mountain system that reaches from the Western Mediterranean to Indonesia. In the Balkans this is mostly sedimentary limestone which was crushed against a resisting central core of hard crystalline rock, the Rhodope massif, bits of which are visible in Thrace and Macedonia. The backbone mountain range of Greece is the Pindus, descending from Yugoslavia and winding eastwards in a series of arcs to the Aegean.

Greece is a land of contrast between craggy rock and sea, silvery olive groves and red soil, golden marble and black cliffs, with a snow-topped mountain here and there.

Greece is bounded on the north by Albania, Yugoslavia and Bulgaria: to the east is Turkey, an ever-uneasy proximity. The Mediterranean Sea becomes the Ionian on the west, and the Aegean on the East. The coastline is about 15,000 km. (9,300 miles) long, and about 85 of her 2,000 islands are inhabited.

The local mountain chain includes Parnassus (8,061 ft), Helicon, Kitheron, Parnis, Pendeli and Hymettus. Athens is situated in the plain of the Kifissos, with access to harbours, wood, fruit, olives, grapes, lead and zinc mines, - long ago silver mines at Lavrion - and of course, marble at Pendelicon.

Climate

Greeks say that the sun shines almost every day, and it's true. Only in the deepest of winter are there one or two dark days. The climate is hot and dry in summer, with temperatures ranging from 70° to 110°F. In August, comes the *meltemi*, the North wind, which cools the city appreciably from the still heat of July. Rainfall is an average 15.4 inches per year in Athens - all between September and May. Winters are cool, but it rarely snows in Athens. October and November are often warm enough to eat out in a sunny corner. In early January there may be two or three weeks of glorious warmth before the chilly wind returns.

Flora and Fauna

Greek vegetation is of Mediterranean type: evergreen and deciduous trees were the natural cover. Though much of the land is now cultivated, botanists delight in the 6,000 indigenous species of native plants. In spring all Greece is carpeted with brilliant colour -

poppies, crocus, iris, anemones, hyacinth and narcissus (both named after mythological characters.) As summer burns on, the green becomes scorched and makes a brown background for the autumn flowers - cyclamen, asphodel and gladiolus. Herbs thrive in the dry soil - thyme, camomile, juniper, oregano, lavender. If you like herb teas, pick your own on the hillsides.

In the city, dogs and cats are everywhere. In the country there are goats, sheep and donkeys, still the best transport on hilly ground for a small farm. Birds like canaries and parakeets are very popular pets. Native fauna are wild goats and hedgehogs, with occasional foxes, wolves, brown bears, and boars in the wild forests. Of birds there are pelicans and storks, herons and many other water birds, as well as eagles, the great spotted cuckoo, and the migrants. Tortoises, lizards, snakes represent the reptiles.

As for the creatures of the sea, Greece is the home of the last of the Mediterranean seals. And of course there are the playful dolphins, and a great variety of fish to study with a snorkel - or at a seaside taverna!

Government

Greece is an area of about 131,944 sq. kilometers and a population of over 9 million. There are ten regions divided into 52 *nomi*, districts for administration. Within each *nomos* are rural districts, rural communities and municipalities, with smaller units called settlements. Greece is a democratic republic (since the 1974 referendum rejecting the King). The President is elected by Parliament for a term of five years. The single house *Vouli*, Parliament, is elected for four years, the last elections were in 1985.

Greece is a member of the United Nations, NATO, and the European Economic Community.

Athens is the capital of Greece and is situated in the *nomos* of Attica. The city is composed of townships each of which is a *"dimos"*, with its own governing body and town centre.

Education

The Greek educational system is like that of other European countries, with the lower school *(Dimotikó)* followed by Gymnasium and Lyceum, then University, Polytechnic, or technical college. Though Athens is once again a centre for scholars, many students continue their education abroad.

Many parents eagerly augment their children's public education with extra private lessons or studies in private schools - especially in foreign languages like English.

Commerce and Industry

Much of Greece is fertile farmland, orchard, and vineyard. Manufacturing industries are food, metals, textiles, chemicals, and cement, while shipping and tourism are important sources of foreign exchange and employment. Most firms are family sized, so that small businesses are the most numerous. There are many associations of businessmen in various enterprises.

Greece welcomes foreign investments. Athens is the country's commercial centre, with her own Stock Exchange. See also BUSINESS).

Religion

The State Church is Greek Orthodox, and very much a part of life. The Archbishop of Athens is the head of the Greek Church. Priests wear black robes and cylindrical hats, with hair long and twisted into a braid in back. They may marry before taking their vows, but cannot then become Metropolitans (Bishops). Passing a church, people cross themselves, right side first, thumb and first fingers together, representing the Trinity. Inside the church, large or small, are icons which are hung with small votive medals, figurines, models, and which are kissed by those who pray. People stop in at any time of the day, as they go about their business, to light a candle, say a prayer, chat with a neighbour.

The church has three sections: the narthex, or vestibule: the nave or main church: and the sanctuary, in in front of which is a screen called *Iconostasi* , and where the altar and icons are kept for the priest to use during service (liturgy). Women are forbidden to pass the doors of the *iconostasi*, and during some services are supposed to sit on one side of the church. Its central doors traditionally show the Annunciation; the right side shows Christ and John the Baptist; while on the left is an icon of the *Panayía* (the Holy Virgin) flanked by an icon of the patron saint. The walls show saints, the apostles above them, and higher still, the patriarchs and prophets. In the dome is usually a representation of Christ *Pantocrator,* Ruler of All, surrounded by Angels and cherubim.

The priest conducts a very formal, chanted liturgy, dressed grandly in gold embroidered robes. Amazingly, at the same time the congregation is chatting, taking wedding or baptism photographs, distributing sugared almonds wrapped in fluffy net. Church is a friendly neighbourhood gathering-place under the blessing of heaven. (see FEASTS).

The Greek People

The Hellenic soul is driven by the search for a balance between the spirit of the isolated village and the ever-changing influences brought by the sea. A profound love of country, of family, and of freedom go hand in hand with sincere pleasure in the company of strangers.

The family is the heart of Greek society. Individual relationships may vary, but everybody expects to maintain the connections, help out the relatives, and never let the family down. Relatives provide security in an uneasy world - your cousin who married a doctor is more likely to be able to help you than a mere stranger, however professional.

Greek life is public, spirited and noisy. There's no word for privacy. You can be lonely, alone, special a private business-person, but not "private". Try sitting alone on a beach... Greeks hasten to

Whaterer the subject, the discussion is serious.

comfort anyone so unfortunate as to be all by themselves. In Mediterranean countries, personal distances are close, and drawing back from a kiss of greeting is hurtful, even offensive.

Tourists were always eagerly welcomed. The Athens of Pericles was intended to attract visitors. The Acropolis was not meant to be left gloriously alone! Greeks are traditionally hospitable, and very curious. They like to know all about you. Where are you from? Are you married? Do you have children? Do you have a house? Where is your family? What work do you do? Do you like Greece? Have you been to My Village? It's always the present that interests them, not the past.

In conversation Greeks speak with voice and body quivering with passionate conviction. Arms are waved and hands chop the air. The uninformed foreigner may be convinced that he is about to witness a massacre, but it is more likely to be an argument about who will have the privilege of paying for dinner.

You will often see Greeks fighting over the bill in restaurants or tavernas. It is considered an honour to "make a table" for as many as possible. Hospitality is of high priority, even if the personal cost is great... This is an expression of *"filotimo"* - an untranslatable term that includes pride, repute, duty, honour, self esteem.

Other Points in the Game of Life: being first aboard public transport; shouting until business is done; queue-jumping; grabbing the taxi, and then allowing a defeated rival to share it (this does not apply to courtships, however); never being wrong, but magnanimous in victory; noticing that you look hot and thirsty and bringing a cool drink from the back of the shop; calling you back to give you your correct change; above all, recognizing you when you return, even months later. Greeks look at you as if you're real.

As a people who have learned to live with the immovable mountains and the irresistible sea, Greeks are full of contradictions. Profoundly religious and profoundly skeptical; hard-working and idle; regarding books as too serious for daily life, though every other man-on-the-street writes poetry; living with one respectful eye on past glories, and one anxious eye on the present. The only thing you can say about Greek characteristics is that whatever you say, the next Greek you meet is likely to be an exception. All Greeks are exceptions. Say they are intensely political and then meet the only Greek in the world who doesn't care... Say they invented logic and then try and make sense of the road system. Ask why the men spend all day in the *Kafenion,* and then observe the long hard hours the grocer puts in, starting at 5:00 a.m. at the market.

Kite-flying on Shrove-Monday is family fun.

There is also the vital matter of *"kefi"*, which the dictionary helplessly calls "mood". Not to have *Kefi* means everything is flat and dull. It's what makes everybody in the taverna suddenly feel like dancing, because the music is so good and the company so pleasant, or what makes people sing while driving, or what makes a party a success.

"Moderation in all things", said Sophocles, wistfully. He was not addressing a temperate people. In fact, it is un-Greek to be wishy-washy.

Meeting People

Greetings

Shaking hands is the formal convention and it is always acceptable. Friendlier greetings produce the kiss on both cheeks. Equivalent to "How to you do?" is "Ti Kánete?", and the correct reply is "Fine, Thank you, and yourself?" or "Kalá, Efhar-ist-ó. Keh esées?". Informally to one person, "Yassoo," or to several, "Ya sas,", which means "to your health" and is also a toast and a farewell.

"Hereteh" is another kind of hello, for strangers or slight acquaintances.

"Good morning", "Kali méra".: "Good afternoon" (i.e., from 3-9 p.m. and can be used all evening!) "Kali spéra". At the end of the evening (which may be well into tomorrow if there is *kefi*), it's "Káli níchta" "Good night".

Personal distance is close rather than far: personal questions are to be expected - best parried with another question!

DO NOT: Raise your hand with fingers extended and palm out, even if you want to buy five of those. It means "Go to the Devil" and is very, very rude.

When dining out the "Dutch treat" system is uncouth, to a Greek. A Hellene would rather pay the bill as a matter of honour than let the company divide the costs.

Wine glasses are half-filled, full glasses are gross. But the host keeps it half full all the time, and will automatically replenish if empty. Don't refuse - just accept, take a tiny sip and leave the rest in the glass, then your host will know you have drunk as much as he can press on you. And hospitality will be satisfied.

Visiting

Siesta hours, between 2:30 and 5:30, are sacred to the Goddess of Rest, and please don't phone or knock at the door during those hours (unless specifically invited to).

Visitors bring gifts, usually a box of pastries, sometimes a bottle of liquor or wine, occasionally flowers. A present for a child of the house is fine.

The hostess offers refreshment to guests almost immediately. A plate with a spoonful of sticky sweet preserves, a glass of water,

and a small Turkish coffee are the most likely. You drink the water first, eat the sweet and put the spoon into the empty glass, then sip the coffee. And try to look as if it's delicious. If you cannot tolerate sugar for any reason, explain that you have *"zácharo"*, (diabetes), which is the ONLY acceptable excuse.

Coffee comes *"Glikó"*, sweet: *"Métrio"*, medium: *"Skéto"*, plain without sugar, which is a little bitter.

Dating

Greek men are eager to date foreigners, Greek women less so. Wearing skimpy tops and shorts in the city usually labels a woman as a foreigner. Most Greek women dress for town. Greek men have thousands of years of experience in X-ray eye penetration of layers and layers of thick embroidery.

Eye contact alone establishes a dialogue, and sometimes unwarranted assumptions. Greek men pursue with enthusiasm. To their credit, they don't sulk or become enraged if refused. (If you do not want attentions, say you are meeting your father or husband).

If a relationship develops, it is more or less expected to be exclusive on the part of the woman.

If you are introduced to the family, he/she is taking it seriously!

The Evil Eye

Like touching wood after making a boast or praising someone, the Greeks say "ftou-ftou", or even spit to ward off the evil eye, the glance of envy that can bring on inexplicable headaches or other problems. Therefore it is tempting fate for example to say that a baby is beautiful. The blue jewels that are on sale everywhere are held to ward off the ill-effects.

Greek Language

The Greek language has a long and fascinating history. The classical language was somewhat simplified during the period of Alexander the Great, so that the administrators far and wide could communicate. Later the Romans regarded the Greeks with great respect, despite the fact that Greece was a subject nation and took works of art, teachers, and words from her: many Greek words were Latinized. Due to medieval monastic scholars, medical and scientific words were preserved in Greek. Psychology is the *Logos* of the *Psyche*, "the word about the soul": atom, mathematics, gymnastics, pediatrician, clone, analogy, fantasy - all are Greek words.

During the long years of foreign occupation, Greeks abroad - never forgetting their homeland - protected and cherished the language based on that of Alexander's empire. The language itself though, was developing all these years, the grammar was simplified and what was spoken at the end of the War of Independence was the language of the people, *"Dimotiki"*. The need though for a standard language in the newly established Greek State prevailed and a refined and literary form of the language, called *"Katharevoussa"*, was restored.

The Greek Alphabet.

It's a good idea to learn the alphabet. The language is not easy and you can manage with very few words, but if you don't know that the bus says *PIRAEUS* you may end up in *RAFINA* by mistake.

Greek language is difficult and its spelling system is different than English. Below are some very important hints to help you read the language and follow the transliteration

- An i is always pronounced /i/ as "viva".
- An e is always pronounced /e/ as in "egg".
- There are no silent letters or eauxes. If a letter is there, it is pronounced.

Written forms	Name	Pronunciation
Αα	Alfa	short a
Ββ	Vita	never mind B. it's V.
Γγ	Gamma	pronounced as y or g as in gear.
Δδ	Thelta	the old "D", pronounced "th" as in them but d in many names.
Εε	Epsilon	short e, as in egg.
Ζζ	Zita	z
Ηη	Ita	i as in "viva". There are several spellings of this sound.
Θθ	Thita	th as in thanks
Ιι	Yiota	i as in "viva".
Κκ	Kappa	k
Λλ	Lamda	l
Μμ	Mee	m
Νν	Nee	n
Ξξ	Ksee	pronounced like X in English
Οο	Omicron	o as in oh!
Ππ	Pee (not pie as in math)	p.
Ρρ	Ro	r. Hard to remember: IT IS NOT P.
Σσ	Sigma	s
Ττ	Taf, not Tao.	t.
Υυ	Ipsilon	pronounced - you guessed it - i as in "viva", except after E or A, when it becomes V... Evreka!?? Yes! With o, it's ou, as in soup.
Φφ	Fee	f
Χχ	Hee	h, unless you can manage ch as in Scottish loch
Ψψ	Psee	ps, but the p is not silent.
Ωω	Omega	o.

The sound of sh and ch are heard and spelled as s and ts. If your name begins with D, you'll see it written startlingly with "Nt", Ντόναλντ Ντακ = Donald Duck. However, ΜΠ= B, as in ΜΠΑΡ= Bar, and TZIN is gin.

Vocabulary

In hotels, tavernas, shops and tourist areas, and in any business that does international trade, someone will speak English. If you go off the tourist routes, you can usually make basic needs understood. In case of real urgency, remember that you can get help from phone number 171, the Tourist Police, any time of day or night.

Meanwhile... The most important word to know is *toualéta*. Works anywhere in the world. Never mind W.C., ladies' room, powder room and all the other evasions. Just say "Toualéta?" as if it's a question and you will be shown where it is. Perfectionists may say "Poo ineh i toualeta?" - "Where is the toilet?" "Hartí i yías" = toilet paper, if you want to get technical.

A few other useful phrases:

ΑΝΔΡΩΝ	MEN
ΓΥΝΑΙΚΩΝ	WOMEN
ΑΝΟΙΚΤΟ	OPEN
ΚΛΕΙΣΤΟ	CLOSED
ΠΡΟΣΟΧΗ	CAREFUL
ΑΠΑΓΟΡΕΥΕΤΑΙ	DO NOT, IT IS FORBIDDEN
ΚΙΝΔΥΝΟΣ	DANGER
ΑΡΓΑ	SLOW
Miláte Anglika?	Do you speak English?
Neh or Málista	Yes
Ohi	No
Then Kat-á-lava.	I didn't understand.
Then Milá-o Elliniká.	I don't speak Greek.
Orísteh	At your service , Here you are
Tha íthela...	I'd like...
Para-kaló	Please (or "You're welcome" in response to "Thank you")
Ef-har-is-tóe (F. Harry Stowe)	Thank you
Pou?	Where?
Eh-thóe	Here
Ti?	What?
Póteh	When?
Potèh	Never (Note change of accent)
Símera	Today
Tóra	Now
Mí!	Don't do that!
Och!	OUCH!
Ísos/ Bori	Maybe
Vo-íthia!	Help!
Sig-nómi	Sorry, Excuse Me (when shoving or standing on someone's corns)
Ti óra ine?	What time is it?
Aftó -	This. (All you need at the grocery store, as long as you have a finger to point with).
Pósso Kostízi?	How much is it?
Hartomándila	Paper hankies
Kleenex	Chlorine Bleach (Brand name)
Serviétes	Sanitary pads (Tampax is Tampax)
Strumfákia	Smurfs

Numbers / Arithmí

1	Ena	8	Októ	15	Deka-pénde
2	Dío	9	Eniá	16	Deka-éxi
3	Tría	10	Déka	17	Deka-eftá
4	Téssera	11	Éndeka	18	Deka-októ
5	Pénde	12	Dódeka	19	Deka-eniá
6	Éxi	13	Deka-tría	20	Ikosi
7	Eftá	14	Deka-téssera		

21	Ikosi-éna	400	Tetra-kóssia
22	Ikosi-dío	500	Penda-kóssia
23	Ikosi-tría	600	Exa-kóssia
24	Ikosi-téssera	700	Efta-kóssia
25	Ikosi-pénde	800	Okta-kóssia
26	Ikosi-éxi	900	Enia-kóssia
27	Ikosi-eftá	1,000	Hília
28	Ikosi-októ	2,000	Dío hili-á-des
29	Ikosi-eniá	3,000	Tris Hili-á-des
30	Triánda	4,000	Tésseris Hili-ádes
40	Saránda	5,000	Pénde Hili-á-des
50	Pen-índa	6,000	Exi Hili-á-des
60	Ex-índa	7,000	Eftá Hili-á-des
70	Evdom-índa	8,000	Októ Hili-á-des
80	Ogdónda	9,000	Eniá Hili-á-des
90	Enen-índa	10,000	Déka Hili-á-des
100	Ekató	500,000	Penda-Kóssies Hili-á-des
200	Dia-kòssia	1,000,000	Éna Ekato-mírio
300	Tra-kóssia		

TEMPERATURE EQUIVALENTS:

0´ C. = 32´ F.
10´ C. = 50´ F.
15´ C. = 59´ F.
20´ C. = 68´ F.
25´ C. = 77´ F.
30´ C. = 86´ F.
35´ C. = 95´ F.
37´ C. = 98.6´ F.
40´ C. = 104´ F.
45´ C. = 113´ F.
50´ C. = 122´ F.
100´ C. = 212´ F.

WEIGHTS

ena kiló. . . . . 1 kilo
missó kiló. . . . . 1/2 kilo
ekató gramária . . . . 100 grams
pendakossia gramária . . . 500 grams

EQUIVALENTS:

1 kilo = 2.2. lbs.
1 litre = 34 ounces
1 metre = 39.4 inches
1 kilometre = 5/8 mile

FRACTIONS

1/2 missó
1/4 tétarto
1/10 dékato

Scene from the war of the Olympians against the Titans: Athena defeating the giant Enceladus. (Greek amphora).

Greek Mythology

Greek myth is deeply embedded in Western civilization. We speak of Oedipus complexes, the riddle of the Sphinx, Delphic oracles, Herculean tasks, Panic, the Midas Touch...

There are hundreds of myths which have formed the basis of paintings, sculpture, poetry, literature, drama, since immemorial times. Mythology is a mixture of history, poetic symbolism, fiction, and wishful thinking, with an occasional shred of the original religious awe. According to some scholars, stories of the seduction of nymphs are often symbolic renditions of the invasion of a god worshipping tribe and the conquest of a goddess-worshipping tribe. Alternative version of myths appear in different places and at different times.

CREATION

Before the invasions of the patriarchs from east and north, European religion was based in worship of the triple (maiden, matron and hag) Moon-Goddess in her many forms, and the family was headed by the mother, through whom property also was inherited.

The oldest stories tell that in the beginning the Goddess of All Things rose naked from Chaos, but found nowhere solid to put her feet, and so she divided the waters from the heavens. Fertilized by the North Wind, she laid the Universal Egg from which hatched everything, sun and moon and stars, land and living creatures. When the North Wind, who is often represented as a serpent, became uppity about being the Creator, she banished him underground, and then made the planetary powers with their tutelary Titans. The first man was Pelasgus, who sprang from the soil of Arcadia.

(We know this story to be true, because it was retold by Homer, and Pliny, Hesiod and Apollodorus, and even the great travel writer Pausanius. There are hints, though, that the Goddess of all Things may have been Night, and that it was Eros, the bisexual symbol of erotic love, who hatched from the silver egg of the Moon...)

With the Dorian invaders came gods, and somebody caught on that it wasn't really the North Wind that fertilized mothers, whereupon the matriarchy lost the psychological edge. Hesiod and Apollodorus and the rest tell us the other creation myth, the one that came to Greece with the Dorians.

Mother Earth was born of Chaos, and bore a son Uranus (Sky). He loved her with rain which made grass, and flowers, and animals. Among their children were the Cyclopes, who had one eye each and who were builders of gigantic walls. Uranus punished these rebellious brothers/sons by sending them to the underworld. There were other children: the Titans, the eldest of whom was Kronos. These delinquents crept up on their father in his sleep, castrated him, and took over the world. But both Uranus and Mother Earth, in their separate ways, prophesied that one of Kronos' sons would grow up to dethrone him - a prophecy that crops up again and again in Greek myth. Kronos wasn't about to accept that, so he ate his children as a preventive measure as soon as they were born. Rhea, the earth-goddess sister of Kronos and the mother of his children, took action. The third boy was smuggled away to grow up in the cave of Dicte in Crete,while Kronos happily ate a rock wrapped in baby clothes instead.

This son, Zeus, became King of the Gods: when grown, he connived with his mother to give Kronos a nasty drink of mustard, salt and honey. Kronos urped up: 1) one stone in baby clothes; 2) Poseidon; 3) Demeter; 4) Pluto, god of the underworld; 5) Hera, later to be Zeus' wife. (See GODS below).

As the tales were told through the centuries of invasions, conquests and combinations of populations, characters merged into one another, and parts of legends were lost or altered. Yet many express historical facts in a poetic form. For many years, Troy and the Trojan War was considered a Homeric fairy tale, until Heinrich Schliemann devoted his life and fortune to proving that Troy - and evidence of a war - were really there, just where the story said.

THE GODS

Eventually the stories gathered around the gods who lived on Mount Olympus, and who conducted a lively social life among themselves while playing with the lives of mortals.

1. **ZEUS** (Jupiter), the king of the gods, was born of Rhea the Goddess of Earth and Kronos (Saturn). His main obsession in life was pursuing females - goddesses, nymphs, mortals, anything in skirts, as well as his Very Close Friends who tended to be beautiful boys. He hurled thunderbolts, ordered the planets, produced oracles. He married his sister:

2. **HERA,** (a word variation on Rhea: Juno) whose birds were the dove and the peacock, her animal the mountain lion. She had the gift of prophecy. Zeus wooed and won her in disguise as a rain-soaked cuckoo. Their wedding night on Samos lasted 300 years... (a metaphor for the subjugation of the Minoan culture in Greece!) Her motto was SCHEME: she plotted punishments - not of unfaithful Zeus, but of the nymphs, princesses, women, nereids and so on, rather unfairly, especially since most of them were pregnant.

above: Zeus, "father of Gods and men", 4th cent. BC. below: Demeter, giving the first wheat seed to an Eleusinian prince. (Athens Nat. Arch. Museum).

SIBLINGS OF ZEUS:

3. **POSEIDON** (Neptune): god of the Sea, a grouchy type with a trident , whose white horses' manes gallop over the sea.

—**PLUTO** (Dis , Hades): God of the Underworld, is known for his abduction of Persephone, the daughter of Demeter, carrying her to his dark kingdom of the dead, and thus no dweller on Olympus he.

4. **DEMETER** (Ceres): Goddess of the harvest, of grain and springtime. When Hades took her daughter, she raged and wept and there was no harvest. It was finally resolved that Persephone could be with her half the year. Demeter allowed the fields to become fruitful again only while her daughter remained with her.

5. **HESTIA** (Vesta): A very nice lady goddess of hearth and home, though unmarried and virgin. Hospitality and keeping the home fires burning were her business.

CHILDREN OF ZEUS AND HERA

6. **ARES** (Mars): God of War, impulsive, violent and brutish. With the goddess of discord,he stirred things up whenever possible just for the hell of it.

7. **HEPHAESTUS** (Vulcan): God of the Smiths, who was lamed and married to Aphrodite. He was ugly and rejected, but talented - made a set of golden robots to do his bidding.

However, Zeus fathered a bunch of other gods on ladies not his wife:

8. **APOLLO:** Beautiful sun-god of music and medicine, who killed the serpent Python that threatened his mother, at Delphi: and so took over the Sacred Oracle.

9. **ARTEMIS** (Diana): Twin sister of Apollo: the huntress, a virgin moon-goddess who refused men, carried a bow and arrow, and had the power to send both plague and healing. She was protector of

children and babies, and the goddess of midwifery. Her emblems were the date-palm, the stag and the bee.

10. **APHRODITE** (Venus): Sea-born Goddess of sexual love. She renewed her virginity by bathing and had a magic girdle that caused every man to want her. She was married to Hephaestus, but deceived him frequently.

11. **HERMES** (Mercury): Mischief-making messenger, a clever thief who invented the tortoise-shell lyre and gave it to Apollo, and who never told a lie. Well, not really a LIE... Prehistoric homes once had a Herm, or male figure, to protect it. His symbols were the winged sandals and helmet and the caduceus, the snake - twined staff that later became a symbol of healers.

above: Venus de Milo; the most famous representation of love Goddess.
below: Dionysus with a Satyr and a Maenad.

12. **DIONYSUS** (Bacchus): God of the vine, orgies and ecstasies, theatre and masks. He conquered more territory than Alexander, but was subject to madness. Married Theseus' discarded love, Ariadne, with whom he had many children.

13. **ATHENA** (Minerva): Born in Libya, daughter of Metis the Titaness, who governed wisdom and knowledge. An oracle declared that in future Metis would bear a son, who would overthrow his father (as usual). Zeus swallowed her whole while she was expecting her first. In due time he got a splitting headache, and Athena, fully armed, leaped out of his head.

Here is an example of a myth describing a historical event: the patriarch god absorbs the wise Goddess, and becomes (rather painfully) thereby the father of wisdom.

Athens was one of her cities: and her signs were the owl and the *aegis*, a shield with the head of the snake-haired Medusa. She was Goddess of wisdom, weaving, war.

Bronze head of Athena, 4th cent. BC. (Athens Nat. Arch. Museum).

Why are there *thirteen* gods of Olympus in this list? Everybody knows there were twelve! According to Robert Graves, "Dionysus ascended to Heaven, and sits at the right hand of Zeus as one of the Twelve Great Ones. The self-effacing goddess Hestia resigned her seat at the high table in his favour glad of any excuse to escape the jealous wranglings of her family, and knowing that she could always count on a quiet welcome in any Greek city which it might please her to visit..."

Lesser gods: Pan, the goat-footed meadow god who guarded flocks, chased girls, and could cause Panic; Satyrs, with goat horns and feet; Tyche and Nemesis, Luck and Retribution; Asklepios, son of Apollo, who became the founder of medicine and had a hospital at Epidavros; the various trinities - Three Fates, Three Furies, Three Graces; Nymphs of the trees,the mountains, the sea, of these there were hundreds, local and international.

Legends about humans also abound. King Midas, who wished that his touch would turn things to gold - until his family became golden statues. Narcissus, who admired his reflection so much that he finally turned into a flower nodding over the silvery water; the original "My Fair Lady", Galatea,who started life as an ivory statue of Aphrodite. Her sculptor Pygmalion desired her so much that the goddess brought the statue to life and they lived happily ever after; and the legendary Theseus, son of Aegeus, King of Athens, and a princess of Troezen. The boy was raised there, and was instructed to take the sword and sandals of his father to Athens when grown. On the way he vanquished a number of such unpleasant characters who infested the roads between the kingdoms as Procrustes. This fellow invited travellers to stay for the night, but if they did not fit his bed precisely, he trimmed their feet off or stretched them out. In Athens, Theseus found that Medea, discarded lover of Jason, was his stepmother. Medea was a sorceress, and did not take kindly to the intruder. But as the youth was carrying his father's sword, Aegeus welcomed him, and Medea's efforts to kill him failed. She then went to Asia Minor.

Theseus, giving the final blow to wounded Minotaur. (5th cent. BC.)

Theseus then set off to stop the annual tax of seven youths and seven maidens demanded by King Minos of Crete. The young slaves were given to the Minotaur, half bull and half-man, to devour. With a little help and a long string from the besotted Cretan princess Ariadne, Theseus was able to track the creature into the centre of the labyrinth in which it lived, and defeat it. Ariadne had betrayed her people, and he took her away with him. He then sneaked off while she slept on the island of Naxos. (Her story ends nicely: the god Dionysus rescued and married her.) On the way to Athens, Theseus forgot to raise the white sail announcing his survival and his despairing father jumped into the sea from Sounion cliff, which is why it is called the Aegean Sea.

Theseus had many more adventures - and wives. He married Hippolyta, Queen of the Amazons, the wedding feast of "A Midsummer Night's Dream", and Phaedra, younger sister of Ariadne; he abducted the child Helen, intending a future marriage, and then went on an ill fated expedition to the underworld. Here he unknowingly sat on the Chair of Forgertfulness for four years, and had to be rescued by Herakles. Theseus would have attained demi-god status like Herakles (whom he much admired), but he had powerful enemies in the Peloponnese. Helen's brothers became powerful in Athens, and the Athenians found his womanizing embarrassing. In classical times it was said that it was he who founded the first commonwealth in Athens.

There are adventure stories about Jason looking for the golden fleece aboard the *Argo,* and his tragic affair with the barbarian witch Medea: about Herakles (Hercules), the bodybuilt hero who sailed with Jason. He performed twelve very hard tasks, with side trips like repopulating a whole island in one night - in the most pleasant possible way.

The oldest known myths describe mysterious great powers - Night, Chaos, Light. Later, the powers were personified. Later still, with the decline in mysteries and divine possession, the gods became less and less distinguishable from humans in character. Greek myths were taken over and spread by the Romans, and thus have found their way into Western culture.

Hermes, presenting the three Goddesses to Paris: Athena in full armour, Hera holding her staff, and Aphrodite followed by cupids.

Myth in Greek Drama

The poet Homer has left us two epics: *The Iliad,* describing the long war at Troy. Paris, a conceited young prince of Troy, awarded a beauty prize to Aphrodite, who promised him the loveliest woman in the world, and never mind her husband. (Aphrodite had a one-track mind.) That was Helen, now grown up and married. Paris duly abducted the beauty. Naturally, Helen's husband Menelaus was obliged to go after her. He had won her from many rival princes, and they had all agreed to accept her choice, and protect her forever from danger. Menelaus called them up, and off they went. The ten-year war involved humans, gods and heroes in a series of insults, battles, revenges and duels. The tantrums of Achilles, the exploits of Agamemnon, Ajax, Odysseus, and many others are told in detail in the *Iliad.*

The *Odyssey* describes the long voyage of Odysseus (Ulysses), who took ten more years to get home after the war, due to seductions, attacks, imprisonments and adventures on the way.

In the end Menelaus brought his Helen home and they lived happily ever after.

The House of Atreus

Menelaus and Helen play a minor role in the tragic story of the doom-ridden family of Atreus, horrors about which playwrights and poets have been writing ever since. Since so many plays are performed about this family, we offer a summary of the terrible events.

Atreus was a king who wanted the throne of Mycenae. He vowed to sacrifice his sheep to Artemis, and when Hermes mischievously placed a golden sheep in the flock, Atreus sacrificed the sheep all right, but kept that fleece. Artemis was not pleased. He got out of that spot with help from Zeus, but it aggravated a vicious running feud with his brother Thyestes the king.

Finally, he cooked and served the children of Thyestes to their father, who understandably uttered a very strong curse. The story grows ever darker: oracles and incest tangled the family so that who was son and who uncle became very confused. Thyestes had raped his own daughter, and begot Aegisthus, secretly raised by Uncle Atreus. Atreus commanded the child Aegisthus to kill Thyestes, who recognized his own old sword in his son's hand. Thyestes, assuming the role of father, ordered the boy to kill Atreus instead. He did. Thyestes got the Mycenean throne. Briefly.

But the king of Sparta forced Thyestes to go into exile, leaving the throne to Menelaus' brother Agamemnon. Agamemnon abducted Clytemnestra, killing her inconvenient husband and baby, and she bore him Orestes and three daughters: Iphigenia, Chrysothemis and Electra. By now Menelaus had inherited the kingship of Sparta, and while he and Agamemnon went off to fight in Troy, Aegisthus stayed at home, brooding and thinking revengeful thoughts. It occurred to him to have a go with Clytemnestra, and dispose of Agamemnon whenever he showed up.

The god Hermes warned him that it was a poor idea, but Aegisthus succeeded in wooing Clytemnestra. She didn't care much for Agamemnon anyway: not only had his courtship been too rough, but he had sacrificed their daughter Iphigenia at Aulis, and on top of everything else, it was said that he was bringing his mistress Cassandra home. Agamemnon landed after his years at war, happy to be back at last. Cassandra, who was cursed with foresight that nobody believed, smelt trouble and spoke warnings, but Agamemnon patted her on the head and went to take a bath. His wife caught him in a towel, where Aegisthus slew him with a sword. Clytemnestra wielded an axe, with which she then dealt with Cassandra.

Clytemnestra's son Orestes was only a child, and away with his tutor; Aegisthus reigned at Mycenae for seven years while Orestes was growing up. He was hen-pecked. He was nervous about the surviving Electra, who is usually depicted as sulking and muttering darkly around the palace. She had no money and was always watched. She continued to send messages to her brother, and fret.

Orestes came at last, and with help from Electra, got into the palace and whacked off the head of Aegisthus. It is said that he also executed his mother Clytemnestra. This act of disloyalty and matricide evoked the wrath of the Erinyes (Furies).

Orestes had to stand trial, and he and his sister were treated as pariahs. Menelaus and Helen came visiting and scolding. Menelaus wanted the pair condemned, but by a trick, Orestes and Electra grabbed Helen as a hostage, and attempted to kill her, since they decided that all their troubles were her fault. Helen was taken up into heaven.

Electra vengefully trapped Menelaus' daughter: the god Apollo sorted out the matter just in time. Orestes went off to the oracle at Delphi, still being harassed by the Furies. He was ordered to go to Athens and embrace the statue of Athena, who would annul the curse. Orestes crept off leaving the Furies asleep (but not for long. Clytemnestra's ghost waked them and set them after him again). He ran for a year all over Greece, finally reaching Athens where Athena summoned the Areos Pagos, the court of wise men, to hear the case. Athena broke a tied verdict with her vote for acquittal

After a scuffle, the Furies calmed down when Athena promised them all sorts of goodies, and moved into a cave under the Acropolis in Athens. Eventually they were turned into the Eumenides.

But the story was not yet over. Orestes was still pursued by remorse - matricide was a revolting crime. The Delphic Oracle ordered him to sail to Tauris (in the Crimea) and bring back the image of Artemis from the bloodstained temple of that wild, savage tribe. In fact, his sister Iphigenia was a priestess at the temple, having been rescued from Aulis long ago. When they recognized each other, Iphigenia helped him steal the cult statue, which was placed in the temple of Artemis of Tauris at Brauron (Vravrona).

A grand reunion of Orestes, Iphigenia and Electra at Delphi brought an end: the three returned to Mycenae, killed Aegisthus' son who had taken the throne, and settled down to staid married life in the palace.

The following classical plays touch on the Trojan War or the House of Atreus: *The Oresteia* trilogy *(Agamemnon, The Libation Bearers, The Eumenides)* of Aeschylus; *Philoctetes, Ajax,* and *Electra* of Sophocles; *Hecuba, Trojan Women, Electra, Iphigenia in Tauris, Iphigenia in Aulis, Orestes,* and *Helen,* of Euripides.

The Theban Cycle

Another group of plays is about Oedipus, poor fellow, again a victim of that recurring prophecy.

Laius, king of Thebes and his wife Jocasta had an infertility problem, and the king went in secret to the Oracle at Delphi for advice. The oracle claimed that a son would destroy him - the same old story - so he rejected Jocasta. Knowing and caring nothing about prophecies, Jocasta succeeded in seducing him back to her. The resulting baby boy was dumped on the mountainside with a nail through his feet (Oedipus means "Swollen feet"). He was rescued and raised by the king of Corinth. Already showing a Heroic Flaw, he insisted on asking about his future. The Oracle said "Go away, you wretch! Not only will you kill your father, you're going to marry your mother, too". Naturally, Oedipus quickly packed and left Corinth, taking no chances on harming his "parents". Limping through a narrow mountain pass, he met an arrogant chap in a chariot who shoved him. He hit back, and there, unbeknownst, went his father.He continued to Thebes, and found the city terrorized by a Sphinx: This creature insisted that everyone who passed must answer her riddle or die. "What is it that has one voice, four feet in the morning, two feet at midday and three feet at night?" Gazing at the bloodstained jaws of the Sphinx - a mixture of woman, lion, snake and eagle - he explained kindly "You're thinking of man, ma'am, who crawls on hands and knees as a baby, walks on two feet as an adult and with a cane when old..." The Sphinx, in a fit of embarrassment, hurled herself from a cliff.

The Thebans acclaimed Oedipus as King, whereupon he was required to marry the Queen. So the terrible prophecy was fulfilled, and the city began dying of plague. When a blind prophet Teiresias (blind prophets are always called Teiresias) called Oedipus' attention to the facts, he was very upset and blinded himself, taking to the road (Homer says he died gloriously in battle). Poor Jocasta, who hadn't a clue about all this, and who had been feeling pretty good about her new young hero-husband, killed herself.

Aeschylus' *Seven against Thebes;* Sophocles' *Oedipus at Colonus, Oedipus Rex, Antigone:* and Euripides' *Phoenician Women, Suppliants, Antigone* are all based on this tale.

Historical and Cultural Chart

The history of Greece goes back to prehistoric times, with its greatest moment of glory in the 5th century before Christ. The following pages offer a unique illustrated chart of Greek history in relation to the rest of the world, with illustrations of contemporary arts, architecture and literature.

World History		Greek History
	40,000 BC	First known human remains.
NEOLITHIC First cities of Mesopotamia	6000-4500	Sesklo and Dimini (northern Greece) settled.
Predynastic Egypt N. America: Paleoindians European Beaker People	4500	Migrations by "Corded Ware" Folk, warriors from Pontic/Caucasus.
	BRONZE AGE	
Upper and Lower Egypt united: 1st Dynasty Hieroglyphic writing First stone buildings	3000	Early Minoan (Pre-Palatial) : Small settlement in Athens.
The Flood Sumerians	2613-2180	"Pelasgians" (Ancient ones) settle in Attica, Corinth
Egypt Old Kingdom Cheops, Pyramids Founding of Stonehenge Sargon II of Akkad	2350-2300	Worshippers of the Great Goddess. Early Helladic Period: Migrations from Near East to Cyprus, Crete, East Coast, Islands bringing trade, crafts and Goddess religion. Early Cycladic Period. First Minoan Palaces (Knossos, Phaestos).
	2133-1603	Achaeans ("Akhiyawans") invade mainland from Danube area with macho gods, horses, Greek language, and the potter's wheel. They found Mycenae, Tiryns, Argos.
Egypt Middle Kingdom	2000	
Egyptian reunification under Mentuhotep II Abraham	1900	Middle Minoan/Middle Cycladic. Achaeans mingle with natives. Cultural mix will result in great "Mycenaean" civilization. Shaft graves hold weapons and jewels, marked by "Stelae", gravestones carved with scenes of war and hunting.
Old Assyrian Empire Babylonian Empire, Hammurabi	1800	
Fall of Babylon	1700	
China: Taoism, 1567-1320	1600	Peak of Minoan civilization Late Helladic Period.
Egyptian New Kingdom 18th Dynasty Colonial Expansion Assyrians dominate Near East: Hittite Empire Archaic Mexico Vedic India Egypt conquers Nubia, Palestine, Syria Amenhotep, Tutankhamen Phoenician alphabet	1500	New Mycenaean aristocracy adopts Minoan styles, bringing in fashions, arts, even trendy newstyle *tholos* (domed beehive) tombs to replace good old shaft graves. Catastrophic volcanic eruption of Thira. Minoan culture fails rapidly, and Crete becomes Mycenaean island. Mycenaeans take Aigina, expand to Cyprus, Rodos. Final destruction of palace at Knossos. Enlargement of Great Palace at Mycenae. Treasury of Atreus.
Egypt, 19th Dynasty Age of Rameses, Moses Iron introduced in Babylonia Chou period, China	1250	Erechtheus, Kekrops, Theseus, kings of Athens. A decline in trade and peace. Cities (including Athens) fortified with "Cyclopean" walls - only a Titan could have moved those stones, said punier pundits of later days. Sea Peoples, island and coast groups, prey on land and sea, disrupting trade routes. Piracy is a way of life: threats to Mycenaean cities and dynasties, the crumbling of civil structure. Hence those forts.
Phoenicia develops culture, colonies, Carthage	1194-1184	Trojan War, events of Iliad, Odyssey - a pirate raid.
		Fall of Mycenaean civilization. "Dorian" Greeks invade from Epirus, block the passage of armies, play alliance games in Peloponnese, and continue as far as Crete. (Ionians, in Attica, Evia and the Cyclades, consider Dorians low, vulgar primitives).

Greek Culture

Prehistoric versions of gods beginning as nature spirits and changing with time, conquests, absorption of other gods, and with developing sophistication.

Spiral decorated pottery.

Fortified villages 6000-4500.

Long narrow houses with pitched roofs called "long halls", or "megarons", as found in Central Europe. Stone battle axes, similar to those of Caspian Sea.

Cord patterns on pottery - giving the name to the Corded Ware People.

Early Cycladic island culture and early Minoan contemporary, but

Early Helladic development is interrupted by invasions bringing Vedic Gods like the trio Mitra/Varuna/Indra, who resemble the Olympians Zeus/Poseidon/Hades.

High Minoan culture (Crete) produces strange tales of bulls and Minotaurs, engineers with flying machines and robots (Daedalus), firmly based in Goddess-worship. Cross-culture shown by story of Theseus (Page 18) and there is no question that there is trade of artifacts and ideas.

The Mycenean myths: (see Mythology p. 20) Surprisingly accurate historically: Troy was found exactly as described by Homer 300 years (?) later. Hero-stories like that of Perseus, who conquered the snake-haired Gorgon, Medusa (with Athena's help), and Oedipus, (page 21) date from this period.

Late Minoan culture influences Mycenaean: (Late Helladic) Designers use Minoan motifs, though stylizing the free natural forms. (see octopus vases). Gold jewels and cups, masks, and large palaces, at Mycenae, Pylos - and Athens' Acropolis.

Linear A Script, Crete, (not yet deciphered) 1700.

Linear B Script, Crete, first written use of Greek language 1400.

Phoenician Alphabet in use for writing Greek: Greek alphabet starts here.

Geometric Period of Vases Stylized design becomes standard while ceramics develop in shapes, firing techniques, and size. Buildings have been ruined, paintings destroyed, but pottery has left us a record of how life was lived in those days.

Iron tools make farming profitable.

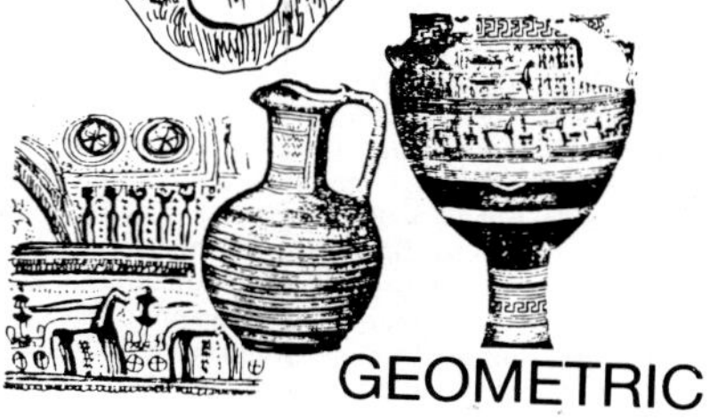

Greece and her People

World History		Greek History
Saul		City States: *Polis* of town and surrounding land, independent and coexisting by treaty (Athens, Sparta, Aigina).
David Solomon Kings of Judah	1000	City-states plant colonies on coasts and islands of Asia Minor, along Black Sea.
	776	First Olympic Games: first sense of Greek identity (panhellenism).
	ARCHAIC PERIOD 722-705	Greek cities colonise Mediterranean, Nile, Italy. Massilia
Assyrian Empire of Tiglath, Pileser III		Sicilian colonies founded by Corinth
Foundation of Rome	700	City-states doing good business. Athens thriving. First navy and first coins, with turtle-symbol, Aigina
Destruction of Babylon Second Assyrian Empire Asshurbanipal Fall of Assyrians The Prophet Jeremiah	650	Ionic Period: Ionic cities line coast of Asia Minor (see events of 1921-22 A.D.) City-states develop through "tyranny" (Tyrants = revolutionary leaders who took dictatorial power) toward democracy
Neo-Babylonians, Nebuchadnezzar Buddha		Draconian measures: fierce code of law by Dracon (see Agora, page 56)
Persian Empire, Cyrus II Confucius Lao-Tze Hebrew Disapora	590	Solon as archon reforms law, politics under pressure from middle class traders. Peisistratid Tyranny in Athens. Peace and prosperity. Art and Commerce thrive while Persians nibble away at Asia Minor bases.
Persian Empire 525-404	525-404	Cyrus incorporates Lydia into Persia
Cambyses, Darius,		Darius leads Persians across Bosporus, takes Macedonia.
Xerxes,		Mainland Greece ignores Persian incursions. Sparta is the only state in a strong enough position to act, and persuades other states to join Peleponnesian League.
Darius II	510	First Great Dionysian Festival in Athens.
		Cleisthenes rewrites constitution, making residence instead of race the basis of suffrage, and gerrymanders districts to break clan influence: equal rights, balanced democracy of *ecclesia* (popular assembly), *boule* (council) and *heliaea* (people's law court): the old aristocratic religious/legal judges, the Areos Pagos, are losing power.

CLASSICAL GREECE (478-336 BC)

During the years from 500 to 400, Athens becomes the political, cultural and commercial centre of the world. Art, architecture, mathematics, grammar, philosophy, science, literature and drama burst into glorious achievement - even though the cities are at war most of the time, first with the Persian Empire, then with each other. The Persians invade Greece and get as far as Marathon (490), where the Athenian army led by Miltiades beats them back... The Persian wars cause Athens and Sparta to suspend their perpetual quarrel, as Persia keeps trying to conquer Athens. Sparta, piqued by missing the battle because of the mid-August religious holiday (August 15?) leads a unique coalition of city-states and leads military actions on land while Themistokles, a brilliant tactician, builds the Athenian navy, plans walls around the citadel, the city and the port.

But the Persians keep coming back. In summer of 480, the Spartan general Leonidas dies heroically protecting the retreat of the army from Thermopylae, luring the Persians to mount an attack on Athens. Themistokles orders the Athenians to wait in a "wooden wall" of ships at Piraeus while Xerxes burns and loots the city. Themistokles then entraps the Persian fleet in the straits of Salamis and sends it home yelping. In 479 the Perennially Persistent Persians are soundly thumped at the Battle of Platea, under the Spartan Pausanias. Themistokles is Commander-in-Chief.

Themistokles now starts those walls around Athens and Piraeus, with Sparta objecting all the way. The port has been long established at Phaleron (Paleo Faliron), in sight of the Acropolis: but Piraeus is easier to defend, and Themistokles includes the road to Piraeus and the port in his Sea Wars defence system. Athens insists that with her great new navy she can protect everybody for miles around. Sparta disagrees. Athens meets with allies on the sacred (and slave market) island of Delos, forming the *Delian Alliance* in 477. A few years thereafter, Athenians ostracize (banish) Themistokles, who dies as a Persian guest. Sparta keeps on with her own coalition, the Peloponnesian League. The final defeat of the Persians occurred in 465 under the command of Kimon at the River Eurymedon.

Greek Culture

Greek alphabet develops by 850.

Greek poetry, like high Greek drama, was always meant to be spoken to an audience. Poets used the material of myth, interpreting and developing the stories. Familiar with the myths, audience could notice and think about such changes. Hesiod: (fl. 800) Didactic Poetry: a passionate believer in the gods as moral images: a collator of myth.

Spread of Ionic lyric poetry: Sappho (600) writes in local dialect (Aeolian).

Art: Archaic Statues of Kouroi and Korai. Youths (nude, meaning heroic) and girls (draped) used as memorials, dedications to gods, later as columns (caryatides). They are stiffly posed with a strange smile, usually painted in vivid colors.

Red-figured vases - very, er, lively

Poetry: Homer writes epics the *Iliad* and the *Odyssey* (see page 19)

Philosophy: Pythagoras founds a group to study mathematics, physics, accoustics and harmony, political theory - and reincarnation. Heraclitus remarks that the world order is a state of becoming and change, rather than static (- future shock?)

Doric temple of Aphaia, Egina

Philosophy: The universe as sphere, the upper half air and light and the lower half dark underworld, Earth a flat disk floating between. Gods and men are subject to laws of existence: men subject to capricious gods as well.

Olympia, Delos, Delphi become strong spiritual centres.

Drama: Tragedy, "goat-song", started as monologue performed with chorus at Dionysos' festivals. Aeschylus (525-456,) who fought in Persian Wars, invents tragic drama, introducing a second actor and dialogue (with chorus): works in which humans lose nobly against the fatal power of gods.

Sophocles: (496-408) Brings in a third actor, making for higher drama. His tragedies express the heroic ideal, working out of fate with dignity.

Euripides, (480-406,) the third great playwright, influenced by Sophists, questioning all in the light of reason - more psychological approach. All these dramatists go back to the older myths for rich material.

Black figure vases from Attica.
First temple of Olympian Zeus.
The Charioteer of Delphi.
The Critian Boy.

ARCHAIC

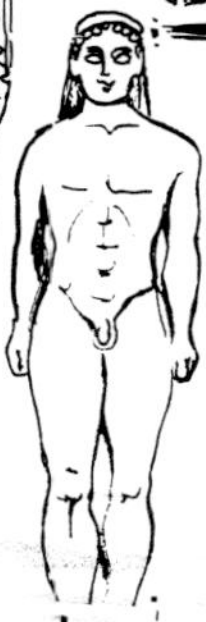

Doric

Ionic

Greece and her People

The Spartans are growling and muttering over Athenian growth, fear the corruption of their youth by flabby democratic principles, suffer a terrible earth quake. With typical Spartan logic, they declare war with Messinia - for the third time - to get their minds off their troubles.

Radical reformers Ephialtes and Perikles are making Athens an ideal democracy. Ephialtes is murdered. Perikles gives up trying to make friends with Sparta, and tries to break up the Peloponnesian League. An overconfident effort to wrest Egypt from Persians ends with the wreck of the fleet.

However, by 454, the Delian Alliance has become the Athenian Empire. Themistokles' long walls joining Athens and Piraeus become a reality (457). Athens now controls Aigina, Gulf of Corinth, Boeotia, Lokris and Phokis, and Piraeus is the major transit port of the known world. Money is rolling in. Perikles moves the Alliance treasury from Delos to Athens, and silver mines are working at Lavrion. Athens is tired of fighting both Persia and Sparta, and an uneasy 5-year armistice is negotiated in 451.

Commands are issued, making currency, votes and loyalty oaths subject to Athenian commissioners. "Democracy" is now maintained by military law, and suffrage is narrowed: power struggles are endless. A respite from the Persians comes with the Peace of Kallias of 448, giving Athens control of the Aegean. Wearily recognizing Sparta's dominance of the Peloponnese, Athens gets Sparta off her back with a 30-year peace treaty in 445.

447-429 Golden Age of Perikles

Reconstruction of Athens: Great public works (see Acropolis) and a running feud with the politician Thucydides, who writes the "objective and scientific" history of his time. Perikles gets this rival ostracized. Kerkyra (Corfu), under attack by Sparta's friends, appeals to Athens for help. Sparta and her allies plan for renewal of war. Both Sparta and Athens choose not to honour the treaty of 445 and set off the

Great Horrible Long Peloponnesian Wars 431-404

The plan is to get all the Athenian allies into the defended city, attack the Peleponnese by sea, and avoid engaging in land fights with the superior Spartan army. But Perikles dies of plague which breaks out in Athens and kills 30% of the Athenians. His successors dither. There is a brief recess - the Peace of Nikias of 421 - but the troubles resume, partly due to the Athenians' lack of commitment.

404: Sparta beseiges and defeats Athens: looting, plague, woe. The long walls to Piraeus are torn down in the reign of "30 Tyrants" under Spartan administration. The Persians are much amused.

403: Thrassyboulos, obviously a very great man, reestablishes democracy in Athens and pays the people to go to the theatre. Bravo, Thrassyboulos!

WORLD HISTORY GOES ON		AND SO DOES GREEK
Celts (Gauls) migrate from Rhine Basin to Britain and S. Europe, and sack Rome	406-396	Athens accepts Persian support to get back at Sparta. Truce-and-fight with the neighbours begins again, though commerce and culture thrive... The Themistoklean walls are rebuilt.
	387 359 338	Phillip II becomes King of Macedonia and gradually consolidates an empire, conquering Thessaly by 352. Athenians hear Demosthenes urge "fight the barbarian!" while Isokrates explains "use the Macedonians to thrash the Persians". Phillip's 18-year-old son Alexander puts a stop to all debate at the battle of Chaeronea, taking Thebes and Athens.
Persia Artaxerxes II to Darius	**HELLENISTIC PERIOD** 339-323	Phillip sets up a pan-Greek council, offering magnanimous terms of friendship and alliance. Athens (with Peloponnese and Thebes) tries a revolt. Destruction of Thebes. So much for revolution. Philip is assassinated.
Egypt under Persia till Ptolemies of Egypt Seleucids of Asia Attalids of Pergamus (in northern Turkey) ruling families, founded by generals serving Alexander from Greece to India		Alexander the Great inherits throne. Helenization of the East: Alexander conquers and resettles Persia: Mass marriages of Persians and Macedonians. Simplification of Greek language for use by distant administrators as far as India.

CLASSICAL

Greek Culture

Bronze Poseidon of Artemision, 460

Rhetoric, the making of effective public speeches, was a necessity for political life and law courts - you could not hire a lawyer to speak for you! Antiphon, (480-411:) Andocides, Lysias (455-380)

Pindar and Corinna, Choral lyric poets.

Herodotus, (ca 484-425) historical narrative of Persian Wars.
Democritus (430-370) - the atom theory.

BUILDING OF THE ACROPOLIS

Parthenon Sculptor/Architect Pheidias; figures are sensuous, strong, graceful, perfectly suited to the perfect building achievement Mnesikles and Iktinos, architects of Propylaia, other temples.
Polyklitos (wrote book about athlete's proportions) and Myron, (The *Discus Thrower)* sculptors.
Polygnotos, painter, who exhibited in Art Gallery on Acropolis
Red-figured vases now elaborately coloured.

Birth of Hippokrates, physician (ca. 447).
Drama festivals of Dionysos: plays of Sophocles, Aeschylus performed Aristophanes: writes Comedies -*Lysistrata, The Frogs, The Birds, Peace, the Acharnians*. Comedy has clownish elements from early Dionysiac rites.

Philosophy: The Sophists and Socrates (469-399) known to us through Plato's *Dialogues*. Famed for walking around Agora, debating Truth, and was sentenced to drink hemlock (poison), for corrupting the minds of the young. Supposedly married to a terrible shrew, Xantippe.
Plato (427-347) was his student, and developed a theory of the Ideal World, which is reflected in the world we perceive. Founded the Academy to pass on his ideas.
Aristotle (384-222) a Macedonian pupil of Plato, who tutored Alexander, returned to Athens to the Lyceum. His students were called "Walkers" (peripatetics) as they talked with the Master in colonnades of Lyceum. First to classify the world in terms of natural science and wrote on zoology, biology, ethics, metaphysics and poetics.

Epidaurus Theatre built 358-330

Praxiteles, sculptor of human figure at peak of sensuousness and discipline.

Parthenon Interior

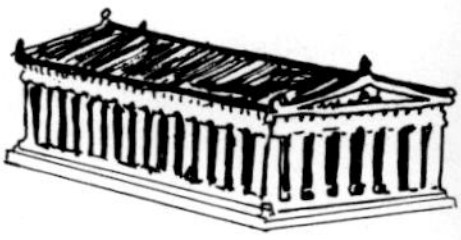

Greece and her People

World History		**Greek History**
	323	Death of Alexander. Athens tries another revolution, fails. Severe measures are taken by garrisons in Athens during wars of succession to Alexander (Diadochian Wars) as the empire dissolves.
The Cleopatras (Ptolemies) Roman domination begins Titus takes Jerusalem	280-278	Invasion by Gauls: repelled by Aetolian League, which with Achaean Alliance, now replaces decadent city-states with rival political structures. Corinth (Achaean Alliance) is puppet of Macedonia, to its later sorrow. Athens makes friends with Rome, remains the foremost centre of culture.
Hannibal crosses Alps	215	First and Second Macedonian Wars with Rome, Rome wins. Rome proclaims herself "Protector of the Freedom of Greece".
Punic Wars Hannibal's suicide 183	197	
	171-168	Third Macedonian War: Perseus, son of Phillip V, tries to liberate Greece and is beaten: Rome annihilates Macedonia and brutally punishes her Greek allies - Epirus, Achaean Alliance, Aetolia.
	168	
	166	Delos a free port: Rodos falls to Athens.
	ROMAN GREECE	
Third Punic War Carthage destroyed	146	Final rebellion of the Achaean Alliance makes the Roman Empire strike back: Corinth destroyed. End of Achaean Alliance. Independence for Athens, Sparta, Delphi. The "Pax Romana" (Roman Peace) Continual "Export" of artworks, a.k.a., looting of Athens
Rome Sulla's dictatorship Spartacus Cicero Julius Caesar	88-86	Mithridates of Pontos stirs up Athens against Rome, a rebellion which is firmly squelched by Sulla, leaving Athens both broken and broke. But the philosophy schools go on and on...
	48-31	Battle of Pharsalus. Mark Antony grants Aigina and Eretria to Athens, making her his HQ for his "Eastern Roman Empire"
Augustus Caesar (formely Octavian) Suicide of Anthony and Cleopatra	31 BC- 14 AD 30	Now a free and independent city, Athens approves of those nice Caesars. "Greece" separated from Macedonia as "Achaea" province, with Corinth as capital.
Roman Empire reunited	Birth of Christ. ANNO DOMINI	
Rome I, Claudius	41-54	Gives Acropolis a grand staircase.
	54	St Paul visits Athens, Corinth.
Trajan Hadrian	117-140	Hadrian rebuilds much of Athens and adds theatres, temples and Roman braggeries to what he regards as his very own Athens. Herod Atticus adds a touch of Sophistication. Athens visited by plague. Pausanias writes his tourist guide.
Marcus Aurelius	170	
Antiochus IV of Syria	245	Goths begin raids from Black Sea and loot Athens.
325-330 of Roman		The Divine Emperor Constantine: Christianity becomes recognized religion of Roman Empire (Edict of Milan 330) Rhetorical schools revival Romans continue to import Greek art.
	393	Last Olympic Games until 1896.
Death of Emperor Theodosios. Roman Empire divided again	395	Emperor Theodosios proclaims Christianity as official religion with capital at Byzantium - sorry, Constantinople. Eastern Rome includes Greece.
Attila the Hun Visigoths settle throughout Europe. Deposition of Romulus Augustus, end of Roman Empire	406-500	Gothic invasion. Eleusis and Peloponnese destroyed by Alaric. Athens looted. Vandal invasions and lootings. Christian church building, often in or over ancient temples.

Greek Culture

Hellenistic Period: classical ideals turn into realism, super-realism, completely-baroque period. Buildings monumental and self-conscious. Athens loses her position as the centre of civilization, as her culture is spread through the known world.

Theatre of Dionysos completed by Lykourgos, 338-26.

Euclid (ca. 300) father of geometry, sophist.
Archimedes (287-212) mathematician and philosopher.
Diogenes, Cynic philosopher.
Greek language is simplified and spread: a great Library at Alexandria of 100,000 scrolls.
Lysippos, Alexander's favorite sculptor.
Apelles, Protogenes, painter 300.
Epicurus (342-221), Zeno (336-263) Stoicism.
Drama: Menander, "Attic" comedy-early sitcoms. One surviving play, *The Misanthrope.* (317) A student of the school of Aristotle.
Boy Jockey from Artemision.
Roman copies of Greek works.
Venus de Milo, ca. 200-100.

146 BC - 1018 AD
This period in letters has suffered catastrophically from destruction of works, largely because the Roman and Byzantine readers preserved only what they approved, letting the others, written on papyrus, crumble to dust or actively destroying them. What remain are mostly minor efforts, with tantalizing references to the greater lost works.

Eratosthenes (276-162) astronomer and geographer:
Galen, medical writings.

The New Testament and many Jewish scriptures were written originally in Greek (due to Alexander).Plutarch - "Parallel Lives" of famous Greeks and Romans.

Lucian of Samosata: the first science fiction story - *Voyage to the Moon.*
Philostratus, "Lives of the Sophists". Love stories, in this period.

Philosophy; Epictetus, (50 b.c.) Marcus Aurelius (121-180.)

Stoa of Attalos, 132.
Hadrian's, Arch 130.
Olympian Zeus, Trajan to Aurelian 160.
Odeon of Herod Atticus.

World History	BYZANTINE GREECE	Greek History
		Byzantium: a Christian empire, using Greek language, Roman law and administration; often in conflict with Arabs, later with Islam.
Merovingian France Saxon England Mayan Old Empire	529	Emperor Justinian abolishes the "pagan" University, - schools of philosophy that were all that was left of glorious Athens, which now becomes a poor provincial town for next 1300 years. An age of monasteries.
Lombardic take-over of Italy from Byzantium Rise of Roman papacy		Slavs loot Athens.
Mohammed	570-532	
T'ang Dynasty, China Pope Gregory I	618-906	War of Byzantium with Persia. Byzantine victory leaves victors exhausted, broke. Those Slavs are back again.
Carolingians: Pepin the Short	700	Emperor Leo III. Iconoclastic controversy, (Are icons graven images?)
Charlemagne	775-875	
Viking raids, European Coast	800	Slavs converted.
Haroun al-Rashid		Basil I emperor: split widens between Roman and Eastern Churches.
		Saracens in Crete; Magyar invaders. Renaissance under Macedonian Dynasty. Saracens sack Thessaloniki.
King Alfred unites England under West Saxon house	900	
Beginning of Holy Roman Empire	750-1200	Bulgars expand into N. Greece.
	1018	Basil II deals with Bulgars.
Hanseatic League		Albanians ooze in from North and Harold Hardraade of Norway suppresses Athenian rebels for Byzantium.
	1054	Final schism with Roman Church. Both churches claim universalism.
Norman Conquest of England	1066	Normans invade Corfu, Thessaly, Thebes: Italy takes Ionian Islands.
The Crusades begin		
	1095	Battle of Mantzikert: Ottomans defeat Emperor Romanos Dionysus.
	1185	Normans conquer Thessaloniki
		FRANKISH AND VENETIAN GREECE
Plantagenets in England Magna Carta, 1215 Latin Empire of Romania The Golden Horde, Jenghiz Khan	1204	4th crusade: sackings of Constantinople (looting Athens en passant). Greece falls to French Crusaders: "Grand Seigneur" of Athens, Othon de la Roche. Venetians hold Crete, Euboea, islands.
	1240	Franks form the "Municipality of Morea" - the Peloponnese.
Sung Dynasty of China Kamakura Shoguns, Japan Start of Ottoman Empire	1261	Constantinople retaken by Byzantines - Greek Paleologos Dynasty: Franks forced to release part of Peloponnese to Byzantium: Frankish Dukes replaced by Sicilians, - after some heated debate.
Early Renaissance	1312	
Ming Dynasty, China Richard II, England Hundred Years War	1389	Florentine Duchy of Athens.
Holy Roman Empire Incas, Peru Aztecs, Mexico	1438	Venetians take Nauplion, and then all Greece and islands: Venetians hold Aigina 1451-1537 and 1654-1718, Ionian islands 1438-1797.
Wars of the Roses	1453	Constantinople falls to Mehmet II: Turks take most Aegean island Last Byzantine emperor: Konstandinos Paleologos Killed defending the city.

Greek Culture

Byzantine Period

Deeply religious art, symbolic, stylized (Saints' images were what they really looked like!) Two main trends: Hellenic/ realistic, and Eastern/symbolic - flat and decorative. Architectural sculpture (sculpture considered a pagan art, remains only as decoration), icon painting, sumptuary arts - jewellery, bookbinding, cups and church furnishings. Church needlework led to domestic (dowry) linens, clothing and household fabric decoration. Cloisonne enamels, ivories.

532-37: Agia Sophia, Constantinople. Anthemios and Isidoros solve technical problem of dome which dominates Byzantine architecture.

726-843: Iconoclastic Controversy: Eastern Christians very strict about images: wars and destruction of many early Byzantine works. Western rationalism and deep individualism of Greek character contrasted with Eastern Christian mystic tendency.

Byzantine attitude on literature: God gave His revelations in Greek, and the holy language must not change. Theological writing of the 4th to 9th centuries: Athanasius, Eusebius, works of Patriarchs: Theophanes the Confessor, Ioannis Chrysostomos.

BYZANTINE

Popular architecture developed many beautiful small churches and houses, and folk painters decorated walls, shop signs, tavernas.

Church decoration culminates always in the Christ Ruler of the World overhead. Examples: Ossios Loukas, Dafni, abroad, St. Mark's, Venice.

Aristotle translated into Latin. Mosaic supplanted by richer and more realistic fresco. Many churches remain from this period - Agia Ekaterini, Agios Nikolaos Rângavas, Agios Ioannis Theologos, Agia Sotiria, all in Plaka: Agii Assomati, Thissio.

Byzantine Music: basically liturgical chant, derived from synagogue music. Chant from the 3d century was preserved: during the 13th century certain chants became coloratura tours-de-force.

Decline of Byzantine, now imitating works from earlier more original period.

Folk arts: From the 12th century, poetry, epics, romances in a uniquely Greek medieval style were written. Political verse took and retains high importance. 10th C. folk epic by Digenes Akritas.

Greece and her People

World History		Greek History
Colonizing of Americas	1500-1600	Ottoman Turks take Athens, and all Greece (except territory held by Venetians)
Elizabeth I of England	1547-1603	
Ivan the Terrible	1571	Venetians defeat Turks at Lepanto
English Civil War	1645	Gunpowder stored on Acropolis struck by lightning. Damage severe.
Mogul Empire, India		
	1687-1688	Venetian Morosini attacks Acropolis and blows up Turkish arms dump in Parthenon. Parts of ancient works used to repair walls, or removed for export shipping and broken up.
Rise of Capitalism		
Baroque Period		
Louis XIV, France		
Stuart Restoration	1715	Turks set fire to Athens, Venetians leave
Catherine of Russia	1718	Peace of Passarowitz, confirming Turkish occupation
American Revolution	1776	
Age of Enlightenment	brings	Tourists who take antiquities
French Revolution	1789	Rule of Ali Pasha
Napoleon	1788-1822	Lord Elgin loots Athens
Regency of George III	1804	
War of 1812	1814	*Filiki Etairia* (Friendship League) a secret Nationalist group founded in Odessa by Greek merchants.
Congress of Vienna	1815	British Protectorate of Ionian Islands
	1821	War of Independence: Peloponnese freed: Capital at Nauplion.
Confederation of Germany		
Industrialization of England		Peleponnese/Athens retaken by Ibrahim Pasha: Damage to Erechtheion.
Bourbon Restoration, France	1826	Fall of Missolonghi, death of Byron.
	1827	Battle of Navarino. A confrontation at this bay in the Peloponnese between the Ottoman Turks, and ships of France, Britain and Russia explodes into a battle, ending indecision about not bothering the Ottomans too much. Decisive defeat of Turks.
Catherine of Russia who has an interest in anti-Turkish activity		
	1828	Exit Ibrahim Pasha and all his ilk. Kapodistrias appointed as first Prime Minister. Assassinated in 1833.
Czar Nicholas I		
	1833	Kingdom of Greece, with Otto of Bavaria as "King of the Hellenes", courtesy of the Great Powers. (London Conference of 1830). Athens reconstructed by German architects, continued looting by archeological tourists.
British Rule, India	1837-1901	Athens becomes Greek capital 1836
Queen Victoria	1843	First Modern Greek Constitution forced out of the king
	1840's	Birth of "The *Megali Idea*" (Big Idea): Greek nationalism / new Greek empire/state
Crimean War	1854-57	Greece supports Russia.
Germany unified		Otto I expelled after a lot of trouble. (unpopular, no children, not Orthodox.)
Italy unified		
Americal Civil War	1863	William of Denmark becomes King George I, marries. Queen Olga of Russia.
		Greece gains Thessaly, Arta by treaty
	1881	
	1897	Turks occupy Crete, and Greece loses war. Treaty demands high indemnities, loss of financial slovereignty.
Dreyfus Affair	1898	Crete gets self-government under Turkey.
Boer War		Crete united with Greece.
Russo-Japanese War		The Cretan Venizelos becomes Prime Minister.
First Russian Revolution	1908	Dodecanese islands become Italian.
		Turkey vs. Bulgaria/Serbia, then Greece: Treaty of London abolishes Turkish claims in Europe. Next, Bulgaria sacks Rumania, Serbia and Greece. Turks regain lost areas.
	1912-1913	George I, murdered, succeeded by son Constantine.
	1914-18	Balkan crises postponed during Great War. King + Colonel Metaxas favour neutrality, while Venizelos favours Allies. This difference makes for political split between pro-and anti-monarchists. Turkey enters War in Nov. 1914.
World War I		
Second Russian Revolution		

1545, Theophanes of Crete paints frescoes at Meteora and Athos.

Rhyming verse introduced by Crusaders

Cretan (under Venice) high culture (16th-17th C.) drama, poetry, romance. *Erotokritos,* epic by Vikentios Koranros.

Drama: *Gyparis, Thisia tou Avraam.*

Art: El Greco (1541-1614) who left Crete for Spain. Theod. Poulakis (1622-75) traditional icons with flair Nik. Kantounis, Nik. Doxaras, religious subjects influenced by Italian Renaissance

Music: Under Turkish occupation, folk songs and ballads of the klephts - armed Greeks living outlaw. Spontaneous poetry with a 15-syllable verse, quite different from the formal poets.

With the war of liberation, poets and painters rallied to the cause: Dionisios Solomos (1798-1857), (Ionian School) the *Hymn to Liberty,* now the National Anthem; Andreas Kalvos (1792-1869), austere Patriotism: both these influenced by Italian poetry; Alexandros Soutsos, Romantic poetry; Aristotle Valaoritis (1824-1864); General Makrigianis (1797-1864): Poet, soldier and hero.

With victory came rebuilding of the new country. In time, Greek architects replaced foreign Kleanthis (Byzantine Museum, Old University, Conservatory) Kaftanzoglou, Eye Hospital, Agia Irini Ch., Arsakion; P. Kalvos, Nat. Arch. Museum, Mitropolis Cathedral (with D. Zezos)

Poetry: Kostis Palamas (1859-1943) and the "New School of Athens,", a patriotic art movement which freed Greek poetry from stilted formalism.

Art: With a few exceptions, painters essentially European in approach, influenced by the academic style of Munich Impressionism after 1900, but Greek in concept. During and after the War of Independence, subjects are frequently patriotic. Theophilos 1873-1934: a Personality himself, naif style. Vryzakis (1814-1878) painter of scenes from the Revolution, often supervised by heaven and showing portraits of all participants. Nikiforos Lytras - school of Munich post-impressionist, Manet-like, interiors and lively figures. Nikolaos Gyzis, very varied oeuvre, from stiff academic to the most free and easy.

Kounelakis (1829-1869) Studied in Russia and Italy, neo-Renaissance.

1896-Olympic games revived, Athens.

1901-New Testament translated into Demotic Greek causes riots with fatalities.

19th CENTURY

Vryzakis

Kounelakis

Lytras

Gyzis

	1915	Venizelos banished. Greece stays neutral.
	1916	Venizelos secedes from Athens and sets up rival govt. in Crete. English/French demand that King Constantine leave: son Alexander succeeds. Venizelos returns as Premier and Greece comes into War on Allied side.
	1919	Allies help Venizelos with invasion of Smyrna. Venizelos goes to diplomatic conferences for next 2 years
	1919-20	Treaty of Sevres (unratified): Greece gains southern Albania, Thrace and mandate over Smyrna. King Alexander dies, some say poisoned. Venizelos loses election. Constantine is recalled. Greek full-scale offensive against Turkey. Kemal Ataturk counterattacks.
Mussolini takes power in Italy	1922-3	Greece loses war. King abdicates in favour of son George II. Greece loses territories in Asia Minor, (settled by Greeks since 1000 B.C.) Treaty of Lausanne decrees exchange of Muslim and Orthodox Christian populations. Over 1,500,000 refugees crowd into Greece. Monarchy is abolished, George II asked to leave.
	1924	Republic of Greece. Many changes of government, pro-and anti-monarchist. Venizelos resigns.
	1928	Venizelos returns from abroad, wins election: Balkan treaties.
The Great Depression	1930	Treaty of Ankara, settling with Turkey
	1932	Economic crises. Government falls: no clear victor in election.
Germany, Rise of Nazism	1935	Restoration of monarchy under George II, after Venizelos' supporters' coup fails.
	1936	Metaxas dictatorship, agreed to by king, leading to fascist regime.
World War II	1939-45	
	1940	Oct 28: Greeks say *OXI* (No) to Italian invasion, though surrounded by Axis, push Italians far into Albania.
		But German invasion succeeds and appoints Italian military governor. Formidable partisan resistance, in spite of famine in Greece. King in Exile. British allies.
Allied Victory	Oct 1944	Liberation of Athens.
Yalta Agreement	1946	Return of George II. Dies 1947. Paul I succeeds
	1946-9	Civil War, bitter fighting between Communists and Government (royalist majority of 1946). Scars remain. U.S. aid via Truman Doctrine of 1947.
	1949	Government under General Papagos.
Korean War	1952	New Constitution. Greece joins NATO.
	1956	Karamanlis elected Prime Minister.
		Lambrakis, leader of Peace movement, murdered. Civil unrest brings government crisis, and Karamanlis departs. Political instability leads to...-
		constitutional crisis with King Constantine and to...-
	1967-74	military Dictatorship of Papadopoulos
	1973	Riots and civil unrest, students' and peoples' protest ends in massacre at Polytechnion.
	1974	Greece partially withdraws from NATO over Turkish invasion of Cyprus. Dictatorship brought down. Monarchy abolished: General election/referendum brings restoration of democratic republic with Karamanlis as Prime Minister.
	1979	Treaty with EEC, taking graded effect over a nine year period.
	1980-1985	First Socialist Government under P.M. Andreas Papandreou.

Greek Culture

Painting

Volonakis (1837-1907) Sea and ships. Savvidis (1858-1927) Romantic landscape.

As the 20th century pervades the world, art and letters become international, even interchangeable. Nevertheless, many Greek artists continue to cherish their unique national heritage as well as absorbing the essence of various contemporary movements.

Painters - Gyzis (1842-1901) Munich impressionist influence. Bouzianis (1885-1959) German Expressionist influence. Parthenis: Romantic, poetic - 30's generation: reminiscent of Redon Maleas: Landscape strange and solid. Papaloukas: haunted knotted landscapes. Kontoglou: (1896-1965) Byzantine throwback: resisted western influence. Gounaropoulos: 1890-8 luminous surreal world blowing in the wind.

1924: beginning of Greek cinema

Architecture: A. Metaxas, 1920-30's Benaki Museum, Ionian Bank, Athenaeum, French Embassy.
Hilton by Vourekas, Vassiliadis and Staikos

Literature: Sikelianos 1884-1951: from new school fo Athens, mystical Kavafi, 1863-1933: history and memory, based in tradition. Kazantzakis 1883-1957: poet (ODYSSEY), critic, novelist, (ZORBA) essayist. Seferis (1900-1971) symbolist poet (1963 Nobel Prize) Elytis: (b 1911) surrealist island poet: (1981 Nobel Prize) Prevelakis (1909-1986) Cretan Critic and teacher, essays, lit. crit. Terzakis A. (1907-1979) Dim. Hadzis (1910-83) Greece past, small town life, working abroad.

Contemporary Painting: Nikos Engonopoulos, personal surrealistic blend. Hadzikiriakos-Gikas (1906-) delicate mosaic landscape. Moralis, (1916-) architectural, semi-abstract, recalls Picasso. Gaitis paints "A Little Man". Kondopoulos: (1905-1975) non-figurative, subtle colour. Sculptor Makris Agamemnon. Engraving: Galanis, A. Tassos, Vasso Katraki, Grammatopoulos

Popular writing: V. Vasilikos. Z. etc Stratis Haviaras, *The Heroic Age*

Music: Composers: Nikos Skalkotas, 1904-49 Innovator in Greek music. Iannis Christou (1926-70), Iannis Xenakis, Dmitri Terzakis. Popular-/Serious Composers: Mikis Theodorakis, Manos Hadzidakis

Maleas

Zach

20th CENTURY

Theophilos

Zoulias

Engonopoulos

Moralis

Gaitis

Zenetos: design for a Cretan village

Tobazis

ATHENS, CITY OF PLURALS

On the borderline between Europe and the Orient, Athens is the first city of the East and the last of the West. Once a group of villages, the modern city is complex, exciting, a time-crazy crossroads between Asia, Africa and Europe. Traffic roars past marble first quarried before Cleopatra kissed Mark Anthony. (She was a Macedonian Ptolemy: the family left The Village 300 years before her birth.) A bronze Hermes is displayed next to the video arcade, along with dresses of a Coptic pattern.

Villages, now local townships, grew up around the centre, with separate local governments, schools, market days. A resident of Pangrati will say he is "going to Athens".

The city of Athena lives cupped by mountains, near natural harbours, and supplied with a lookout hill with a flat top ideal for a fort. The Greek word for the high point of the city is *"acropolis"*. Before the castles there were look-outs and of course, a place of worship to the guardian spirits. A long time later this temple was rebuilt as the Parthenon, dedicated to the patron goddess Athena.

The history of this city is long and bumpy. What you see today is almost all modern, laid out and built since the Greek War of Independence by German architects working for King Otto and centered as always on the Acropolis. Athens has been the capital of Greece since 1834, but not until after World War II did the population of the country move in huge numbers to the city. Escape from the poverty of the countryside, escape from the political troubles of the Civil War and the search for a better education and quality of life pulled thousands into the city - where you have the chance to make enough money to own a car. This influx caused some too-hasty building, during the post-war recovery. Of course, the country has all that fresh air, and now you need the car to get away from Athens. (These are the folk who discovered logic?). Now the city is restoring the lovely old buildings one by one, and creating shady pedestrian walks from traffic-jammed alleys.

Of course, most Athenian residents' souls *really* live in the Village: on holidays, Athenians return home and the city is wonderfully empty of people. And cars.

But the past is still so tangled up with the present that it doesn't seem to be willing to lie down decently. In one day, you may walk on a Roman road, visit a palace where people lived 3,500 years ago, and trip over their broken dinner plates; see a performance of "Midsummer Night's Dream" set in Athens when it was a Frankish Duchy, and played in a theatre built before Philip of Macedon was born, eat a dish whose recipe came with the Turks five hundred years ago, and sleep in a hotel built last month. The past does not die. It twists and dances through today. The 11th century Byzantine church is holding services as you pass and a couple of Italian tourists are holding hands on a Roman bench.

Athens is a city full of surprises. Neat sensible plans go round the corner and come back and step on their own tails. Geometry takes strange forms, as does logic, because the straight road leads you in a circle, parallel roads meet and the crooked winding road may bring you to your destination almost before you started out. Or not. It is a place of contradictions and paradoxes, none of which are mutually exclusive. Questions cannot be answered "yes" or "no" - only as "sometimes", "maybe", "on Thursdays", "tomorrow", or "we hope so". This can inspire some delightful, unplanned, entertainments.

Beaches; fun fairs; sports; art galleries; concerts in the open air; Chinese opera with acrobats; dancing bears: buskers, mimes, dancers peforming in the street; waiters skittering across a busy thoroughfare with trays of iced drinks for tables in the park; buses with steps 3 feet high; Roman mosaic steps... You can discover almost anything in our unpredictable city, under the ruined beauty of the Acropolis. *ATHENS LIVES!*

CITY OF THESEUS: Acropolis and vicinity

The first travel writer, Pausanius, wrote about his visit to Greece in 173 A.D. His reports are generally accepted. But even he wrote about events that were already history, or sometimes rumor, to him. The public buildings of the Acropolis and Agora have been pulled down and rebuilt again and again with the same bits and pieces for thousands of years. And all the while, ancient and classical evidence was removed by art fanciers from Roman times to the 20th century. Even plain broken pottery, so helpful to the archeologist, was carried off as souvenirs. 19th century scholars thought nothing of taking home any portable object of study, and in any case were relying on deductions or educated guesswork. The work of Schliemann, who proved that Homer's poems were based in fact and not fairy tale myth - has brought about a new respect for the reflection of historical events in mythology. Only with the age of scientific archeology, and the deep excavations made after World War II in the Agora and the Keramikos cemetery (see page 61) has solid data begun to emerge, and serious steps toward the preservation of irreplaceable antiquities been taken. Sadly, the combination of atmospheric pollution and an annual trampling by 3 million pairs of feet took a dreadful toll of the marble surface.

The Greek government and UNESCO are taking measures to rescue these world treasures: some have been removed to atmosphere-controlled museums, the Parthenon and other buildings are closed to trampling feet, and protective roofing and scaffolding have had to be provided.

Fortress Acropolis

The Acropolis with its commanding position is the focal point of modern Athens, as it has always been. Citadel of kings fifteen centuries before Christ, refuge in times of war, admirable vantage point from which to address the Gods of Olympus: on this rock the people built their shrines and temples while they lived and traded on the fertile and well-watered land below. When the Cyclopean walls of Mycenae and Tiryns were breached and Pylos devastated by the Dorians, Athens stood firm. Displaced populations swelled its size from prehistory until today.

The rock of limestone is 320 m from East to West, 156 m North to South and 156.2 m. high. It contains springs, and water can be seen streaming from the sides in winter.

The history of Athens and the history of her Acropolis are closely entwined. The first settlers were probably worshippers of the fertility or Mother goddess. The north side of the citadel shows evidence of early religious rites, about 3,000 B.C. These settlers were followed by the Bronze Age "Pelasgians".

The Achaean invasions of 2000-1800 BC brought patriarchy, hunters, herdsmen, and a hierarchy of macho gods and a taste for gold. The combination of cultures became the great Mycenean civilization, from which evolved most of the structure of Classical Greece. Athens was a fortified town, with "Cyclopean" walls - pairs of facing walls of undressed stones so large that only giants like the Cyclops could lift them into place, with a core of rubble and clay filler 15-22 feet thick.

The first legendary king of Athens was Erechthonius/Erechtheus, son of Mother Earth and Hephaistos, raised by Athena, half man and half serpent. Kekrops is said to have been his son, and likewise endowed with a snake's tail. He is credited with introducing monogamy, the reorganization of the tribes of Attica (see p. 18) and the replacement of blood sacrifice by vegetarian offerings - all historical events. He also gave evidence in the case of Athena vs. Poseidon . The Athenian kings wore the golden

serpent as their amulet in honour of this ancestor. And in the late 13th century, a king's palace called by Homer "The Strong House of Erechtheus", was built: palace and walls indicate that Athens was already a military and political force to be reckoned with.

Like King Arthur, the figure of the hero-king Theseus (see page 18) was credited with the social and political reforms that came with the Achaeans, as well as epic deeds. He is considered mythological, but who knows? So many legends are based in history.

And always, the goddess Athena, Protectress of Athens, watched over the Athenians clustered around the Acropolis.

The Dorian invasion brought the destruction of the Mycenean forts. Athens, the only state to ecape destruction became the centre of a city-state, the *polis,* which meant the city and the surrounding common lands. City-states, *demoi* were independent, coexisting by a complicated web of treaties and alliances. The Acropolis was then a religious center rather than a fort, for the next thousand years.

Government changed over the years from monarchy (one king) to aristocracy (government by hereditary nobles) to archonship, (government by officials for one-year terms) to oligarchy (reign by a privileged few) to tyranny (not unlike the kingship, though not hereditary) to democracy (supported however by slavery so the citizens had time for politics). (See page 56)

A period of colonising and trade made Athens a powerful centre. With her increased size and strength the influence of Athens began to spread thoughout the Mediterranean.The invasion of the Dorians was not the end but the beginning of the spread of Greek civilization. As the city traded and prospered, the temples grew in size and beauty.

Political confrontations in the 6th century BC evoked the "tyranny" of Peisistratos - not necessarily a bad thing: this absolute ruler was a reformer and continued to improve his city. Athens annexed Elefsis and Salamis. The Acropolis became a place of worship and the site of many temples. Athena's Hekatompedon (which means "100 feet" presumably a measurement), and other smaller temples, were built along with a great altar for Athena.

In 480, while the Athenians took cover in their ships on the orders of Themistokles, the Persians sacked and burned the city, destroying most of the marble sculptures of the archaic period. Many small bronzes hidden then for centuries are now in the Archeological Museum. The Persians also made a mess of the newly-laid terraces and foundations of an early Parthenon.

Many holy places were purposely left in ruins for thirty years, a generation, because of an oath taken after the Battle of Plataea: We Must Never Forget Rotten Persian Perfidiousness in Burning our Undefended City. When the North wall was rebuilt, parts of the old Temple of Athena and the older Parthenon were incorporated as reminders.

While Themistokles started to put walls all around everything, the top of the Acropolis was repaired to accomodate the frenzy of building that took place under Perikles. His Classical building spree ended with the Erechtheion.

The Parthenon, begining of 19th century.

The years after the birth of Christ brought several sharp changes. The great staircase built by "I, Claudius" covered ancient ramps. Revered by the Romans, desecrated by successive conquerors, Athena was finally abandoned and her city had dwindled to a village before the Greeks once more gained mastery of their fate.

In the third century a new front gate, now named for its French discoverer Beulé (1852), was added. By the 6th century AD all the temples had been converted to Christianity, and within the next 300 years Athens was looted many times: the great statues had been taken to Constantinople. The "Frankish" occupation of Athens began in 1204 (Montferrat and Otho de la Roche), and their Dukes lived in the Propylaia. By 1403 the Parthenon had become not only a church but the Frankish Cathedral.

In 1456 the Turks took over. As Athena had been replaced by the Virgin, the Virgin was replaced by Allah as the Parthenon became a mosque, complete with minarets.

Some years later, the Temple of Nike was removed to accomodate a battery of cannon. Franks (now Venetians) were trying to retake the city.

On 21 September 1687, Venetian troops led by one Morosini set up cannon on Philopappou Hill. The Turkish powder store was kept in the Parthenon. Morosoni commenced firing, and there was a direct hit on a powder keg. The Acropolis burned for 48 hours. The Turks were so shaken by the explosion that they quit... temporarily.

The noble Morosini then removed sculptures from the west pediment and smashed them. He soon abandoned his Athenian venture. By April the Turks had retaken the citadel. They rebuilt their mosque inside the ruins of the Parthenon. The maze of little streets and huts grew up again.

In 1801 Lord Elgin obtained permission to measure, copy, and take a few carved stones. Large parts of the surviving sculptures were removed and taken aboard an overloaded ship, which sank. Eventually, with great effort, the cases were retrieved and brought to an unappreciative England. It was a period of classical architectural revival and antiquarianism. There were many visitors, many of whom took a little something home - a head, a torso, a scrap of stone.

Finally, at the end of the War of Independence, Greece had the citadel of Athens once again, and in 1833 when Athens became the capital, haste was made to remove the crustation of Turkish houses from the famous hill.

In 1875, the archeologist Schliemann paid to have the Frankish tower removed. Since 1876, the Greek government has supported excavations and research, and lately, an immense effort to ensure the preservation of the marbles from pollution. There is also a drive to retrieve the architectural sculptures from England.

The Marble Crown - Buildings of the Acropolis

Site: 07.30-16.
Sun.: 09.00-13

After a gradual climb up deep marble steps, we enter by the **Beulé Gate** (named for the French archeologist who found it in 1852) which was added as an extra defence in ca. 267 AD. Its gateway is lined up with the central door of the Propylaia.

The ascent has often been redesigned. The Late Archaic ramp of the Panathenaic Way is represented by a few polygonal wall remnants. In Classical times this ramp was widened to match the width of the central part of the Propylaia. By Pausanias's day (175 AD) an 80-yard marble staircase had hidden the stairs begun by the Emperor Claudius in 52 AD. At the foot of the steps, just below the Beulé gate, was the shrine of Aphrodite Pandemos, protectress of harlots.

Halfway up the steps on the left is a terraced landing and the base of the Monument of Marcus Agrippa (2nd c. BC). The 29-foot plinth originally held a representation of a quadriga (4-horse chariot). Plutarch reports that Antony and Cleopatra stood there until they blew over in a high wind the year before the real ones died, 31 BC.

A stairway to the spring called **Klepsydra** began here, emerged underneath and followed a gully to the late Roman wellhouse. The spring attracted Neolithic settlers, and became the centre of a nymph-cult. A well-house was built in 460 BC in the small cave from which it flows. Though the roof had fallen in, Mark Antony took water from this well by command of an oracle, in 37 BC. He was then Consul of Eastern Rome (Greece). Water from this spring was piped to the Tower of the Winds (see p. 71) and thus "clepsydra" became a synonym for water clock.

The ruined well-house was later rebuilt and sealed with cement, except for a staircase connecting it with the fortifications above. Frescoes were added when it turned into the Church of the Holy Apostles in Byzantine times. By 1822 the well-house and staircase were buried, though the spring bubbled into a Turkish fountain down the hill. Not knowing that the source was accessible, the besieged Turks surrendered the Acropolis owing to lack of water, whereupon the Greeks found and repaired Klepsydra. In 1826 it was enclosed in a bastion, and supplied the Greeks during the siege of 1827. From here to Propylaia we mount the modern zigzag ramp, not unlike the Mycenaean entrance, to the wood-protected classical stairs.

Infotip Admission to the Acropolis is separate from admission to the Ancient Agora, and also from the South Slope-Theatre area. Make sure you are going in to the site you want!

12
13
14
8
7
4
3
6
2
5
1
15

ACROPOLIS Diagram

1. Beulé Gate
2. Klepsydra
3. Propylaia
4. North wing. Art Gallery
5. Temple of Athena Niké
6. Temple of Artemis of Vravrona (Brauron)
7. Chalkotheke
8. Parthenon
9. Site of Present Museum
10. Temple of Rome and Augustus
11. Temple of Pandion (A hero)
12. Altar of Athena
13. Erechtheion
14. House of the Arrephorai
15. Odeon of Herod Atticus
16. Stoa of Eumenes
17. Asklepion
18. Theatre of Dionysos
19. Odeon of Perikles
20. Tripods, Choregic Monuments

Propylaia

Propylaia is a monumental gateway designed by Mnesikles. It was meant to extend grandly across the whole width of the Acropolis, parallel with the Parthenon. It doesn't: it's lopsided. The Propylaia was begun as soon as the Parthenon was finished (437-432), in a flush of enthusiasm which was squelched by the war with Sparta and lack of funds. On top of this, priests of the temple of Artemis of Vravrona (see Mythology, page 16) objected strenuously to the intrusion of a new wall into their sacred precincts just behind the Propylaia. So plans were altered and readjusted and the job was never quite completed. The cost of 2012 talents was paid from the treasuries of Athena and Hephaistus, from selling old building rubble, rent of houses and private funds and contributions. (Perikles was unjustly accused of spending the Delian treasure on this project, which seems to have brought on a good deal of unseemly wrangling, what with one thing and another.)

It has been used for all kinds of purposes: the bishops' residence in Byzantine times, the chancery of the Duke of Athens, the palace of Nerio Acciaoli. Later, during the Turkish era, the Turkish commander covered Propylaia with a cupola and stored gunpowder in it, even though he too was living there. Perhaps he was depending on someone to keep it safely damp...

...They forgot to, because when it was struck by lightning (1640) the gunpowder exploded and the architraves of the east portico and two Ionic columns fell to bits. When Morosini bombarded it the west facade and the great ceiling were demolished.

Except for its Eleusinian blackstone decorations it is made of Pentelic marble, like all extant buildings of the Acropolis. The Central Hall is 78 ft long, 60 ft wide, with Doric hexastyle porticoes facing east and west, and wings on either side. Up 4 steps and 65 ft wide, the West portico on the left leads to a vestibule. Spaces between the columns align with the 5 doors.

Running through the central hall there was a famous ceiling, coffered and painted blue with gold stars, supported by 18-foot marble beams resting on Ionic columns. This ceiling seems to have survived until 1687. An inner colonnade supports the ceiling as the Propylaia incorporates the rise of the ground. Here Mnesikles used Ionic order columns which could be tall without losing grace. One of those Ionic columns. 33.5 feet high, has been restored, with a scrap of the famous ceiling. Two complete Doric columns remain with a height of 29 ft.

In the north wing a frieze of triglyphs and metopes is still to be seen on the architrave, and the walls of the back room still stand. Its art gallery (Pinakotheke) exhibited the works of Polygnotos, a painter of 450 BC. The south wing had to be smaller because of the sanctuary of Artemis Vravronia. It has no rear chamber, and has been slightly chambered on the SE corner to accomodate those priests of Artemis.

Temple of Athena Nike

The tiny (12 x 18 ft) TEMPLE OF ATHENA NIKE stands on the south wing of the Propylaia on a clifflike platform, which was once a Mycenaean outwork. The altar and contents of the original temple were lost in the Persian raids of 480. In 449 a new temple was planned, and designed by Kallikrates (a contractor who also worked on the Parthenon) but due to differences of opinion his design was modified, and finally built by 424. It was reconstructed in the 1830's and again, just before 1914 rebuilt with a strengthened bastion.

It stands on a base of three steps and has an Ionic portico of four columns either end. A high relief frieze surrounds the whole building. Four sections are cement casts of originals in the British Museum. Gods who have lost their heads occupy the East front, and Athena with her shield. Battle scenes decorate the other sides - Plataea, Boeotia and Athenians fighting Persians. Once there was a marble statue inside, with the Goddess holding the pomegranate of fertility in her right hand and her war helmet in her left.

"Athena Niké" means "Athena of Victory": Niké, Victory, is a winged goddess, but Athena, Our Lady of Victory, is naturally not winged. Pausanias claims that the Athenians had stripped Athena Nike of her wings so she would stay put in Athens. A calumny. A band of winged Victories attend Athena on the relief of the parapet surrounding the Pyrgos (platform).

Legend claims that it was from here that Aegeus the father of Theseus maintained the watch for his son's ship, returning to Phaleron harbour from his adventures in Crete. If the sails were black, as they had been on departure, it meant that Theseus had failed: if white, he was victorious. Theseus forgot and left the black sails. His father thought his son was dead and threw himself off the rock. Other versions say this happened at Sounion.

Temple of Artemis of Vravrona (Remains)

From the Propylaia and bearing to the right Pausanias says, "There is also a sanctuary of Brauronian (Vravronian) Artemis, with its statue by Praxiteles. The goddess gets her name from the country place Brauron, where her ancient wooden cult-statue still is. They call her the Artemis of Tauris..." It was said to be the very same that Iphigenia and Orestes brought back from Tauris (see Mythology, page 20). This temple dated from the time of Peisistratos.

The *Chalkotheke* (bronze storehouse) stood between here and the Parthenon. This could have been a sculpture gallery - or an arsenal of spears and swords.

Emerging from the shade of the gateway, it is suddenly clear how the city nestles among the pine-covered hills. Here, high above the modern city, the traffic is unheard. It is easy to feel the ancient sense of a holy place, and a safe retreat.

A continual rise in the ground leads to the steps of the Parthenon. The marble surface of the path was scored with deep cuts to afford a foothold in Classical times.

INFOTIP Watch out. It is still slippery.

Statues stood in those square pedestal-depressions along the way: one was of Perikles; and another, the 30-foot gold-helmeted Athena Promachos (Champion), contemporary equivalent of a flashing red light, signaled her presence to ships sailing up from Sounion. This statue, by Pheidias, was meant as a celebration of the victory at Marathon. Eventually it was taken to Constantinople where in 1203 a drunken mob, blaming her beckoning gesture for the imminent arrival of the Fourth Crusade, destroyed it.

The Parthenon

The PARTHENON was the home of the cult statue of Athena the Virgin - and the ever - increasing treasury.

In spite of the broken columns, missing roof, fallen walls, the temple remains a supreme expression of harmony, art and mathematics. The appalling desecrations it has sustained tear the heart with a sorrow that intensifies its beauty. Against a blue sky the marble of a shattered column is delicately modulated ivory; on a cloudy day they turn gold, glowing against the gray: on a day when the atmospheric pollution is heavy and brown, the columns become iridescent.

The building of the Parthenon was one of those rare occasions when everything went right, everybody on cue and giving his best performance, the right time and place, the right financing - even though the original architect, Kallikrates, was dumped from the project when Perikles (the activist reformer) came into power, and Iktinos was given the commission. Nobody argued about Pheidias: he was the best of architectural sculptors. He, his rivals and students all worked on the carvings.

It is a triumph of subtle optical illusions, the width, spacing and shapes of the columns have been designed to seem taller, lighter and more tapered than they really are. Columns are slightly swollen in the center *(Entasis)*: even the base *(Stylobate)* is curved rather than straight.

Parthenon: the East Pediment.

It was constructed of Pentelic marble, probably with a wooden ceiling: The friezes and metopes (friezes interrupted by geometric motifs) were picked out in bright blues and reds and golds, as were the complex reliefs of the pediments. Inside, the ceiling was panelled in dark blue with gold stars - an accurate night sky - zodiac circle - constellations?

(For the numerically minded, it is 8 columns wide by 17 long, making 46 in all, and measures 95 x 213 ft. The columns are 6.25 feet at the base and 34.5 high, with 20 flutings apiece and 10-12 drums. The apex of the pediment, 59 feet from the top step. Originally there were 14 metopes at each end and 32 each side, making a total of 92. These are scattered from the British Museum to the Louvre to the Acropolis Museum.

The western facade was actually the back. The original West Pediment showed the legend of the contest between Athena and Poseidon over Athens (See·Erechtheion, below), the legendary first king Kekrops on the left with his daughter, and a woman representing the Kallirois spring on the right. Behind the columns of the facade was the wall of the chamber behind the temple, which was used as a treasury

The Sacred Way (Iera Odos) ran along the northern colonnade to the pronaos - the ante - temple -, past the double set of columns with the inner Ionic frieze in which young men and their horses are preparing for the Panathenaic procession.

When the Parthenon was converted to Christianity this pronaos was destroyed, traces only remain. There were paintings on the walls, and votive offerings were left here. An outer Doric Frieze showing Athenians warring against Giants, Amazons, Centaurs is almost obliterated, parts having been taken to the British Museum or the Acropolis Museum.

The Eastern pediment was over the main entrance, which faced Hymettos, and showed the birth of Athena. Most of the originals were appropriated by Lord Elgin and are now in the British Museum.

Pheidias, as Top Man, had the privilege of carving the gold and ivory Athena for the inner cella, the "Chamber of the Virgin", which contemporary writings acclaimed as one of the masterpieces of the world. According to evidence pieced together from contemporary accounts and later copies, this statue was of gold plate over a wooden inner core and 39 feet high, including pedestal. Her face and hands and feet were ivory, and the pupils of her eyes were jewels. She wore a long dress, and an *aegis* (breastplate) of the snake-haired Medusa in ivory. Her right hand held Victory (a small goddess thereof) and her left a gold-tipped spear. On her helmet was a Sphinx, with low relief carved griffins on either side. Centaurs and Lapiths battled on her sandals. The shield leaning against her legs showed the battle of the Amazons and the Athenians. A self-portrait of Pheidias in this carving and one of Perikles caused a scandal - blasphemy! On the other side of the shield was a battle of giants. Even the pedestal had a story on it, this time Pandora's birth. All the gold work was designed to be quickly detachable in case of emergency. Poor Pheidias was eventually accused of stealing the gold from his own creation.

The only way to enter the Temple was through the great doors and antechamber on the Eastern end. The statue stood at the far side of the inner chamber, lit by votive lamps, her golden armor flashing through the smoke of incense and sometimes the reek of sacrificial slaughter floating through the doors. One wonders if worshippers dropped in with their offerings of statuettes, oil, or flowers and chatted with their neighbours under her benign gaze, as worshippers do today...

Nero Acciaioli, who took Athens from a Sicilian duke in 1386, celebrated his victory by building a huge "Frankish tower" 90 feet high on the southwest corner.

It is no longer permitted to go inside the Parthenon.

North-West corner of the Temple.

left: The Calf-bearer. right: The Eutycides Koré, a masterpiece of 5th century BC.

Acropolis Museum

Continuing around the Acropolis, we come next to the **Acropolis Museum** which contains a superb collection of archaic and classical sculptures. Owls and snakes were sacred to Athena, and a great Owl greets Museum visitors, while others guard the doorways of the rooms. The 6th c. BC was a period of development in sculpture, as in politics and economics. A piece showing lionesses killing calves remains from this period.

During the Archaic period themes from myth and an emphasis on the human replaced contesting animals. The first marble statues appear: the Calf-bearer (Gallery II, No. 624) is one of the earliest. Here are pediment sculptures, still brightly coloured, showing Herakles having an argument with cheerful sea serpents. From the same temple comes a marvellous rendition of a bull in extremis, vanquished by the claws of two lions.

When the Old Temple was rebuilt (525 BC) marble was used on the pediment of the building: and whole bevies of marble "kores" - maidens - were dedicated to Athens, and are to be found in the Museum. Their dresses are enthusiastically pleated, patterned and often coloured. The word *agalma* - statue - comes from a verb meaning "to rejoice": the kores were joy-gifts to the goddess. Gallery IV shows a variety of these girls with quite distinctive differences. Their heads were once protected from bird droppings by iron shades. The same gallery displays the "Rampin Horseman" the oldest known statue of a rider, with an incredible coiffure.

A huge Athena from the pediment of the Old Temple, with a flowing cape trimmed with snake-lace, and disposing of some giants, dominates Gallery V. In an alcove are some small objects found on the Acropolis and nearby in the 1950's.

Slab from the west frieze of the Parthenon.

The great Classical period of Perikles and the Parthenon brought the finest sculpture of all time. From the stiff poses of the previous century, figures acquire flowing balanced grace. The Ephebes (underage youths), and the pensive Athena relief (Nos. 698, 689, 695) demonstrate phases leading from the archaic to the high classical. Then, in Gallery VII, we find fragments from the pediment of the Parthenon - Kekrops and his daughter, whose bodies express their relationship with complete clarity; Poseidon, Selene the Moon Goddess with her horses; a Centaur battling with a Lapith, and fine heads of horses are followed by a large gallery containing Parthenon friezes. All these are attributed to the designs of Pheidias, though other hands worked on them.

In the same gallery are some parts of the Erechtheion frieze, showing the contrast of coloured marbles, and lovely small plaques from the Nike temple by different artists.

Marble converts to gypsum in the presence of sulfur and the caryatid maidens from the Erechtheion, now safely in a climate - controlled case, have already suffered from the fume-laden air.

Outside the Museum was probably the masons' workshop, where roughed out carvings were completed and paints mixed. Looking over the ramparts, see on the south slope the theatres of Dionysus and Herod Atticus: on the Hill of the Muses to the west is the peculiar Monument of Philopappus, a rich Syrian. From there, where cannons were installed, those Venetians shot at the Parthenon.

Near the Museum we find columns from the tiny temple of Rome and Augustus, a Roman mini-version of the Erechtheion. On the highest point of the Acropolis are marks of the former temple of Zeus Polias: and then the 19th century **Belvedere**, where the Greek flag flies till sunset when it is very solemnly taken down by a guard of honour of Evzones to the strains of the National Anthem. From this viewpoint, one can see the slopes of Hymettos, once topped by statuary, now by a radar station.

On the north side between the Belvedere and the Erechtheion are traces of earlier buildings and the spot where the Altar of Athena Polias (of the city) stood: but the main feature is the Erechtheion.

Erechtheion

According to prehistoric legend, Poseidon and Athena fought over fertile Attica, especially Athens. Poseidon struck the Acropolis with his trident and brought forth the spring of sea-water called Erechtheis, while Athena planted an olive tree. The agrument was referred to Olympus for decision and it was ruled that Athena had offered a better deal to the population. Poseidon stomped off in a huff, but he had many worshippers. The temple was named either for the spring, or for Erechtheus, the early king of Athens.

It is now impossible to decipher the plan of the interior. In 406, when it was barely completed, there was a fire. There were two main chambers for cult statues, one of standing Athena with shield, and one of Poseidon. This Athena was carved in olive wood, and every four years was ceremonially re-dressed in the Sacred Peplos, a robe newly rewoven, at the Panathenaic Festival. An eternal flame that needed oil only once a year burned before her.

Fire, storm and warfare caused continual reconstruction. In the 6th century it became a church and the in side was rebuilt several times. In 1463, the church became the harem of the Turkish commander.

In the nineteenth century, the culture vultures descended and began to "rescue" antiquities; the long War of Independence caused damage and storms knocked great chunks of it to rubble. In 1903-9 the exterior was almost completely restored.

Porch of the Karyatides on the Erechteion.

The Erechtheion is built on several levels, basically a rectangle with a porch on each side. On the East there are five Ionic columns supporting a plain pediment: the sixth column was "rescued" by Lord Elgin. These columns are 22 ft high by 2.5 ft at the base. The back wall was removed to make the Christian alterations. Stairs descended from the North porch to a paved court. This porch had Ionic columns, a grey marble frieze, panelled ceiling and decorated door. Deeper down were the serpent guardians of the temple. Other steps lead to the Pandroseion, an area with a small temple containing the sacred olive of Athena. The original tree survived many disasters and was planted near an ancient waterpipe, clearly meant to water Something Important, and has been replaced several times. Yet another precinct was sacred to Kekrops, the first Athenian king, built around the block over the tomb of the king. The West facade was restored to its 1st century B.C. form in 1904. It was a high basement; three windows; columns joined by a low wall.

The South Porch is the one with the caryatides, the maidens who hold up the roof on their heads. In 1827 only three damaged ladies remained. These were restored, but recently they have been replaced by copies in fiberglass and removed to the museum for safekeeping from atmospheric pollution.

Imagine this temple with its high-relief frieze almost all around it, made of white marble on dark grey stone. The capitals of the columns were painted gold and red and blue, and the ceiling was again dark blue with gold stars. The steps and small chambers inside must have given it a mysterious atmosphere: incenses and chanting, and probably some competition between the devotees of Poseidon and of Athena...

Strolling back to the Propylaia, the foundations of the **House of the Arrephorai** are on our right. Pausanias describes these: "Virgin girls live not far from the Temple of Athena in the City: the Athenians call them the Bearers. For a certain time they have their living from the goddess: and when the festival comes round they have to perform certain ceremonies during the night. They carry on their heads what Athena's priestess gives them to carry, and neither she who gives it nor they who carry it know what it is she gives them. In the city not far from Aphrodite-in-the-Gardens (undiscovered) is an enclosed place with a natural entrance to an underground descent: this is where the virgin girls go down. They leave down there what they were carrying, and take another thing and bring it back covered up. They are then sent away, and other virgin girls are brought to the Acropolis in their places..." This ritual may have been a fertility rite involving symbols like bread or eggs, or perhaps the Sacred Peplos of Athena. Two possible stairways have been discovered, one descending from North to South, and one going West to East with a Turkish period top flight, which leads to a covered Mycenaean stairway going 110 feet down to a spring.

Between this site and the gate stood the chapel of the Frankish dukes. Before reaching the Propylaia, cross an ancient drain to the cisterns, probably left from Justinian, 530 A.D.

Areopagus

Just below the Acropolis gates is the Hill of Ares, a rocky promontory whose slippery steps can be ascended today (with the right footwear). Here met the Areos Pagos, a council of nobles who were a combination of supreme court, curia, and senate. Here Orestes was tried for the murder of his mother, Clytemnestra.

St. Paul was summoned here to explain his teachings. He was not on trial but given a hearing as a matter of public interest. His famous sermon on the Unknown God so impressed an Areopagite senator that he was converted to Christianity and eventually became St. Dionysius (St. Denis).

The Ancient Agora

ɔen: 08.45-15.00
ın.: 09.30-14.30

ıtrances:
drianou Street
ateia Thission
ıot the station),
ıd below
cropolis.

Below the Acropolis to the north are the ruins of St. Dionysius' Church of the 16th Century, situated just above in the town centre of Athens - the ancient Agora. An open space dotted with cypresses, statues and ruins lying in long grass, it is a peaceful place to stroll. Once, intellectual, commercial and political life was centered here. The Agora was the city's main shopping centre, political forum, meeting place. The name comes from similar words - "to buy" and "to talk". Athenians were and still are people whose heart is in public life: Athenian men still live on the street - or cafeneio - more than in their houses. Here was the place to which all roads led, the Panathenaic way from the Dipylon, the Sacred Way to Eleusis, the road to the Academy, the road to Phaleron or later Piraeus. Shady colonnades, benches, statuary, and of course, temples and shrines, sprang up.

As the place of public buildings, the history of the Agora is mixed with Greek political history, while the history of the Acropolis goes from military to religious (and back). The Acropolis was "the city *(Polis)*" and the Agora and houses were the Asty.

In Mycenean times, the area was a burial ground. Later, the open space was used for dramatic presentations and athletics.

Before the 7th c. BC, under kings and aristocrats, citizens and peasants had a hard time of it. Those in debt could be enslaved by their creditors. Peasants and craftsman could not vote. Archons, the

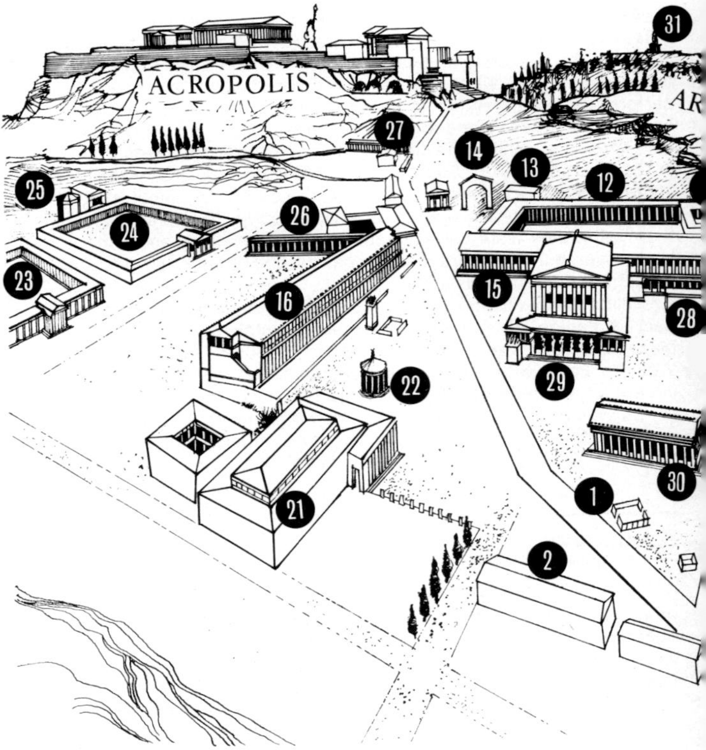

officials elected for one year, weren't much better, and retired archons were automatically admitted to the Areopagos (court/senate), which waxed fat and powerful.

But times were changing. Newly rich traders, knights and landowners were beginning to challenge the old ways. The punitive laws of Dracon (621 BC) corrected some of the abuses of power. A generation later in Solon's day, the lower classes were able to participate in the Boule (Parliament - a council of 400) and the People's Assembly, the *Ecclesia*.

Civil rights went to their heads, apparently, because there were thirty years of squabbling and anarchy thereafter, not sorted out until the advent of the tyrant Peisistratos. His heir Hippias really was a tyrant, and was dumped. About 508 BC Kleisthenes reorganized the state. Three Districts, each containing ten "trittyes" were now called a tribe - but instead of letting them be made up of neighboring areas, they were combined of one each from Town, Coast and Inland, which meant there were now ten completely new "tribes" whose former rivalries and loyalties were no longer operative.

With 50 representatives from each of the ten tribes, the *Boule* Parliament became a council of 500. Officers elected by lot took 5-week turns as *prytanis* (chairman). They elected an *epistates* (chief) who governed with a committee of 9 *proedroi* (presidents) and a secretary. "Ostracism" was established as a way for citizens to get rid of an offending personage for ten years, and the Agora was fenced off with wooden channels where voters passed to cast their secret ballots - names scrawled on scraps of

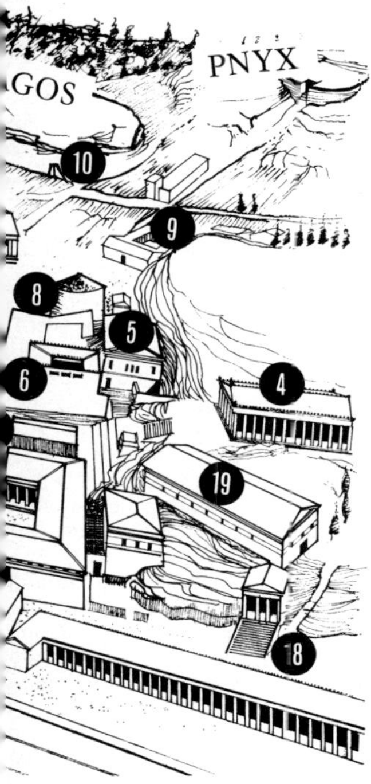

Ancient Agora Diagram

Classical Period

1. Altar of the Twelve Gods
2. Stoa (?)
3. Stoa of Zeus Eleftherios
4. Hephaisteion (Thission)
5. Boulefterion (Council House)
6. Metroon
7. The Heroes
8. Tholos
9. Strategeion (Generals)
10. Shrine
11. Heliaia (Law Courts)
12. Stoa, later part of Square
13. SE Fountain House
14. Mint
    Socrates Prison

Hellenistic Period

15. Middle Stoa
16. Stoa of Attalos
17. Royal Stoa
18. Temple of Aphrodite Ourania
19. Arsenal (?)
20. Temple of Apollo Patroos

Roman Period

21. Basilica
22. Monopteron
23. Library of Hadrian
24. Roman Agora
25. Tower of the Winds
26. Library of Pantainos
27. Eleusinion
28. Temple
29. Odeon of Agrippa
30. Temple of Ares
31. Monument of Philopappou

pottery. Hundreds of these shards have been found in the Agora and Keramikos.

Even generals were subject to election: each tribe had to vote annually for their war chief. These were not only in charge of the army and navy, but also political magistrates.

The round, domed Tholos (479 BC) was the HQ and dining room of this Council of Five Hundred. At the end of the **Tholos** was the Parliament, Boulefterion. This building was replaced again and again: the present ruin is 5th century B.C. (The files were kept in the Mothers' building, the Metroon: the latest version is from the 2nd Century B.C. built on ancient foundations.) East of the Metroon was a long pedestal which held bronze statues of The Ten Heroes whose names were given to those tribes created by Kleisthenes. Later others were added as more tribes developed. Public notices - printed with charcoal on white painted boards - were mounted at their feet. Two tripods also perched here.

Even under the Roman conquest the influence of Athens was great. Near the Metroon was the great drain constructed in Kleisthenes' time. (A headless statue of Hadrian was found here, believed to be contemporary with his reign, it bore a sculptured decoration showing a crowned Athena standing on the wolf which was suckling Romulus and Remus - surely the finest tribute ever paid to a subject city.)

When the Persians came ravaging in 480 BC, down went most of the contemporary building. Afterwards, the west side was repaired and new public buildings went up during the Perikles Push era. (Perikles was elected general every year from 443 to 429: by the time he died the powers of the Areopagus had been transferred to the Assembly.)

At the corner of the market place stood a stone inscribed' "I am the borderstone of the Agora". Near this stone, at the shop of Simon, the cobbler, Socrates was wont to spend his time in friendly discussion (the cobbler was perhaps a poet like the sandal-maker in Pandrossou today).

It was in the Hellenistic and Graeco-Roman periods that most of the buildings still visible were constructed, though the Altar of Zeus was carved in the 4th century BC but placed in situ in the 1st. **Apollo Patroos** of the Ionians was where public officials took their oaths: his statue by Euphranor is in the Stoa Museum, his temple was built in the days of Alexander, 330 B.C. Older remnants of shrines to Zeus and Athena of the Brotherhoods adjoin.

But when Sulla took and ravaged Athens in 86 BC, the Agora area was (of course) laid waste. From 20 BC to the 2nd c. AD, a new building era began. Agrippa (Marcus Vipsanius) built a concert hall (Odeon) in 15 BC: new temples and the Library of Pantainos were added. By 100 AD, Roman and Greek Agoras were joined with a mall.

The Gothic Barbarian invasion of 267 AD put an end to it. The Stoa of Attalos was built into a wall, and the Agora, now outside the wall of the shrunken city, was abandoned. From 400 AD to 500 AD another burst of activity produced a Gymnasium for the University, and later the conversion of the Temple of Hephaistos to Christianity. It was again forgotten. In the 11th century Athenians began once more to settle there, until it was again a busy town center. The Church of the Holy Apostles was built in 1000.

No sooner had the settlement beenreestablished than Athens was invaded from Nauplia and again ruined. Again came the barbarous hordes, and then the area was deserted: the water drains silted up, the ground level was buried. Slowly it was resettled in the late 1600's, only to be wrecked again during the War of Independence in the early 19th Century.

When Athens became the capital of the new nation there were a few houses. As people began to flood into the city, buildings went enthusiastically up all over the place, and the Agora was a small village by 1931 when excavations by German, American and Greek archeologists began to reveal the treasures under the silt.

Stoa of Attalos

On the eastern edge of the Agora is the Stoa of Attalos (about 140 BC) restored with materials from the original quarries by the American School of Classical Studies, an astonishingly beautiful building. To walk its length today is to know how welcome this cool shade is in the burning summer sun. It was a shopping arcade from which Athenians watched processions like the Panathenaic, perhaps sipping cooled drinks at small tables belonging to a wineshop.

Today the Stoa is a Museum housing thousands of items found in the Agora, and special exhibitions. Admission is included with the ticket to the Agora.

The Stoa is two stories high, 382 feet long and 66 ft wide with a colonnade of 45 Doric columns downstairs and Ionic upstairs. There were twenty one shops on each floor: and of course, there were statues.

The ground floor displays sculpture found on the site. The "Patroos Apollo", statues of the "Iliad" and the "Odyssey" which probably adorned the lost library of Pantainos may be found here, among the graceful classical figures. Ten shop-areas are arranged in chronological order from the Neolithic to the Turkish Occupation with many everyday or political objects - make-up cases, voting discs, *ostraka* (some of which are written with the names of Themistokles, Kimon and even Perikles, of whom somebody apparently had had enough), a clock for timing legal arguments in court, even a child's potty. A head of Nike shows traces of the gold leaf hammered finish. A shield taken from the Spartans at Sphakteria (425 BC), coins and ovens and pottery and portraits - all the detritus of a busy city centre over two and a half millenia...

Partial view of the Agora, with church of Agioi Apostoli and Hephaistion.

Hephaistion

On a rise to the west of the Agora stands the temple of Hephaistos, god of metal workers, which was completed after the building boom on the Acropolis. The HEPHAISTION was wrongly identified as a temple to King Theseus instead of to the god of ironmongery and volcanoes (who must be much better-tempered than he appears: chap had a lot to put up with - lameness, ever-loving Aphrodite for a wife, people mixing up his temples...)

This temple is the most complete Doric hexastyle building remaining. It has been attributed to Kallikrates, architect of the Sounion and Rhamnous temples. The peristyle consists of 6 by 13 columns. it is built of Pentelic marble with Parian marble sculptural decoration. The optical tricks of size and shape used on the Parthenon were used on the Hephaistion: but since the columns are smaller and the enteblature heavier, and the whole thing shorter, it doesn't attain the floating quality of the Parthenon. The metopes show nine-twelfths of the labours of Hercules, and the eastern metopes show eight of Theseus' adventures, which is why it was thought to be the Theseion,where Theseus was said to be buried.

The eastern wing still has its coffered ceiling, as well as an Ionic frieze of heroes in battle. The cella (inner chamber) was altered by its conversion to St. George's Church in the 7th century. For a while in the 19th century it was a Protestant cemetery - an epigraph of Byron adorns the memorial of George Watson. Graves were dug into the marble floors, probably in the middle ages. The plants outside the building represent the same herbs that were always there...

Descendants of the metal workers who worshipped Hephaistos still ply their trade in the area, and his name is still celebrated in the central street of the Monastiraki Sunday morning flea market - Ifestou. This continued use of the area for over four and a half centuries may account for the fact that the Hephaistion is the best preserved in the whole of Greece. Who would treat this temple with disrespect with the smiths wielding their hammers close by?

The open, grassy temple area was the centre of great rejoicing in the year following the end of Turkish rule. A contemporary account tells of people arriving from far and wide, singing and dancing on the grass. The trees and shrubs that now cover the area were planted later and were chosen to replace those mentioned in ancient records.

The Sacred Way (Iera Odos) and the Panathenaic Way, leading from Acropolis through the Agora, passed out of the city at Keramikos.

Leaving the Agora at Adrianou Street and turning left it is a short walk to Keramikos, passing the 12-Century church of Agion Assomaton on Ermou Street.

Keramikos

Entrance:
148 Ermou Str.
Elektriko and
Bus Stop Thissio
Open: 09.00-15.0

In the Keramikos area the potters, like the smiths, were well supplied with water. The name is ancient - Keramos was said to be the son of Dionysos and Ariadne - but ceramic has come to mean pottery everywhere.

The area was divided by the city walls and, as it was customary to bury the dead outside the city, the roads leading away from the gates were lined with tombs. Many beautiful pottery jars have been found in the Keramikos graves and were used as monuments. Many later stone monuments were made in the shape of the ceramic vases.

Those whom the city wished to honour were buried here, in magnificent tombs, outside the city's most important gates.

The smaller one was known as the Sacred Gate, the beginning of the Sacred Way (Iera Odos) leading to Elefsis where the mysteries of Demeter were held.

The larger double gate led directly to the Academy, of which Plato was a senior professor.

From the entrance bearing right is a mound from which to survey the grounds. To the right is a 200 yard section with two spaces for the gates. Down at the walls, one can peer though gaps at the several accretions of the inner wall, layers of Periclean stone, grey acropolis stone from Konon,Demosthenes' white limestone, ending with Justinian's contributions to the city's fortifications. Alongside the **Sacred Way** is a sluggish stream, Eridanos. The lower parts of the precinct are swampy; watch for frogs as you step over the water on the bridges provided. A tall stand of brilliant orange lilies crosses the field of vision against the green of the alga on the water. The stream was enclosed in a channel alongside the Sacred Way and used to carry waste from the Agora.

To the right are new excavations. To the left is the large **Pompeion** used as a dressing room and storage space for the great processions and festivals. There is evidence of a space enclosed by 13 columns by 6, with small rooms on the north and west: dining rooms, dressing rooms. The gate shows the metal clamps holding the marble in place - quite unnecessarily, since those blocks haven't budged in 2500 years - and the places for the door hardware. Beyond this is the **Dipylon**, the great double gate used by most of the traffic... A wide road led from the Agora. Facing away from Athens, on the right is a fountain house, then the remains of the two mighty towers that guarded the entrance. From the Sacred Gate the road led to the precincts of Elefsis and another branched off to Piraeus.

Following the road back toward the Church of Agia Triada, we begin to see signs of pedestals and plinths. Down under the church is a partially excavated monument hung over with a curtain of greenery, and disappearing into the darkness under the road above.

Bearing left around the church and across the stream again, we come to the Street of the Tombs, lined with pedestals bearing all kinds of funerary monuments to wealthy Athenians. The Monument of Dionysus of Kollytos sports a wild bull, high on a pillar stele: next to him is a fine dog. This road ends with steps, which lead under a busy road so that no excavations can be made at present. A cross street holds the tombs of the actors Makareus and Hieronymus: many of these are family plots , with representations and stones to various family members.

The **Oberlaender Museum** of Keramikos has on display the Dexileos Monument, several stelae and relief sculptures, and terra cotta figurines and vases found in the tombs. Important finds include an early pot depicting a horse (labelled the ur-pferd), and a Phoenician bowl which is one of the oldest Near Eastern objects found in Greece. Some charming statuettes with their arms overhead are meant to hold offerings, and there are some toys and mementoes from the graves of children. The labels are in German and Greek.

Stelae in Keramikos cemetery.

The Academy of Plato

From the "Dipylon" (Double) Gate of Keramikos a broad road led directly to the Academy. The modern roads called "Salamis" and "Platonos", at the rear of Keramikos, roughly follow the route. This road passes a square called Platea Akademias Platonos, but the site is half a mile further on.

West of the railway stations is an area called "Kolonos" which is named for the hill where Oedipus took refuge.

Bus No. 051, Athens/Platonos, departs from Menandrou 53, north of Omonia: ask for the Academy as this is not the terminus.

Athens had three gymnasia whose origins are lost in time. One of the most important aspects of a young man's life was gymnastic training, and the sports and games which were so popular were not merely for fun. Cities were always vulnerable to attack and when the need arose the citizens turned soldier - or sailor if the battle was at sea. The Pan-Hellenic (Olympic, naturally) games which took place at Olympia every four years were of great importance - so much so that warring cities declared a temporary cessation of hostilities while their young men competed. It was always the hope that a spectacular win by one's own man would give a boost to morale and, of course, be a psychological blow to the enemy.

The gymnasia were situated near shrines outside the city and all a young man's education took place there. Solon passed a law imposing the death penalty on anyone who stole clothes from them. The exercises and competitions took place in the nude and theft must have become an intractable problem to call forth such a penalty.

The gymnasia in Athens became famous also as schools of philosophy. The largest of these was dedicated to Akademos (Hecademos) and gave the world the name by which the highest learning became known.

In the fifth century BC it had grown sufficiently in size and importance for there to be a water shortage. Kimon, extending the amenities of the city, had a stream diverted to provide flowing water and created running tracks and shady walks. "The young man of healthy body and mind" wrote Aristophanes in CLOUDS, "will go down to the Academy, and beside the sacred olives will run off races with his modest friends, fragrant with bryony and apragmosyne, delighting in the springtime when the plane whispers to the elm." A delightful prospect!

In the following century the Academy reached the peak of its fame under Plato, who lived by Kolonos hill, a quarter of a mile to the east. According to an account by Aelian, Aristotle made himself so unpleasant to Plato in his later years that he left the shady grove where he was wont to philosophize and returned to his own garden. Xenocrates, on hearing of this, turned Aristotle away and restored Plato to his customary place. Academic rivalry is, by this account, no new phenomenon!

Excavations are in progress in the Academy area, where Platonos crosses Alexandreos and beyond, much of the foundations have been discovered, including a brick floor in almost perfect condition.

The Academy was reconstructed in Roman times and much of the remains now being excavated belong to that era. However, the boundary stone found on the eastern edge, at the side of Aimonos Street, dates back to the 6th century BC. This road formed the north-east boundary and still follows its original course, ignoring the present-day street grid sytem.

Philopappou

From the main gates at Keramikos the walls rose south to Philopappou Hill. The road over the electric railway cutting follows the approximate line. On the other side of the railway is Eptahalkou,

Monument of Philopappus.

a little back-street which has recently been paved with marble - the authorities of Modern Athens being also proud of their city. On the left, the tiny church of St. Athanasios perches high on a rock.

Across Eptahalkou, continue down a couple of blocks to Iraklidon, recently humming with traffic from morning till late at night but now slumbering in tree-lined tranquility. The tarmac has been removed to reveal the Victorian tram-lines which lie exposed on the rough surface between the mature trees, and make one think one has stepped accidentally into Athens of the 1800's. A substantial section of the wall has been revealed below road level and it can be traced again on adjacent Philopappou Hill, though you may have to dodge among the bushes to find it.

The original walls were extended and reinforced by Themistokles at the time of the Persian wars. He first fortified Piraeus (beginning in 493 BC) for use as a port in place of Faliron which was hard to defend. The greater part of the city of Athens was then refortified - somewhat hastily - and finally the two were united by a pair of parallel walls, known as the Long Walls. The city walls were completed by Kimon. The Spartans demolished them in 404 but they were rebuilt by Konon in 393. Lycurgus modified them and adapted Pnyx Hill for use by the Assembly. Some rebuilding was also done during the Justinian period but much of this must have sunk below ground by the time Sulla stormed the city in 86 BC, for though he levelled the walls of the city which had defied him, many courses remained to be rediscovered - as they frequently are today.

Philopappou lower than the Acropolis, covers a much greater area and has three summits. On the most northerly, the **Hill of the Nymphs** is Greece's earliest Observatory and the Seismological Institute.

The adjacent hill, the **Pnyx** or narrow place, was adapted as the meeting place of the Ecclesia, an administrative body which had the power to summon the necessary quorum (5.000) of citizens in order to enact legislation of the day. The citizens were busy people, not always ready to leave their work at the drop of a sandal. It was the custom to send slaves through the streets with knotted ropes and red paint. Anyone found still in the town was in danger of being daubed with paint and having to pay a penalty.

The meeting place was a vantage point which now serves as a natural theatre for the Sound and Light show, featuring of course the Acropolis.

The highest point of the Philopappou, the **Museion** (hill of the Muses), is crowned by a peculiar monument erected in the early second century AD as tomb and memorial to Caius Julius Antiochus Philopappus, a Roman consul. The steep climb is worthwhile. The view of the Acropolis from here is magnificent, backed by the mountains which hem in Athens from every side. To the south, Piraeus, the sea and islands are visible on a clear day.

Hidden among the trees at the foot of this hill, near the church of St. Dimitrios Lombardiaris, is a delightful refreshment pavilion.

Apostolou Pavlou Street, between Philopappou and the Acropolis, marks the finishing point of the Acropolis Auto Rally, where drivers who brave the worst of the European winter end their endurance test, usually in brilliant sunshine.

This is also a good spot from which to walk to the tiny modern theatre where the Dora Stratou dancers perform regional dances collected from all over Greece

The theatre, idyllically set in a wooded grove, can be easily reached by following the signs, first along the wide paved road, then turning off to the right and following a path through the trees. A romantic approach to the theatre, but not novel - you will be following the custom of the ancient Greeks, who trod similar paths to the theatre of Dionysus, on their way perhaps to a first performance of one of the plays of Sophocles or Aristophanes.

Acropolis, South Slope

As we cross the road, the Parthenon directly ahead, a marble path leads up to the **Herod Atticus Theatre** (popularly called the Herodion) where performances are given from June to October as part of the Athens Festival. Herod Atticus, patron of the arts, sophist and epicure, built it in 162 A.D. making the Stoa of Eumenes connect the old theatre of Dionysos (see below) with the new theatre which he built to honour his wife. Its shape is precisely semicircular, with a stage wall of several stories of Roman arches. The height of the stage wall and the topmost row of seats were the same, making a tidy half-circle box to contain 32 rows of seats for 5000 people. As a concert hall, it would have been roofed. At one time this theatre was made part of the medieval castle.

A summer night performance in Herod Atticus Theatre.

Here begins the archeological site of the South Slope. There is a gate on Dionysou Areopagitou, below the Acropolis, opposite Mitsaion Street, and another above the Herodion which also offers access to the Acropolis site (separate ticket).

The **Stoa of Eumenes** led eastward along the back of the Acropolis. 535 feet long and built by that king of Pergamon in 197-159 B.C. (His brother Attalos succeeded him, and built the stoa in the Agora). This one was a promenade for theatre-goers, not intended as a shopping mall; it had two stories, with Doric columns outside, Ionic columns inside and Pergamene on the top floor. Its arcades can still be seen. In front of the Eastern end was the Choregic Monument of Nikias of 319 BC, when he wanted to celebrate the victory of his pet choir. Some of the material from this monument was incorporated into the Beulé Gate.

On a terrace above the stoa the Asklepion, a shrine to the patron god of doctors, was established in 420 when the cult came to Athens from Epidaurus.

The **Theatre of Dionysos** was built even earlier in the 6-5th centuries in a natural hollow on the south slope of the Acropolis. Unlike the Roman theatre, the seats were closer to a 3/4 circle; the orchestra was round and the stage area was close by on one side. Between auditorium and stage were the parodoi, entrances for the chorus. The cult of Dionysos was brought from Eleutherai near Thebes by Peisistratos, and theatre and temple were originally one - Dionysos was god of ecstasy, wine, masks and magic. At the very back a monument was erected by Thrasyllos in 320. Sixty-four rows seated 17.000 spectators in three sections. The front rows were all of honour and there was a special seat for the priest of Dionysus, of course. Behind him was a throne for Hadrian. Marble slabs paved the orchestra, and in the later Roman period walls were built to protect the spectators from the wild animals, and cement was fixed to the inside so that a seabattle performance could take place on water.

There are present plans to restore and use this theatre, which was new when the great tragedies of Aeschylus, Sophocles and Euripides were first performed in it. It hosted drama, poetry, choral competitions, treats for VIPs, cock fights, military exhibitions, displays of prizes from subject states, and the ceremonial discharge of orphans from state care.

To the right was Perikles' rectangular Odeon built in 446 BC and used for rehearsals and for musical performances.

Theatre of Dionysos.

CITY OF HADRIAN : Roman Athens

Though the Romans carted off statuary and other goodies to embellish their own villas n Rome, to have despoiled Athena's temple and destroy Perikles great works would have been to them a barbaric act of vandalism. On the contrary, wealthy Roman patrons built new temples and theatres to the glory of the gods and of themselves, and the use of the citizens. The theatre of Herod Atticus was bigger and grander than anything that had preceded it, the Tower of the Winds sported a weather vane and a public clock.

Hadrian's Arch

However, the Parthenon, in all its many colours dominated this famous city - Roman-occupied but not truly a *Roman* city. Hadrian decided to try to rectify matters by creating his own city to promote his personal glory and fame. The matter must have got under his skin - because on the ceremonial arch through which one entered his new grand scheme he had inscribed on the side, "This is Athens, ancient city of Theseus" and on the other. "This is the city of Hadrian and not of Theseus".

The new city contained villas, aqueducts, baths and other public buildings and, of course, temples. Predictably the most important of these, dedicated to the highest Olympian god, just had to be the biggest if not the most beautiful in Greece. This was built on foundations just inside the Arch and these already existed.

Temple of Olympian Zeus seen through Hadrian's Arch.

Temple of Olympian Zeus

The pleasant well-watered site had struck the Athenians as a good place to build no less than 700 years earlier Peisistratos began it but work stopped when his son Hippias, who succeeded him, was exiled. Hippias joined the Persians and was with them when they fought the Athenians at Marathon.

When Themistokles mobilised all the able-bodied to rebuild and extend the existing walls, much of the partly built temple went into them. The remainder waited until Syrian King Antiochus resumed building in 174 BC. The entablature was never placed. Again politics intervened and work stopped until Sulla conquered Athens in 86 BC and carried off the columns and capitals to Rome for use in the Capitoline Temple.

Over two hundred years and a few plans later Hadrian finally got it together in 130 A.D. He had the original base paved with marble and topped it with a double colonnade of huge Corinthian columns - 104 in all. The base measured 118 by 45 feet and was about 90 feet high using the same optical tricks as the Parthenon to further exaggerate the height. A gold and ivory statue of Zeus (a copy of Pheidias statue at Olympia) was installed, and of course, a huge one of Hadrian himself.

Outside the precincts of the Temple on the north side are remains of several 4th century houses, a Roman bath of 130 A.D. and traces of Themistokles' walls.

Temple of the Olympian Zeus.

On the south side flowed the Ilissos River, from springs near Kesariani on Hymettos. Once vitally important to Athens, it flowed through meadows near the present Royal Olympic Hotel on its way to Faliron. Much shrunk since Classical times, its course has been built over by roads. There was a spring called Kalliroi, and the name stuck, even to a modern street.

There are remains of three temples; one dedicated in second c. BC to Kronos and Rhea, father and mother of mankind; a larger Doric temple to Apollo Delphinios; and an archaic structure called the Law Court of the Delphinion.

Many other unidentified ruins lie within the area bounded by the Themistoklean wall (a Roman extension was built to enclose an area which now includes part of the Zappion and National Gardens, rejoining the original wall north of Syntagma Square).

Bounded now by endless streams of traffic, the Ilissos area has recently been screened by the planting of trees and flowering shrubs by the City authorities and has become a much pleasanter place to visit. In a lane by the side of the temple the noise of traffic miraculously recedes and the scent of jasmine is overpowering.

The Olympic Stadium

Returning to Vass. Olgas, turning east and crossing Vas. Konstantinou brings one to the Stadium, dating from 330 BC when it was used for the Panathenaic Games.

The ancient track was "one stade", 60 (Greek) feet, with a row of pillars down the center. Four of these square columns with the head of Hermes have been discovered.

Herod Atticus (who was born in Attica) restored the stadium for the games of 144 A.D. Greek games were replaced by Roman holidays and 1.000 wild beasts were brought here to be baited. In later years the marble was removed and the site left a ruin.

With the renewal of Greece as an independent state a new benefactor, Ernst Ziller, began to clear the site. King George I of the Hellenes gave some financial help, and the first modern Olympic Games were held here in 1896. The marble was this time replaced by a wealthy Alexandrian Greek benefactor, Georgios Averof. (A recent film shows the 1896 games).

CITY OF THE ATHENIANS: Plaka and Monastiraki

Summer and winter Plaka is full of life. Athenians enjoy business and bustle, love to see and be seen, know what is going on, meet friends, talk to strangers and, if they are men, chat up the girls. In Plaka they can do all those things at once.

So can the visitor. Plaka has many fascinating corners to explore, colourful shopping areas and numerous tavernas, restaurants and snack bars.

This part of old Athens, with its crazy street plan, is roughly bounded by Filellinon and Nikis to the West and by Mitropoleos and Ermou to the North, all of which run from central Syntagma Square. The third boundary is the Acropolis itself.

Leaving Syntagma Square by Nikis street, noted for fast food, travel agents and English bookshops (one with a second-hand department, a boon to the travelling bookworm), turn right into traffic-free Kidathineon which leads to Filomousou Square where

Traditional Greek Kafenion, in the heart of Plaka.

you can start the day with a solid breakfast or spend the evening in one of the many tavernas and bars. Here or in the surrounding streets you can get your watch mended, do your laundry, or, for very little cost, rent a room with a balcony overlooking the square. The square is a popular place for rendezvous and busy the whole year round.

A few yards, a turn or two, and Plaka has a different face. From the square walk down Farmaki to the beautiful old church of St. Catherine, in a sunken square. When a service is in progress the magnificent chants pour out through the open doors and the worshippers' candles flicker under the trees. Palms wave high above, and beyond, on a lower and yet earlier level, stand two marble columns from Roman times... here where you walk people have walked through many centuries.

Strolling down Plaka in a bright afternoon.

Turn right into Lysicratous by the taverna with a painted wall, toward **Lysicrates Monument** built when his choir won a tripod (meant to hold an urn for libations), at the Theatre of Dionysos in 334 BC. These competitions were very popular and the trophies were highly prized. It was customary to erect them near the theatre or on Tripodon, the road which led to it from the Agora, and dedicate them to one of the gods. The bases ranged from a simple pedestal to elaborate confections which were minor temples in themselves. This lone survivor of over 200 was constructed with marble from three different sources on a base of Piraeus stone - evidently the stonemasons were well stocked to keep up with the constant demand. Many bases have been uncovered and reburied for here in Plaka it is impossible to turn a spade without finding what someone left here 20, 200, or 2,000 years ago.

Walk up now towards the Acropolis and into **Anafiotika.** The road skirting the hill has been extended to allow easy access to the Acropolis. From this road, steeps and steps twist up and down among tiny old houses, built at all angles on the rock as space allowed, and almost every minute space not built on contains a tree, little tubs of flowers or a creeper rioting in glorious cascades of colour.

When the Royal Palace was built and the Acropolis being cleared of Turkish houses, workers came from the island of Anafi which had been devastated by an earthquake. The displaced families were offered the land now occupied by Syntagma Square, but they were used to mountain terrain. The upper slopes above the old town were bare and the islanders preferred to build their new homes on these rather inhospitable rocks. They built at night and the story runs that land that could be built on in one night could be claimed by the builder. A family working together to build a house (as Greek families still sometimes do) could probably put up quite a lot of masonry in one night and, as before, material was to hand. Recent work has revealed a piece of mosaic floor in use as a step - evidence of Roman building or simply a piece of decorative stone carried away from an abandoned site? Many of these 19th century houses have been pulled down to make the new access possible. The Acropolis that caused them to be built has dealt many of them the final blow.

Walking along the new road towards the Acropolis one reaches the twelfth century church of the Metamorphosis, the old University, and a fine old mansion housing the Kanellopoulos Museum, both dating from the last century. From here Panos or Klepsydras streets lead steeply down to the Roman Agora - the centre of commercial life in Athens at the time of St. Paul. There can be little doubt that he talked with people here in the market place. Athens has always been a place of the people and the Tower of the Winds, standing on the edge of the Roman Agora, was a public clock.

Roman Agora, with the Tower of the Winds.

Roman Agora

The Roman market (365 ft x 315 ft) is below steet level, within an enclosing wall - part of it remains still unexcavated. It was paved in marble, and is thought to have consisted of Doric colonnades with shops. Inscriptions on columns giving the names of the shopkeepers have been found in place. Columns of 8-10 feet are still standing.

The Tower of the Winds

This marble tower, about 44 ft in height, was built to house a water clock or clepsydra 80 yrs before Christ. Its purpose was forgotten until a copy of a work written by Vitruvius, the celebrated Roman architect, was discovered in 1486. It was surrounded by small houses and only the upper part remained above ground level. The Turks converted it into a chapel and the Dervishes of the Bektashi order were reported as "dancing round to two little drums, crying to God and Mohammet' when performing their religious dance.

Designed by Adronicus Cyrrhestes of Syria who erected the tower as a monument to the people of Athens, it predates the Roman Agora on the edge of which it stood - possibly the reason for this site being chosen for the market. The agoranomium, or market overseers office, was built next to it.

On the south wall of the main tower was a stone water cistern which provided the power and regulated the clock. It was supplied by water piped from the spring on the Acropolis, being first fed into a settling tank in order to remove any impurities which might affect the accuracy of the mechanism. The overflow fed a fountain inside the tower where the clock itself was situated.

Not much trace remains of the eight sundials which originally decorated this octagonal building and the bronze triton (half man, half fish), is no longer indicating which way the wind blows, but the reliefs representing the winds to which he pointed are still visible and in remarkably good condition.

North	Bearded man blowing a conch shell	South	Beardless man holding an urn of water
North-east	Bearded man with shield full of hailstones	South-west	Beardless man holding part of a ship
East	Young man bearing fruit and ears of corn	West	Young man scattering flowers
South-east	Bearded man wearing a mantle	North-west	Bearded man holding a vase

Continuing down Panos (which is interrupted by the Roman Agora site), brings one to the precincts of the Library of the Emperor Hadrian which held many thousands of scrolls - Athens was an important city to the Romans too. Excavations continue on the site, which is at present closed to the public.

The remaining pilastered wall of the Library is on the right, facing Areos (a small street leading to Monastiraki Square). Once similar walls enclosed a huge court with "a hundred splendid columns". Five main rooms in a block were along the cloister on the east side. The central chamber or main library was a large central recess with four small ones on each side - probably the stacks or reference rooms. The courtyard was likely to have contained a long pool, perhaps with fish, and statuary. In 410 a lecture hall was built at one end, and in the 6th century a basilica which still later became a church. By that time, the area had been covered over, and was used as a bazaar.

Plaka's main thoroughfare, Adrianou Street, ran through the bazaar and was split to accommodate the excavations (1885 on), causing a detour through Dexipou, a bazaar-like street which has changed little over the centuries. Tiny shops and booths sell basketware and cane furniture, boots, heavy clothing, and all sorts of wonderful things made from old tyres. Sidewalks are for goods and the street is for passing traffic (on wheels or on foot) in the old style. You may well be surprised to find this rule still holds good in many parts of the modern city where the passing traffic is thick and fast!

Turning right into Areos brings one past an old mosque into Monastiraki Square, with a little 10th century church, a derelict mosque and a electric train station in front of which street traders sell nuts, fruit, ice-cream, and whatever else is in season. Ifestou on the left and Pandrossou on the right are both lined with tiny shops but the merchandise is very different. All the crafts are represented here and the deep, narrow fronted shops are veritable Aladdins caves - storehouses filled from front to back, from floor to ceiling and to overflowing with goods of all descriptions -

Monastiraki Bazaar. Anything can be found in these Alladin caves.

piled high with brassware, copper, enamelled ware, marble, onyx, shirts, dresses, icons, basketwares, worry beads, chess and tavli (backgammon) sets, leather goods, handwoven bags and rugs. Here are the goldsmiths and silversmiths whose exquisite displays draw like magnets. Leather craftsmen make sandals on the premises and will fit them onto your feet.

The Hellenic Popular Handicrafts Industry in Pandrossou has coffee and light snacks as well as a permanent display of handicrafts and embroideries from all over Greece.

A right at the end of Pandrossou will lead back into the heart of Plaka and the colourful main street, Adrianou. Or go left and follow Mitropoleos or Ermou Streets back to Syntagma.

A vast expanse of shining marble surrounds the Cathedral in Mitropoleos. It stands with its tiny predecessor which was built in the 12th century using any piece of carved stone that came to hand. Further up is the microscopic tiny Agia Dynamis (17 c.) which stands rather incongruously under the Ministry of Education building.

INFOTIP:
The bank in the square and the post office at 60 Mitropoleos, both open on Sundays during the summer.

Ermou Street was cut straight through the old city in the rebuilding after Independence. The two parts are now joined only by the Kapnikarea church which was in the way of the new road. King Otto's father, Ludwig of Bavaria, pleaded for it and it now stands islanded in the middle of the traffic.

You may have spent a whole day in Plaka and feel the need to go back to your hotel now to freshen up - but do come back, Plaka is just beginning to wake up...

The restaurants and tavernas are just opening their doors for the evening and are looking out for customers. At this time of the evening if you walk up Miniskleous you will be enticed with offers of free aperitifs, invited to inspect the premises, see the view from the roof garden, study the menu, note the low prices, inspect the food - and this they will do in your own language, and rarely guess wrongly what it is, though if you don't reply in English you may find it all repeated again in German, just in case.

Stroll around and see how Plaka changes at night. Now you will find the tables set out in the streets in places it would be impossible to sit in the heat of the day.

Tavernas spread out into the street and round the corner, in the squares or wherever there is space for a table. Higher up, where the streets get steeper and space is at a premium doors are thrown wide to open the taverna to the summer night, and tables are placed inside, outside and often on the roof. The entertainment here is usually more elaborate than the strolling guitarist, and often includes Greek dancers in their traditional costumes. Musicians are already in full swing, the dancers limbering up. On the opposite side of the street a different group of musicians is playing a lively Greek song, while round the corner comes the plaintive sound of an amani from the eastern islands.

It is when the tavernas begin to fill up in the evening that the Plaka really comes into its own. In every part of Athens there are tavernas and restaurants but it is here in the heart of the old town that they are most popular. Greeks and tourists wend their way through the old streets, up steps and down inspecting the tavernas, the food and the entertainment provided before finally deciding which one they will patronise tonight.

Naturally, when three or four tavernas stand on the same corner, each with its own musicians, it does get a little difficult to distinguish exactly what is being played. However, this is of little consequence to the untutored ear and one can always concentrate on the dancing. This varies quite considerably between one island and another. Outside influences also have their effects - belly dancing is not really Greek! yet always seems to be included.

You will find the dishes are all translated into English, and sometimes French and German as well but with all these languages at your command you may still be mystified by some of the items. Don't worry - just go in and see what's cooking - as the Greeks do. If you like the look of it, try it. You can still enjoy it even if you can't pronounce it!

If a quiet evening is what you have in mind, you will find that too. Not every Greek taverna has music and there are many tucked away in quiet and picturesque corners.

The night clubs and non-traditional night life have now been closed or moved to other areas, the traffic banished and the streets made more attractive with restoration of many of the older houses. Many Athenians, especially younger ones, walk about here at Carnival time in fancy dress - either on the way to a party or just out with friends for a meal and an evening out. They carry plastic clubs and have mock-fights - the rule is not to 'attack' anyone who is not in fancy dress and this is usually observed though everyone runs the risk of having a paper squeaker blown in their ear. At Easter time the Athenians are usually away in their villages but Plaka puts on a special Easter spread, roast lamb and red eggs for all comers on (Greek) Easter Sunday mid-day.

For those seeking quietness, a beautiful, picturesque corner in Plaka.

GUARDS AND GARDENS : Syntagma

SYNTAGMA SQUARE is usually the first place that visitors to Athens get to know and from which they take their bearings. On the natural rise to the east is the **Parliament** building. Down in front of it the Evzones in their familiar uniforms keep guard not on the palace but on the tomb of the Unknown Warrior of Greece. On the wall behind them are bosses commemorating the more recent battles in which Greek soldiers have fought, both during and since the War of Independence. The famous name of El Alamein can be easily read even in Greek.The guard is ceremoniously changed every hour. On Sundays at 11:00 the new guard is accompanied by a guard of honour in full uniform and a military band in splendid array.

In Syntagma or the streets surrounding it are luxury hotels, airline offices, airport buses, travel offices and taxi rank, banks and 7-days-a-week Post Office. The National Bank of Greece has all day exchange services, 7-days-a-week opening, **Greek National Tourist Office** information and hotel booking desks.

Kiosks sell all the world's news, cigarettes, sweets, biscuits, batteries, aspirins, films, pens and almost everything else you might need at short notice. There are quick film developers, restaurants, coffee bars. Almost the entire pavement at the lower end of the square is taken up with tables and comfortable chairs from which to take refreshment and watch the passing show.

A place of contradictions, none of which are mutually exclusive.

In the square itself one can distance oneself a little from the noise and relax under an awning, with a lightly frosted campari served by immaculately dressed waiters who look cool in crisp white shirts when the rest of us are melting from the heat. Sit near the fountain amid the orange trees, oleanders and cypresses and close your eyes. You are sitting in the Garden of Muses where Aristotle taught. Keep your eyes closed and let the traffic's roar become transposed into the murmur of bees on just such a day as this...

By the side of the Parliament building are the **National Gardens** designed originally for Queen Amalia. Shaded by tropical trees the walks twist and turn like a maze and every few yards brings you to a junction. It can take only a few minutes to walk through the gardens if you know the way back to the traffic and tumult - or a few hours if you just want to wander at peace in the cool shade, breathing healthier air than can be found in many country areas. A stream runs through the gardens and if you explore you can find rustic bridges, a duck pond, a mosaic floor from a Roman bath, a zoo, a cafeteria and a small botanical museum.

If you have a child to amuse there is a tiny cottage library where the children can read books in Greek or English, listen to stories or play chess or other boardgames (grownups please wait outside). When inactivity palls there is also a newly re-equipped childrens playground to delight any child.

At the rear of the National Gardens is the **Presidential Palace**, like the Parliament Building also guarded by Evzones wearing their familiar kilts. Their barracks are at the end of the road on the corner of Herodou Attikou street and Vass. Sofias Avenue. Over the years they have worn a track in the pavement as they clop constantly back and forth.

Between the National Gardens and the Temple of Olympian Zeus is the **Zappion Exhibition Hall** , gift of two cousins whose statues flank the grand entrance. Used during Greece's term as President of the European Community as a meeting place for Heads of State, the beautiful building is not always open to the public. If there is not an exhibition on it's worth asking to look inside. The Zappion is surrounded by its own small park which includes a garden restaurant with evening cabaret, and an outdoor cinema.

HIGH LIFE: Likavitos and Kolonaki

On this Athenian hill,
islanded in air,
pull the green growth of pines
above the last roof,
the stair that climbs red earth to rock,
you'd see the whole thing spin
concentric like a top.
It's possible within
this orbit not to know
the limits one has set
oneself. The mind may leap
on truth and hold it, get
to grips with God - for God
is light and here the light
is palpable...

from "On this Athenian Hill" by Jennifer Couroucli (c) 1969, Chatto & Windus, The Hogarth press

Athens' highest hill, close to Syntagma, is **Likavitos**. Said to be a stone dropped by Athena on her way to the Acropolis, it rises to a peak which overlooks the Acropolis itself. The summit can be reached by a 'TELEFERIK' which cuts through the hill, but this does not start near the bottom and can only be reached by steep roads or by a series of five flights of steps . Topped by a small chapel to St. George and a restaurant this eyrie has an effect on the spirit which cannot be described. Go in early evening and watch the sun set and the lights begin to flicker on from Piraeus to Kifissia and from Hymettos to Parnes.

On a lower ridge to the north-east is a modern open-air theatre where plays and concerts are performed throughout the season. The air here is cooler than downtown and this is an out-of-this world place to spend an hour or two with the stage immediately below and, beyond it, the city viewed as if from a flying saucer.

Bus No.023 from Kaningos or Academias runs to Likavitos via Kolonaki.

On the lower slopes above Syntagma is high life of a different flavour, in elegant **Kolonaki** named for a small Roman column standing in the square. The politicians and the cognoscenti gather in smart cafes to drink coffee; fashionable ladies meet to exchange gossip and, above all, to be seen in this trendy neighbourhood. In the surrounding hilly and often narrow streets are many small boutiques, antique shops and fashionable restaurants and bars.

On this cosmopolitan hill are many of the foreign embassies, the British Council (Kolonaki Square), the French, British, and American schools of Archeology, and the Gennadios Library.

From Syntagma, passing the foot of Kolonaki on Vas. Sofias Avenue are the Benaki, Byzantine and War Museums and, further along, the National Gallery and the Hilton Hotel.

Across the street from the Hilton is the vast Evangelismos Hospital, in front of which is a park; on the northern end of this park is a secluded taverna serving meals, snacks, sweets and coffee among the trees.

Continuing in the same direction, just before the American Embassy is a green and wooded hillside. Eleftherias Park has more than meets the eye. Walk up the steep tree-lined road and you will find another unexpected open-air restaurant and bar hidden in a grove, an exhibition hall and a minute open-air theatre. If a feast of song or an Indian dance evening is scheduled there during your visit, you may enjoy getting off the beaten track a little.

A NEW BEGINNING: Syntagma to Omonia

As the agora was the centre of Athens in ancient times, Syntagma (Constitution) Square is the centre of Athens' modern history.

After the War of Independence, not only monuments had been wrecked. Many of the four thousand Athenians saw their roofless dwellings huddled around the Acropolis crumbling in the autumn rains. Even the churches were piles of rubble, while the suburbs were infested by brigands.

With the establishment of Athens as capital in 1834, the city rapidly expanded.Political manoeuvres by returning Greeks, proud patriots, and financial control by Britain, France and Russia molded this period of Greek history. The new Bavarian king of the Hellenes, knowing not a word of Greek and only 17 years old, entered into his new job enthusiastic but helpless.

King Otto's Council of Regency solicited architects to get the city in shape, after the desolation of occupation and war. It was to be a new version of the days of glory. Neo-classicism was the European rage; and what better than to reintroduce the classical motif into the home of Classicism? There were proposals to put the Palace on the Acropolis, raze the Plaka, construct grand houses among the shanties. Plans by Leo von Klenze laid out Athens on a triangle formed by Ermou, Stadiou and Pireos Streets, skirting the existing town. The king's palace, a university, hospitals and administrative buildings were built on new roads and squares outside the old city limits.

Otto's palace towered above the surrounding buildings. The regents' achitects were Ziler, Boulanger, von Hansen, von Garthner. (Of course, nobody had asked the Greeks who had fought the long bloody revolution if they wanted any of this new Frankish occupation).

The Constitution of 1843 was proclaimed from the new palace, which is now the Parliament building, and the Square was named.

Opposite the palace an annex was built for guests of state, which later became the Grande Bretagne Hotel (where Churchill narrowly escaped being blown up by a bomb in 1944).

Delighted to be rid of the Turks, the Greeks soon found themselves under a monumental bureaucracy, heavy taxation, and a heretic ruler - Catholic, not Orthodox. They demanded reform.

Otto was forced to quit after the Crimean War, and in 1863 the foreign powers in London appointed George of Denmark - another boy of 17 - who reigned for 50 years, while Greece developed from a shattered ex-colony to an independent power.A new constitution in 1864 made a "democracy under monarchy".

George was assassinated in 1913. His son Constantine was popular for leading a campaign to reclaim Greek territory from Bulgaria. But after all, the Kaiser was the king's brother-in-law, and his pro-German sentiments were unpopular with many Greeks. Pressure from the Allies and Eleftherios Venizelos (Cretan patriot and frequent prime minister) brought Greece into World War I on the Allied side.

In 1922, as a result of the failed effort to free the Greek cities of Asia Minor, came the agonizing exchange of populations with Turkey, i.e., Greeks and Turks were repatriated no matter how long their families had lived in the other country. A million and a half Greeks arrived as refugees and were settled in Nea Smyrni (New Smyrna), Mihalakopoulou (a drained swamp), Nea Ionia, Nea Philadelphia, and other areas. With them came cultural changes - music with an Eastern influence, business practices, a habit of financial success; agriculture, trading and industry got a lift.

By World War II, Greece had become a united nation in spite of the basic political split between monarchists and anti-monarchists, which went into abeyance while under attack from Italy and Germany. On 28 October 1940, the Italian Ambassador demanded surrender from Prime Minister Metaxas, who said NO. The Greeks united passionately behind this NO, and beat the Italians back. But in April 1941, the Germans were in Athens. Overwhelming odds forced a surrender, though the war was courageously continued by partisans.

The War was followed immediately by a bitter civil war. Peace finally came in 1949 and foreign aid helped rebuild once more. Athens went into another phase of expansion which has not yet ended, radiating out into the surrounding hills from the modern centre, Syntagma.

From here Stadiou and Panepistimiou (University) street, link Syntagma Square and Omonia Square.

In Panepistimiou the most important new buildings were erected. After leaving Syntagma the first major building on the right is the arched **Iliou Melathron** (Hall of Troy) designed for Heinrich Schliemann by Ziller (1878). The mosaic floors and the painted walls and ceilings have a Trojan motif. Used for many years as Court of Appeals, the house is currently being restored and will be open to the public in 1986. This elegant house was described by Kaftandzoglou as "An incurable leprosy". Kaftandzoglou was joint architect of the Roman Catholic Cathedral of St. Denis, which is just a couple of blocks down the road, and also the Eye Hospital in the same block.

Next comes the academic trilogy. First to be constructed was the **University** building (1839), designed by Christian Hansen in neoclassical style with a circular staircase leading to the entrance. This stands back from the road and is flanked by two other buildings, the **Academy of Sciences** and the **National Library.** The University was designed to be the central and most important building in the street, but the group seems a little unbalanced. On the right the Academy building stands well forward of the University, and the two large wings flanking its main entrance each have two pediments ornamented with sculptures, as has the central pediment. Two huge Ionic columns support the statues of Athena and Apollo, below which stand statues of Socrates and Plato. The building facade is painted and gilded and is ornate and eyecatching. The architect was Theofil Hansen, younger brother of Christian. One can only wonder if sibling rivalry was responsible for so great a contrast. The National Library designed later by Theofil is modest by comparison.

KEY TO THE MAP

1. N.T.O.G. Information Office

ARCHAEOLOGICAL SITES

2. Acropolis	D2
3. Areopagus	C1
4. Ancient Agora	C1
5. Keramikos	C1
6. Pnyx Hill	D1
7. Herod Atticus Theatre	D2
8. Theatre of Dionysos	D2
9. Hadrian's Arch	D2
10. Temple of Olympian Zeus	D2
11. Stadium	D3
12. Roman Agora	C2
13. Hadrian's Library	C2

MUSEUMS

14. Nat. Archaeological	A2
15. City Museum	C2
16. Nat. Historical	C2
17. Benaki Museum	C3
18. Cycladic Museum	C3
19. Byzantine Museum	C3
20. National Gallery	C4
21. Popular Art Museums	C2
22. Kanellopoulos Museum	C2

PUBLIC BUILDINGS

38. Parliament Building	C3
39. National Gardens	C3

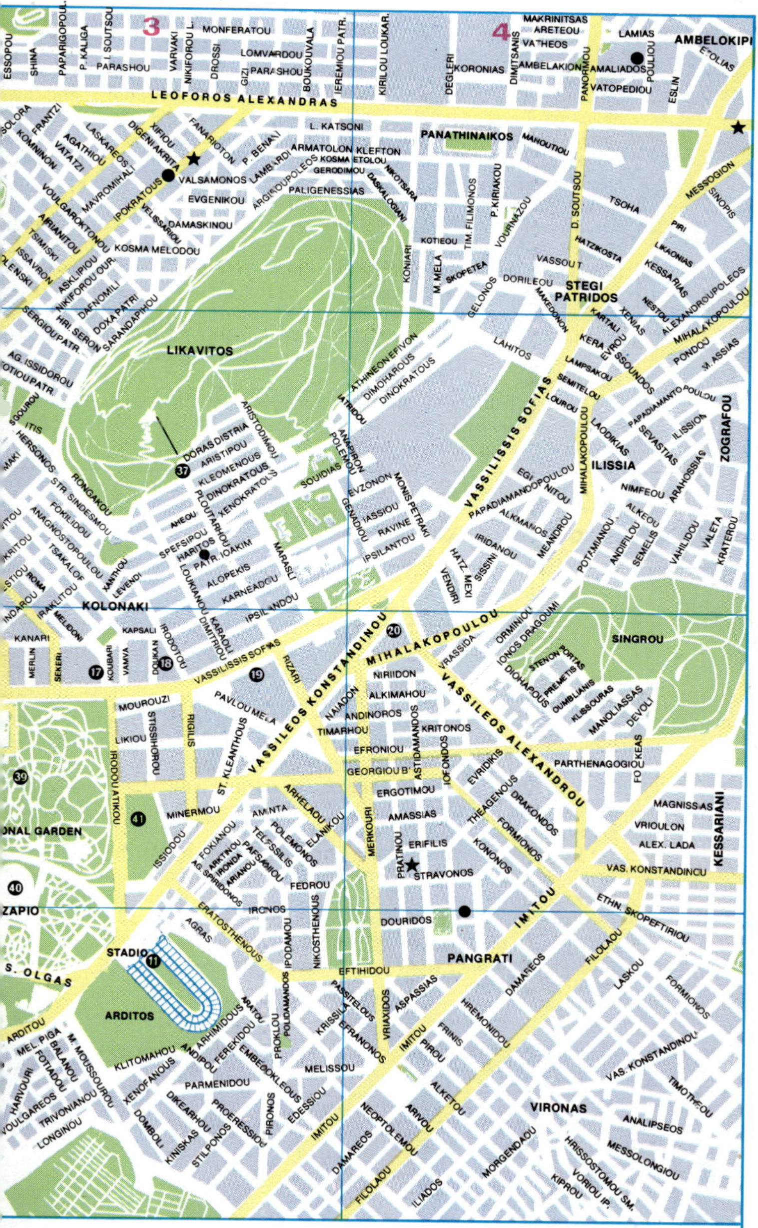

Zappion Exhibition Hall C3
Presidential Palace C3
Schliemann House C2
Academy B2
University B2
National Library B2

ZANTINE CHURCHES

Agii Apostoli C2
Agii Asomati C1
Agia Dynamis C2
Kapnikarea C2
Agii Theodori C2
Agios Nikodemos (Russian Orthodox) C2
Agia Ekaterini D2

OTHER CHURCHES

30. Mitropolis Cathedral (Greek Orthodox) C2
31. St Denis (Roman Catholic) B2
32. St Andrew's (Evangelical) B3
33. St Paul's (Anglican) C2
34. Synagogue C1

COMMUNICATIONS

35. Larissa Station (Europe & Northern Greece) A1
36. Peloponnesos Station A1
37. Lykavitos Funicular B3

● Post Office
★ Telecommunications (O.T.E.)

The University is outside the normal jurisdiction of the police and the forecourt is used for small private demonstrations and by unlicenced street vendors, often students and other young people selling jewellery and paintings.

At the rear of the University building, in Akademias, is the former city hospital, now a Centre for the Arts. On the lower ground floor is the tiny but fascinating Theatre Museum.

In front of the University the short promenade of Korai street leads to Stadiou, parallel with Panepistimiou and also connecting Syntagma with Omonia. Below Korai, in Plateia Klafthmonos, a section of the old (Themistoclean) city wall is to be found. On the left hand side of the square the City Museum is housed in a modest mansion that was the first palace of King Otto. Further down is the 12th century church of the two saints Theodori, who are always inseparable.

Further back along Stadiou, towards Syntagma, is the National Historical Museum, where relics of the War of Independence include Lord Byron's helmet and sword.

MARKET PLACES: Omonia to Fokionos Negri

Omonia

At the opposite end of Stadiou from Syntagma is the other of the city's two great squares - **Omonia.** The hotels here are less expensive. Everything - and much more - that is on sale in Syntagma can be bought here and cheaper, and there is an air of hustle and bustle as people spill out of the escalators and rush off in all directions. To the left is Athinas Street, leading back to Monastiraki Square. The men who stand in the street with little glass-sided show-cases are buying and selling gold (rings, watches, jewellery, coins).

Between Omonia Square and the market on Athinas Street is small Kodzias Square. Here are elegant refurbished neoclassical banks, and the unfortunately proportioned City Hall. The square was destined to become an underground garage, but, as so often in Athens, the excavations became archeological within days. The area produced statuary from Roman tombs and older graves are being unearthed below.

Omonia Square: Busy round the clock.

Further down Athinas is the meat and fish market built in 1880 on the neoclassical pattern - a basically handsome building not enhanced by butcher's stalls below. It is a large block with outer corridors for the sides of beef and lamb hanging on display, poultry and pork, while within is a block lined with fresh fish stands. It is always noisy and active. Inside are tavernas: around the edges are shops for cheeses, sausages and groceries. Opposite on Athinas Street are the colourful fresh fruit and vegetable stalls. This point marks the edge of the old town and from here to Monastiraki small workshops and wholesalers operate in a maze of narrow streets.

> **INFOTIP** Wash fresh fruit and vegetables, even if you peel them. They have probably been sprayed.

Returning to Omonia, the next two streets lead to Piraeus, and to the railway stations. There are many eating places round the square and under it more shops, a post office and the main station of the single-line electric railway. Men gather here to discuss every weighty matter under the sun and the man with the silver samovar sells Salepi, a thick drink made from grapes.

A second Post Office in Aeolou (leave the square again by Stadiou and take the first left) has week-end opening.

Patission/Fokionos Negri

Past the Post Office the street name changes officially to 28th October but, like many streets in Athens, it has changed its name once too often and the Athenians ingore the official title and call it Patission (the road to Patissia).

Half a mile to the north of Omonia next to the Polytechnic, is the handsome building housing the National Archaeological Museum, and the Epigraphic and Numismatic collections (see page 119).

Two blocks beyond, behind the bus station at Platea Egyptou, is Pedion Areos, a vast park with several open-air restaurants. The main road into the park is lined with busts of the heroes of the revolution. There is also a memorial to the Commonwealth forces who died here in World War II.

Further north, about two miles from Omonia, Fokionos Negri swings off at an angle to the right. Unprepossessing at first sight, this road opens quickly into a wide, pedestrian avenue lined with coffee shops and restaurants, with tables set out under trees and amid fountains in the central area. There are many fashionable boutiques for both sexes and small shops selling interesting bric-a-brac. This is a great place to shop-and-eat, either for lunch or for an evening saunter.

ATTICA

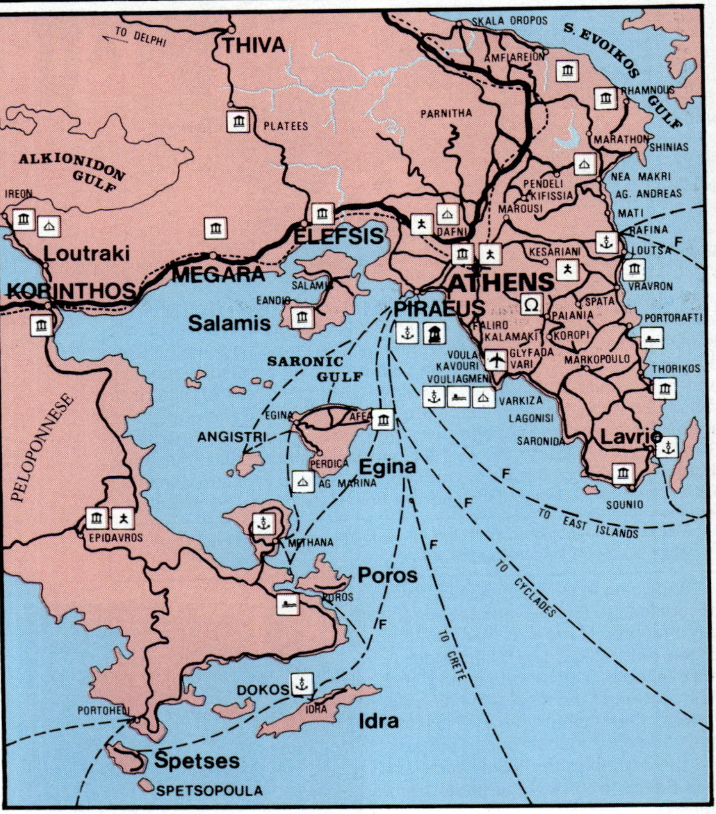

KEY TO THE MAP

- National Road (Toll)
- Major roads – Minor roads
- Railway
- F Car Ferry
- Ferry
- Archaeological Site
- Byzantine Site
- Camping
- Beach Facilities
- Airport
- Cave
- Port with yacht supplies

A STEP FURTHER: The Outskirts

Kifissia

Bus 538, 539 from Kaningos Sq. or electric train.

This former provincial town, which has now become a northern suburb, has been a very popular residential area for most of recorded history. Rich Romans, Turkish Beys, temporary monarchs and Alexandrian millionaires have been among the residents.

Kifissia is popular with Greeks too, both those who live in the elegant villas and those who drive out to get away from the summer heat and pollution for a while. Even without a car the trip is an easy one; this is the terminus of the electric railway and takes less than an hour from Athens centre. The journey is pleasant and the train passes through Maroussi, the ceramic centre of Athens, past numerous olive groves and the "Irini" (Peace) sports stadium where Greece hosts the European games in its turn.

In Kifissia patient horses wait outside the station to take passengers for a gentle trip in an *Amaxaki* around the tree-lined avenues.

Beyond a neat park where the big annual flower show is held in May, is the town centre. Kassaveti Street is lined with shops and eating places. Ice cream bars, grills, tavernas and restaurants are plentiful in this pleasant inland resort, and the local shopping centre attracts much attention, even on Sundays when window shopping is a popular way to spend an hour. There is a roof restaurant, and ten pin bowling on the lower floor.

A little further along this road, housed in an elegant villa, is the Goulandris Natural History Museum.

Elegant villas are the norm in Kifissia, our old friend Herod Atticus built one here, his courtier Aulus Gellius sang the town's praises. Chelebi, a Turkish travel writer, wrote about it and so did Byron's friend, Hobhouse. It was only at the end of the last century however, after serious steps had been taken to stamp out brigands, that the wealthy came out in great numbers to build villas - described by Osbert Lancaster as "extravagant examples of twentieth-century domestic architecture without rival in Europe".

Nowadays Kifissia is a sociable place with night life in abundance. Both in the centre and on the outskirts (Drosia, Ekali) there are many restaurants and bars with an international atmosphere including some traditional English pubs and German beer-houses (Old Times, Alt Berlin). The International Club at the Semiramis Hotel has excellent facilities and a good social environment.

Pendeli

Bus 411, 415, 421, 422 from Nat. Arch. Museum (rear)

Near to Kifissia, but further east the settlement of Pendeli spreads out over the mountain famous for its marble in classical times when it was used for the finest and most luxurious work. The lower slopes are scented with pine trees and the summit houses a modern observatory.

With small cafes tucked away amongst the trees this is an idyllic place for pleasant walks and there are tavernas nearby to cater for healthy appetites. If you have a car take the Dionysos road to "Agios Petros" which stands high up on the mountain. The comfortable motel boasts sweeping views. The road winds on down to the little coastal resort of Nea Makri.

Parnitha (Parnes)

Bus 738 to Teleferik from Platea Vathis

Due north of Athens Mount Parnes, at 8,000 ft. is the highest mountain in Attica. The Mount Parnes Hotel at its peak has a swimming pool, restaurant, bar, night club and casino. The summit can be reached by a cable car and the views over Attica and to the north are breathtaking.

Driving up by car one passes a little church. Nearby one may be assailed by the smell of fresh meat grilling and discover souvlakis are cooked in the open and fresh honey and yoghurt are on sale. The Athens Mountaineering Association caters for walkers and a chalet is located at Bafi on the southern slope with heating, electricity, showers and food. The area is popular with walkers and is part of a National Forest, and a protected area for wild animals. Healthy appetites are catered for in various places along the way by a large number of tavernas.

In late springtime, when the snow is still hanging around the peaks, a gentle descent from the summit brings one from winter through the masses of spring flowers. By the time the foot of the mountain is reached the air is warm, time to take off that jacket and enjoy a leisurely lunch in the sun!

A children's playground in the highest point of Attica

Kesariani

Inside the city limits of Athens, just beyond the universit campus, is a mountain with a dramatic history, now a place of peac and freshness.

Mount Hymettus (Imitos) is one of the hills that surround an enclose the central plain of Attica. At sunset it is diffused with unique violet glow. Once it was the site of marble quarries.

Situated high in a ravine, the Monastery of Kesariani was firs founded in the 12th century where once an ancient temple o Aphrodite stood. Built beside a spring, source of the Ilissos, th waters from its fountain are reputed to cure sterility.

The monastery remained independent of the Turkish governmen of Athens, with a school and library of its own. In the 18th centur it was abandoned; the library was moved to Athens and wa destroyed in the War of Independence.

The buildings slowly fell apart, and wild things grew on th mountain until the German invasion of 1940. Here on the quie hillside, anything green was scavenged for food. The Germans use the hill as a place of execution; and the Civil War of the late 40's le it a barren, rubble-strewn wilderness.

The Friends of the Trees undertook to restore the site, an women slowly sifted the stones to retrieve those of the monaster rescuing the 17th and 18th century frescoes. Tiny trees wer planted on the mountain slopes and tended, until today there is whole forest of examples of every colour and shape and specie The monastery has been lovingly repaired, and the fountain strippe of late additions down to its original ram's head pipe.

Part of the monastery is too fragile to explore, but one can g into the church of St. Anthony and the old refectory with its whit walls and chimney, and into the charmingly flowered courtyard. Behind the monastery is a shaded spot with tree trunks sawn to make seats for family picnics. Water is pure and plentiful, but take your own food.

Further out and higher up is the small monastery of Asteriou, 11th century, also restored. Yet another Byzantine Church, St. John Theologos, is found on the way down.

The summit once held a statue of Zeus at 3,770 feet, towering over the city. (Now it belongs to Ares: at the very top of Hymettos is the radar station and part of the mountain is a military restricted area.)

The bus 224 from Kaningos or Akadimias terminates at the bottom of the mountain. About a 35-40 minutes walk up a sloping (not too steep) road brings you to the monastery. Walk up the hill past the cemetery and under the main highway. Turn right at the fork.

The church of Kesariani monastery.

GOD AND NATURE: Dafni and Elefsis

Dafni

The Monastery of Dafni was built on land long held sacred. Previously the site of a temple to Apollo, stones from the old temple were incorporated both into the monastery and the battlemented walls surrounding it. The monastery was founded in the 5th or 6th century and dedicated to the Virgin Mary. It fell into disrepair and was rebuilt towards the end of the 11th century, only to be sacked by the Crusaders in 1205. Othon de la Roche ceded it to the Cistercian Monks.

It was re-occupied by Orthodox monks in the 16th century but they abandoned it again during the War of Independence, when it was used as a barracks. Following this, the strong fortifications were thought to make it suitable for a lunatic asylum. The inmates were rehoused nearby and restorations began in 1893, but it was only after World War II that extensive work was carried out on the church and cloisters. The earthquake of 1982 shook the foundations and structural reinforcements had to be made before it was again opened to the public.

The cruciform church is famous for its exquisite mosaics, some of the best-preserved in Greece.The dome, supported on re-cycled classical pillars, is decorated with a stern and unforgiving looking *Pantocrator,* Christ the all-powerful. Immediately below are representations of the prophets and the saints. Other mosaics represent the annunciation, nativity, baptism and transfiguration of Christ. Saints face each other across the arches.

Four frescoes on the lower walls are well-preserved, but there are scratches in the plaster which reveal scraps and seeds from the chopped straw used to strengthen the plaster when it was applied. The good condition of the remaining plaster indicates that this ancient method of reinforcement was effective.

Look to your laurels: Dafni, usually translated as laurel, is in fact Laurus Nobilis L., more commonly known as the green bay tree. 'Oil of Bay' is an extract of this tree, which is indigenous to Greece, and the aromatic leaves are used as a flavouring in meat dishes. This is the laurel which was used to garland the victors in the games, and was dedicated to Apollo. 'Baccalaureate' means laurel berries.

The tree still grows within the monastery grounds.

The green wooded area next to the monastery is used for the wine festival in August (see FESTIVALS), and the tourist pavilion there is open all the year round.

Bus No. 228, 229, 864, 880, 853, 854, 855 from Platia Eleftherias (Koumoundourou) Pireos Street.

Dafni Monastery. The Church.

Elefsis (Eleusis, Elefsina)

Past Dafni along the coast and opposite Salamis is the ancient precinct of Eleusis. Eleusis was happily located with the bay strategically near, and until 600 B.C. rivalled Athens and Megara. In Theseus' day it was already subject to Athens, who built a wall to protect the harbour.

The fertile Thriasian Plain was sacred to the stern goddess of the Earth and Harvest, Demeter, from time immemorial. The tale tells of her daughter, Persephone or "Koré" - the word which still means "Daughter" and also describes the archaic young-girl statues - who was playing by the sea one day. Suddenly the earth opened, and from a cave emerged the God of the Underworld, who seized the girl and dragged her to his dark kingdom. Her mother, nearly mad with grief, wailed through the world searching for her, causing the plants to dry up, the corn to wither. This famine was known as the "Wrath of Demeter".

Demeter came to Eleusis disguised as an old woman, and stayed to care for the Princess' baby son. One night, the princess recognized the godhood of her nanny, who promptly required that they build her a temple. Demeter was still too angry with gods and men to return to Olympus: eventually, what with famine and cold, Zeus ruled that Persephone was to be allowed to visit her mother. But since she had eaten six pomegranate seeds while below the earth, she must stay with Pluton for six months of each year, when the earth would be cold and barren.

Demeter graced Eleusis with her Mysteries, rites that no one ever revealed, since the punishment would be death. Aeschulus was almost killed by an angry mob for telling a little too much in one of his plays. There are also some indignant speculations about them from early Christians - with prejudice.

General view of the Ancient Site in Eleusis.

The temple covered a large area near the bay of Eleusis, near the cave of Pluto . The Lesser Mysteries were annual and held in February, and served as a sort of initiation. Every four years there was a nine day celebration in September, beginning with sacrifices at Eleusis. A great procession of initiates, priests, and Eleusinians then moved towards Athens along the Sacred Way, Iera Odos, passing through the gate at Keramikos and going across the Agora to end at the Eleusinion, below the Propylaia. Here they invited Athenians to join them. A baptism at Faliron, sacrifices and rituals were followed by the return procession to Eleusis. At the sanctuaries on the route, the procession halted and chanted, much as they do now during the Good Friday processions (see Festivals). As the torchlit procession came to the narrow bridge over the Kephissus, the Eleusinians met the marchers, wearing disguises, and teased them with accusations and abuse from which no official or dignitary was immune.

When they reached the gate of the temple, they were greeted by dancing maidens, then went in to ceremonies of vigil and purification. During the Nights of the Mysteries, they believed they were meeting the gods of Olympus. Certain very sacred objects were displayed: nobody knows what. Nine days after the first rituals the celebration was ended.

By Alexander's day the site had become less important, but the Romans reconstructed the temple, added gates and courtyards, built bridges and spread the word of the cult. (The Museum has models of both Classical and Roman versions of the Sanctuary). Until nearly 400 years after Christ, loyal worshippers kept the faith and tended the sacred place. Finally, Alaric and the Visigoths burned the sanctuary and every priest, and the Byzantine Emperor Theodosios II banned it in 395 A.D.

Archaeological studies were begun in the late 19th century. There is a small museum holding statuary and ceramics found at the site. So many of the figures are headless that one envisages a righteous Cromwell knocking off their heads with a club. Among the Kores and Demeters is a handsome giant caryatid, a tray with a demonstration of olive oil processing, and in a case in the far room, a tiny bronze portrait which really looks like the Goddess.

The site was used for huts in Medieval times; a barracks during the War of Independence. In the 20th century, the town of Elefsina became a huge industrial zone and shipyard. (In some weather it is clear and pleasant, if the wind shifts the pollution is - awful.)

Above the sanctuary is a hill with pines, prickly pears and grass which might be a good spot for a picnic: there's a fine view from the top. When leaving the site, turn right and go towards the sea, where boarding at the bus terminal gives a chance to get a seat for the 50 minute trip back to Athens. There's also a cafeteria at the shore.

COAST OF APOLLO: The Attic Riviera

Athens' south east city boundaries reach from Faliron down to Vouliagmeni. Beyond the city the coast stretches down to Sounion on the southernmost tip of Attica, dotted with beaches, bays, small resorts and hotels. Each area has its own character and facilities and this is the most popular area for holidaymakers. It offers a rich variety of opportunities for sea and other sports, eating out and entertainment of all kinds.

Faliron Bay

Bus 132 from Othonos St. Syntagma Sq.

Leaving Athens by wide Syngrou Avenue, passing the race-course on the right, the coast is reached by a spaghetti-like delta of new road systems. The last building on the left is the Planetarium.

Turning left at the end of Syngrou, to the south-east, Faliron Bay is on the right site of the ancient harbour of Athens and of the very busy modern Flisvos Marina. Flisvos is the embarkation point for the island cruises. Of course, passengers are taken there by coach from Athens.

The Battleship Averof is moored here.

Kalamaki

Bus 103 from Akadimias

Not at first appearing to offer much in the way of entertainment this quieter area has tucked-away bars with romantic candle-li tables and soft music.

Alimos

Bus 103 from Akadimias

The coast road now passes the marina of Alimos and the Lun Park Rodeo funfare, which make this a lively area, and continues o past the Olympic Airways terminal and Hellinicon Airport. Th airport also serves the Greek and the American military bases.

On the seaward side of the road is a large youth sports centre the tiny church of Agios Kosmas (on a small spit of land), and th Oceanographic Insitute.

Glyfada

Bus 128, 129, 150 from Zappion

Continue south-east along the coast to Glyfada, popular with the airmen from the base and with many thousands of holidaymakers who seem not the least perturbed by the continuous arrival of aircraft throughout the day.

Glyfada is the largest holiday resort on the coast and offers a large selection of restaurants of international standard, pizzarias, coffee shops, ice cream parlours, discos, night clubs, pubs and fast food establishments. Konstantinopoleos Street has a continous line of steakhouses.

There are two ultra-modern shopping centres and many tourist shops, green parks and waving palms, all within a stone's throw of the well-patronised sandy beaches and four yacht harbours. Naturally Glyfada is a popular choice for evening and late night entertainment.

Visitors may use the 18 hole golf course and visiting rugger players are ecstatically welcomed by the members of the 'Spartans' rugby club (no high kicking allowed when planes are landing). Other rules and venue, ask at Flannagans.

Voula, Voulagmeni

Voula Bus 122 from Zappion
Vouliagmeni Bus 417, 152, 153 from Zappion

Varkiza:
Bus 116, 117 from Zappion
Lagonisi:
Every 30΄ min from Pl. Egyptou

A short walk brings one to Voula's Asteria beach with superior refreshment facilities, showers and toilets. Voula is well supplied with beaches and there is a second resort beach on its further periphery. Here it merges with Vouliagmeni, also well supplied with beaches. Kavouri, part of Vouliagmeni, has a rocky shore and offers good swimming to those who like to get away from the more crowded areas.

Vouliagmeni also has a lake in which to swim - very healthy if a little cold. The less hardy may prefer to bathe at the Spa which is famous for its therapeutic waters - taken externally. The lake offers a pleasant promenade, especially in the evening when the lamps are lit.

Past Vouliagmeni the coast road continues on through Attica to Sounion, through **Varkiza** and **Lagonisi.** Here, as elsewhere, Attica is closely linked with Athens which is its geographical, political, social and commercial centre - as it has been throughout history. This south-eastern coast road is well supplied with excellent modern hotels, many with self-catering bungalows.

A visit to Sounion is a must for most visitors to Athens and the journey along this road with its vistas of sea and islands, villages, mountains, green pine trees, rocky outcrops and sandy beaches would be worth making for the views alone. It follows every twist and turn of the shoreline, rounding headlands and retreating at each inlet until the very tip of Attica is reached.

Sounion

At the very tip of the tongue of the Attic peninsula is a small rocky promontory which commands a view of both the Saronic Gulf and the approaches to the north-eastern coast of Attica. Both have always been vital to the defence of Athens, making Sounion of strategic importance throughout history. Here stand the still splendid ruins of the temple of Poseidon.

Built about 444 BC, and of similar proportions to the temple of Hephaestos in Athens, it is thought to have been designed by the same architect. The town which stood here was fabulously wealthy and regattas were held here in honour of the God. Not so honourable are the thousands of autographs which have been carved into the marble. Even Lord Byron apparently couldn't resist the temptation. Obviously in those days no-one was looking - but don't try it today!

The oldest discovery here was two graves from the 3rd millenium BC, and there was an Athenian cult dating back to the 7th century BC. Both Athena and Poseidon were worshipped at this dramatic meeting point of Athens and the sea. It was surrounded by a strong retaining wall with a monumental gate and colonnaded stoas, and votive offerings have been discovered dating from the 7th c BC. It was rebuilt during the Periclean Push after its destruction during the Persian invasion. It had 6 x 13 Doric columns. Once again, the Lapiths battled with Gods and Giants on the frieze. The columns are delicate against the sky, and many recommend seeing this temple at its best at sunset.

At the top of the low hill to the north was the Sanctuary of Athena, a sacred site since the 9th c. BC. In the 5th century an Ionic temple was built, but during Roman times the sculptured stone was removed for use in the construction of the Agora.

Open daily. Bus from Platea Egyptou, every hour. Buses follow alternate routes, via coast or inland. Journey time about 2 hours.

HEART OF ATTICA: Sounion to Skala Oropos

The return journey from Sounion through the Messogia (inland Attica) runs through coastal Lavrion, site of the ancient silver mines which contributed much to the prosperity of Athens in classical times. **Thorikos**, four kilometres further north, was a city in Mycenaean times. The acropolis was on a conical hill at the foot of which most of the remaining ruins are to be found including the theatre, which was built using the natural contours of the land, giving it an irregular shape, and which included a temple of Dionysos. To the north-east are two vaulted tombs from the Mycenaean period.

The main road continues north from Lavrion to Markopoulon. East of Markopoulon is Porto Rafti on the coast, a lively resort with nice beaches. Inland the road runs through Koropi where much of Attica's retsina is made, and Paiania.

Paiania

Paiania, on the eastern side of Mount Hymettos, is the site of the Koutouki Cave with a massive array of stalactites and stalagmites. The special lighting is part of the show and for the nervous it should be noted that at one point the lights are dimmed almost to extinction for a dramatic 'dawn' scene. The 'dim-out' is only momentary but even the coolest have been known to wonder at that point how they would get out if the lights really did fail. A small torch in the pocket might help to give one a feeling of confidence.

Only four kilometers from Paiania, but the entrance is halfway up the side of Mount Hymettos and there is no shade. Not recommended for walkers in summer, though the walk down is pleasant.

Open daily. Bus no 303 or 310 from Thission.
See also Vorres Museum

Exploring Koutouki Cave

Vravron (Braurona), and Loutsa (beaches)

The small town of Loutsa is pleasant and has extensive treelined beaches. There are cafes and tavernas in the town and by the sea.

The Loutsa A bus (no. 304) turns right and continues along the coast to Vravrona, inhabited since neolithic times and site of a temple dedicated to Artemis Vravronia. When leaving the bus, the bay can be seen on the left. To reach the site, continue along the road for about one mile. The museum can be seen across a bamboo thicket before the site comes into view, but it is necessary to follow the road around the rocky outcrop hill or cross the sands to gain access to it (the land is marshy).

Iphigenia, daughter of Agamemnon, was said to have been a priestess at the temple. In the classical period Athenian girls between the ages of 5 and 10 served an apprenticeship at the temple.They wore saffron coloured robes and were known as 'little bears'.

Vravron Museum & Archaeological site, Vravrona, 0294-71020

Daily: 09.00-15.30
Sun.: 10.00-15.00
Closed: Tues.

Contains finds from the site of the sanctuary of Artemis, pottery from the local Acropolis (Helladic), and vases and stelae from various necropoli in the vicinity. Unique are the olivewood vases not found elsewhere in Greece.

There is a fish taverna overlooking the sandy bay. City buses 304, 305, 316 to the coast, No. 304 to Vravrona, from Thission bus station. It is possible to board the buses at Zappion or near the Hilton, but they are almost invariably full on leaving Thission.

Temple of Artemis in Vravron.

Rafina

North of Loutsa the small port of Rafina is an alternative port for some of the Cycladic islands. Ferries run daily to Andros, Tinos and Mykonos (check with National Tourist Office for times), also across to Karystos in Evia. The little town is modern and the quay is lined with fish restaurants. The cliff path between Loutsa and Rafina (7 km) makes a pleasant walk.
Continuing northward brings one to the small coastal villages of Mati, Agios Andreas and Nea Makri with plenty of beaches and lots of night life.

Marathon

Site of one of the most famous battles: between the Greeks and the Persians, the mound covering the Athenian dead lies between the village and the sea. In a valley to the north of the site lay the country estate of Herod Atticus, a man of many properties, who was born and died here. The museum includes pots from the extensive Neolithic settlement at Nea Makri about 2 miles to the south, and popular today for swimming.

Bus from Platea Egyptou, to the Greek Warriors Mound approx. every 30΄ min.

Rhamnous

Further up the coast is the now isolated Rhamnous, site of a once famous temple to the goddess of destiny. Nemesis measured out both happiness and misery, taking special interest in those who considered themselves to be masters of their own fates. Her temple was built on a marble platform facing the sea, near an earlier one to Themis, who personified law, equity and custom. This small temple was never completed.

Nearby a fortified town guarded the straits of Evia.

Uninhabited except by shepherds, and not easily accessible, Rhamnous now stands isolated and beautiful. Nearby Shinias has a pine shaded beach.

Bus from Platea Egyptou to Agia Marina (4 km to walk) 2 or 3 times per day.

Amphiareion

Situated inland in a wooded valley in the north of Attica, the temple of Amphiareion was once an oracle and spa. Prophet-warrior Amphiareos perished when his chariot was swallowed up by earth. His cult was similar to that of Asklepios, the power of healing being attributed to both.

Bus from Pl. Egyptou approx. every hour,

Worshippers coming to seek the cure slept in the incubation hall, wrapped in the skin of a ram, which they had sacrificed to the god. Supplicants also threw gold and silver coins into a fountain. The theatre was large and well-attended. Musical contests were held here every 4 years from 332 BC.

The buildings used by patients and their families were extensive and foundations of houses, a large stadium and theatre indicate a substantial town. Many additions were made by the Romans. Bus from Platea Egyptou to Skala Oropos.

It is possible to take the ferry from Skala Oropos to Eretria in Evia, thence by bus to Halkida, returning by bus or crossing the bridge over the 'mad waters' of Halkida for the train to Athens.

FOR A DAY

Athens is well situated for many excursions outside the limits of the city and province.

Delphi: The "navel of the world", a large site spreading over steep Mt. Parnassus, 3 hours from Athens. Here was the Oracle who advised so many of the kings. There is a splendid ancient theatre, with a spectacular backdrop of valley, mountain and sky, among the shrines and temples. High up in a peaceful stadium lizards soak up sun where athletes once o led themselves and tied back their hair to run. (See TOURS), or take a bus from Liossion Bus Station.

Mycenae: The ruined palace of Agamemnon (see Mythology, Page 22) including both the most ancient shaft graves and a superbly preserved "beehive" tomb as well as the famous Lion Gate. For many years people have refreshed themsleves at the Belle Helene taverna, named for Helen of Troy. Tour Operators offer several trips including this site, or take a local bus from 100 Kifissou Avenue, or a train.

The 'Tooth Train': Historical sites and good bathing beaches abound but there is also one trip which is a must for train enthusiasts and even non-enthusiasts who enjoy something a little out of the usual.

In reach of Athens for a one-day trip is a little rack and pinion railway running from Diakofto on the northern Peloponnese coast. Built in the late 19th century, it rises 2,399 feet up a natural gorge to Kalavrita which was previously without any means of transport, other than the donkey. There is now a road but the railway remains the only form of transport open in the winter when the mountain is heavily covered in snow.

Vertiginous precipices, splashing waterfalls, raging torrents, criss-crossing bridges, rock tunnels with little arched 'church' windows, this journey really has everything and takes 70 minutes, if the driver does not have to stop too often to wait for walkers to get out of the tunnels.

Peloponnesos Railway: Diakofto is on the narow gauge, single line Peloponnesos railway which runs to Patras (for the ferry to Brindisi), then continues down the coast to Kalamata, returning through the mountains by way of Olympia. The round-trip takes 18 hours but can be taken in stages. When the guard checks your ticket, tell him where you want to get off and he will mark your ticket accordingly. The ticket is valid for one month and costs about $ 7!.

A
B
1
2
3
4
5
Nikea
Karavas
Lefki
Ag. Dimitrios
Tabouria
Drapetsona
Keratsini
Hatzikiriakio
PORT
Drapetsona
Marina
Ormos
Afrodidis
Leof. P. Rali
P. TSALDARI
G. KONDILI
TZAVELLA
KOUNTOURIOTOU
28 OKTOVRIOU
LEOF. THIVON
AKTI KONDILI
AKTI POSID
EL. VENIZELOU
AG. PANTELEIMONOS
ANDR. MIAOULI
25 MARTIOU
PALAMA
VIRONOS
PROUSIS
IFESTOU
KYPROU
AKTI XAVERIOU
ZOOD. PIGIS
PROPONTIDOS
IKONOMOU
MIAOULI
2

D
E
Pireos
Leof. Fleming
Kaminia
Leof. Athinon
N. Kanelopoulou
Leof. Possidonos
Moschato
N. Faliro
Pr. Ilias
Mikrolimano
Kastela
Vas. Sofias
Georgiou
STALIS
Zea Marina
Vas. konstanti nou
Sachtouri
Freatis
Nilos
Moutsopoulou
Piraiki
Kalipolis
Saronic Gulf
MIKONOU
THIRAS
KITHNOU
KITHRON
SOLOMOU
OMIROU
KEFALINIAS
VALTETSIOU
ELIKONOS
KITHERONOS
PARNITHOS
SOUIDIAS
DODEKANISOU
N. FATSOULA
DA. IMPRANTI
MIKRAS ASIAS
ATH. DIAKOU
SKILITSI
DISTOMOU
PILIS
EVAGELISTRIAS
EL. VENIZELOU
KARAOLI
DIMITRIOU
TSAMADOU
SOTIROS DIOS
BOUMBOULINAS
MERARHIAS
SKOUZI
FILELINON
H. TRIKOUPI
KANTHAROU
AFENTOULI
EVERGETON
MAKRIGIANI
APOSTOLI
KOTZIADON
PAPANIKOLI
SKOULOUDI
LEOF. ZANNI
L.V. PAVLOU
DRAKOU
AKTI THEMISTOKLEOUS
MEMORANDUM
1.Railway Station to Peloponnese-C3
2.Railway Station to Northern Greece-B3
3.Electric Train, Piraeus, Athens, Kifissia-C3
4.Football stadium Karaiskaki-D2
5.Theatre-D3
6.Yachting Club-E3
7.Telephone-Telegram Services (O.T.E.)-C3
8.Central Post Office-C3
9.Alien's Bureau-C3
10.Municipal Theatre-C3
11.Town Hall-C3
12.Departure point for the Aegean Islands-C3
13.Departure point for Salamis Island-C3
14.Departure point for the Saronic Islands-C3
15.Tourist Police-C3
16.Departure point for foreign Lines-C4
17.Port Authorities-C4
18.Central Customs House-C4
19.Archeological Museum-D4
20.First Aid Station-C3
21.Naval Museum-D4
Stadium of Peace and Friendship-E2

SOMETIMES ON SUNDAY: The Piraeus

For most tourists Piraeus is memorable for the number of ships constantly moving in and out of the port or just lying at anchor. There are frequent services to Egypt, Israel, and other Mediterranean countries; huge white cruise ships call daily to spill their passengers into waiting coaches; cargo ships unload near the railheads and, of course, ferries leave constantly for the islands.

Boats depart daily for Rodos (Rhodes), Crete and Aegean Islands. Ferries and hydrofoils run frequently to and from the Saronic Gulf islands and there is a constant to-ing and fro-ing of little boats to nearby Salamina (Salamis).

Most tourists in transit use the electric train which whisks them into the centre of Athens in less than half an hour. They rush on, glad to leave the crowded quayside, without realising that Piraeus is not a suburb of Athens but a city in its own right with many facets and a unique and interesting character. Resisting strenuously any attempt at a take-over by Athens the Piraiots are proud of their city, of their working origins and culture, which in the 20's and 30's gave rise to the Rembetika music, soon taken up by other working-class communities. This side of Piraeus became known to the outside world in the 60's, through the film 'Never on Sunday'. Piraeus has changed since then but is still a lively and independent place.

Islanders coming off the boats have other calls to make before taking the train or bus. First a visit to the nearby taverna or coffee bar which is owned by a native of their own island. Here they thankfully put down the extra sack or parcel they have brought from the island, which may now have reached its final destination or is simply left here to be called for. Then come the little coffee cups and the serious matter of the moment, passing on the island news - to be told again in turn to any other islanders who live on the mainland and who call in when time permits. This is the island 'post office', luggage depository, and general gossip shop.

Possibly this essential service is what helps to keep the Piraeus Sunday morning market busy all the year round. The market can be found by following the railway line back a couple of blocks. Its stalls spread out into a dozen neighbouring streets. Almost anything can be bought or sold here on a Sunday morning. Birds, live or stuffed, fish, fruit, souvlaki, socks, radios, cheap booze, gas cylinders, old furniture...

Many people visit or pass through Piraeus many times and never see more than is visible from this point. The town proper is built on a double Peninsula with a narrow neck and it is only by exploring this peninsula that one can begin to see the wealth of variety it has to

Aerial view of Piraeus with its port in the backround

offer. The main street, named after the heroes (and heroines) of the Polytechnio runs down the centre of the "humpback" peninsula and the shops and central squares are here, together with the impressive neoclassical City Theatre.

Perhaps the best way to discover Piraeus is by making a circuit of the seafront. Leaving the electric train station and turning left along Akti Kalimasioti, first come the quays from which the ferries leave for Thira (Santorini), and Crete. A few yards along is Karaiskaki Square, from the far side of which buses leave for both the airport terminals. To the right of this bus stop is the Flying Dolphin departure point for Aegina while on the left, in Akti Miaouli, is the departure point for the ferries to the island. On past the big ferries are the smaller express boats and the smaller ferries. Next come the little boats for Salamis.

Here the coast road turns at a right-angle near the cathedral church of the Holy Trinity, into Akti Miaouli. Continue past the Dodekanese ferries, the cruise ships, the international quays and the Customs House to reach the impressive Exhibition Hall of the Port of Piraeus, hosting some of the larger exhibitions in the Athens area.

The outer point is taken up by the Naval Station and it's a good idea to walk on past the Exhibition Hall, leave the sea where the coast road takes a right and walk uphill a little way to Hatsikyriakou Street to take the 904 bus. This will take you across the peninsula to Akti Themistokleous, where the old defensive wall can be seen following the coast for a considerable distance.

From here on, the journey is along the coast of Freattys where the huge yacht harbour of Zea Marina is situated, and where the bus leaves the coast after first circling the small outer harbour which houses the Naval Museum (see page 119). The museum can be reached from the slip road which is also the approach road to the quay for the Flying Dolphin hydrofoils.

Round the point is the main harbour - an almost circular basin full of yachts of all sizes and ports of origin. In classical times Zea housed 196 ship-sheds, fanned out round the bay.

Harilaou Trikoupi Street, with its broad green central strip, runs uphill from the nearside of the bay. Here the Archaeological Museum stands next to the remains of a 2nd c. B.C. Hellenistic theatre of Zea of which little remains.

Naval Week is held annually starting on the first Sunday in July, including nautical sports, boat races, and exhibitions in both Zea and Mikrolimano. The fleet is at home to visitors and the week ends with a spectacular firework display.

Zea Marina

Still circling the coast, next comes the small fishing harbour of Turkolimano (its official name, much ignored, is Microlimano). This pretty bay is lined with fish restaurants, the tables are set under brighly coloured awnings along the shore beside the fishing boats which bring in the catch. Probably you will find the fishermen mending their nets, while one or two caiques are circling around, indicating in sign language that they are for hire for a short trip. The restaurants are very select and rather expensive but very popular with Athenians who like to get out of the city. Turkolimano can be reached from Zea on the No. 20 trolley bus.

The trolley skirts the harbour from the heights of Kastella (ancient Munychia). The views from here are magnificent, there are excellent restaurants and the open air Veakio Theatre specialises in visually spectacular shows, such as the Don Cossacks, and dance groups from such diverse places as Poland and Brazil. The lights can be seen all down the coast, as well as those of the ships anchored in the bay. From the cheaper seats on the upper tier you will be able to admire the view at the same time as watching the show.

The 904 and 905 buses follow circular routes, both from the electric station at Piraeus. The no. 20 trolley runs between the Piraeus and Faliron stations. The no. 901 bus from the electric station passes the theatre. Special buses run to the theatre from Athens on performance nights. Check when booking.

Nearing completion is the Peace and Friendship Stadium, one of the most modern in Europe, occupying an 8-acre site at the western end of Faliron Bay. From the Faliron electric train station you can see its white curved wing. The stadium seats up to 16,000 spectators and is fully equipped for track events, athletics, weightlifting gymnastics, volleyball, table tennis, basketball, tennis, ice skating and ice hockey. There are exhibition halls and conference rooms restaurants and snackbars.

The complex has separate accommodation for gymnastics fencing, table tennis, wrestling, shooting and squash. Athletes in training have everything from saunas to library at their disposal, and the media are well catered for.

Separate open air sites include sports facilities, exhibition areas, refreshments and a childrens playground. Adjacent is a new marina for small yachts.

The gymnasium is open to the public and gymnastic instructors conduct free one-hour sessions at pre-arranged times between 9-11 and 3-5 daily. Phone 412-4024 for information.

THE SARONIC ISLANDS

Greek Islands have each a character so individual that no two are exactly alike, even in the same group. Probably this is more true of the Saronic Gulf islands than any others. These islands are so close to Athens that it's possible to visit three of them on a cruise and still be back for dinner! For a modest price you can leave your hotel in the morning, tour the islands and return in time for dinner. Lunch on the ship is inclusive.

If you prefer to be independent take the ferry or Flying Dolphin hydrofoil. The island you choose to visit will depend on your own taste. The following is a brief description of the different islands to help you choose.

Saronic Gulf Services

1. Steamer and Ferryboat Services

From Piraeus to:	Daily frequencies	Duration of trip
EGINA:	12-13	1.30
POROS:	5	3.00
HYDRA (IDRA):	1	3.30
SPETSES:	1	5.00

For information call the Piraeus Port Authority, Tel.: 4511311.

2. Fast Hydrofoil Services

Though a bit more expensive, supplement the steamer services listed above. For Egina, the service operates from the main port of Piraeus. For Poros, Hydra, Spetses, they sail from the Zea Marina, next to Piraeus. For information call, 4527107 (10 lines) and 4523612.

From Piraeus or Zea to:	Daily Frequencies	Duration of trip
EGINA:	12-13	0.35
POROS:	8-9	1.00
HYDRA:	10-12	1.15
SPETSES:	10-12	1.50

Egina (Aigina, Aegina)

EGINA (0297)
Police Station: 22931
Municipality: 22409, 24215
OTE: 22135
Port: 22328
Hospital: 22251, 22209

Egina, the largest island, is the closest to Athens and very popular with Athenians, many of whom own houses there, where they spend the hot summer months in the fresh air. Many residents work in Athens and commute, so services are plentiful. Add an enormous number of tourists, both Greek and foreign, and one tends to expect the worst! Fear not, among the luxury yachts there are still fishing boats and little caiques selling fruit and vegetables, and the fish market has not been banished from the harbour front. Facing the harbour are Egina pottery shops, ice cream parlours and tavernas, and a wine shop where you bring your own food to be cooked while you sample retsina from the barrels. The people are friendly, the prices reasonable, the island is beautiful and there are pleasant beaches.

Egina was once a powerful state, trading throughout the Mediterranean. Her merchants built a temple to Zeus at the founding of the city of Naukratis on the Nile. About 650 BC. the island became rich enough to mint silver coins (with a tortoise motif), the first in Europe, which were used throughout the Greek world. So many foreign merchants were attracted to Egina, both for trade and to find capital for their ventures, that a special law court was set up for them. A special physician was appointed to deal with public health.

A rival to Athens, the island beat the city in battle in 880 BC. In spite of an alliance with Persia, with whom she had strong trading ties, Egina joined the Greek alliance and sent a powerful fleet to fight at Salamis in 490 BC, acquitting herself so well that the island was given first choice of the spoils after the Persians were defeated. But under Pericles the Athenians returned to attack. At the outbreak of the Peloponnesian War islanders were deported, returning when the Spartans were victorious.

Colonised by the Romans, the Franks, the Catalans and the Venetians, sacked by Barbarossa, repopulated with Albanians and then retaken by the Venetians, the island was ceded by them to Turkey in 1718. Temporary capital for two brief years after independence, the first modern Greek coins were minted there, the motif this time being a phoenix.

Most ferries sail direct to Egina town, which is a delightful place to spend a day, wandering around the village, enjoying coffee and delicious pastries, swimming, visiting the remains of the temple of Apollo and museum with its wealth of local treasures, riding in an *"amaxaki"* behind a patient horse and dining at one of the many tavernas.

Turn left when arriving for the bus station (in front of the post office) if you wish to visit any other part of the island. Souvalla, in the north, is a pretty village with beautiful surrounding countryside. Some Egina ferries make a brief stop there. Aghia Marina, with magnificent beaches, pedillos, surfboards, tavernas, bars and craft shops, has its own small boat service from Piraeus. This is the usual port of call for the 'three islands cruise ships.

Four kilometres inland from Aghia Marina is the temple of Aphaia, which forms a unilateral triangle with the Acropolis and the temple of Poseidon at Sounion. The setting, on the summit of a pineclad hill, is breathtakingly beautiful. From here the bus route into Egina runs through groves of pistachio trees, grape vines, olives, figs, almonds and pines. For a simple 'do-it-yourself' tour take a small ferry out to Aghia Marina and have a swim before visiting the temple. Then take the bus into Egina and explore the town. You should have plenty of time to enjoy a harbourside meal before returning to Piraeus. Or, if you succumb to the island's undoubted charm, stay overnight. There are a few discos, but generally speaking Egina is an island for the holidaymaker who likes peace and quiet - and oh, so near to Athens...

The Temple of Aphaia (the Invisible)

It was taken many years to identify the deity of this temple: at one time it was considered to be dedicated to Zeus; when the 5th century pediments were found, it was clearly Athena's. Since the early 20th century it has been attributed to a minor Cretan goddess who fell into the sea while fleeing from the unwelcome passions of Minos. No sooner had she been rescued by fishermen than one of them went for her (some things never change). By now they had landed on Egina, and calling upon her goddess Artemis, she vanished. The fisherman wondered for a while, then the islanders gave her a temple. Eventually, this cult was blended with Athena's.

The forested hill conceals the beauty of this building until you are nearly upon it, except for some glowing columns overhead. This is one of the few two-story Doric temples still standing, and the sun casts complex shadows on the golden stone.

It has six by twelve columns, gracefully inclined inwards. A two-story stoa enclosed three sides of the cella where stood the ivory and gilded wood wooden cult statue. Some red plaster can still be seen on the floor, and yellow stucco still adheres to cracks in the walls.

Outside the temple itself are remains of altars, the priests' houses and the propylon (entrance) with columned rooms and a courtyard, which leads onto the terrace.

Unfortunately, the usual plundering occurred and the pediment sculptures and "seventeen complete statues and the fragments of at least ten more" were sent to the Munich Glyptothek in 1813. These portrayed battles surrounding the figure of Athena. Heroes from Egina - Achilles, Ajax Telamon, fought with Herakles against the king of Troy and the pediments were dedicated to them. The western pediment had thirteen statues, Athena with warriors; the eastern pediment was struck by lightning soon after it was built, and the fallen heads and torsos are in the National Archeological Museum or the Aegina Museum.

Check the ferry times to Piraeus when you get to Egina , they vary from day to day.

Make a pleasant trip along the coast to Perdika (Partridge), a very small but pretty fishing harbour with tavernas along the sea front. Small caiques ply between here and the tiny island of Moni with beaches, camping site and peacocks. There is a small entrance fee.

There is also a caique service from Egina to the small island of Angistri, but its sandy beach has no shade and the thermometer registers temperatures more suitable to cooking than to sunbathing.

Poros

Thickly wooded Poros is effectively two islands joined by a narrow spit of sand. The strait between it and the mainland is like a calm inland sea. The temple of Poseidon stands just above the

monastery, a short walk from town between forest and sea. This and many sandy coves can be reached by caique.

The temple of Poseidon here was the traditional sanctuary for fugitives. Demosthenes fled here in defeat in 322 BC, but he was followed and eventually committed suicide by biting his poison-filled quill pen.

Very close is Galata on the Peloponnese mainland from which ply a constant stream of ferry boats. Visit Trizina, birthplace of Theseus, or just stroll through the peaceful lemon groves.

POROS (0298)
Police: 22462
Municipality: 22250, 23089
OTE: 22299
Port: 22274
Health Station: 22600, 22266

Hydra (Idra)

Favoured by artists, shipowners and the jet set, famous for Italianate architecture, gabled roofs, international hotels and gay night life: Hydra.

The harbour of this traffic-free island is lined with restaurants, bars, jewellers' shops and art galleries. Thick with old sea captains' mansions, windmills on the horizon, white chapels and prickly pears, the island has long been popular with artists. There is an international branch of the Athens School of Fine Arts housed in the fine old mansion of the Tombazi family.

Visit one of the three monasteries on donkey back or take a small caique to the old naval arsenal of Mandraki, with its sandy beaches. Swim at Bariami where an old sea cave has been converted into a swimming pool or climb to Eros for a panoramic view of the island and its beautiful setting. Take your gayest clothes if you are having a night out on the island.

HYDRA (0298)
Police Station: 52205
Municipality: 53003
OTE: 52339
Port: 52279
Hospital: 53151

Spetses

If the gentle atmosphere, intricately cobbled streets and horse-drawn carriages of this quiet spot induce you to believe that nothing exciting ever happened here, visit the house of Bouboulina. The famous patriot who captained her own warship in the War of Independence was born here and led a rumbustious life.

SPETSES (0298)
Police: 73100
Municipality: 72225
OTE: 72399
Port: 72245
Health Station: 72472

Lascarina Bouboulina was born (May 1771) in the prison in Constantinople, where her mother was visiting her dying father. Because Catherine of Russia took a keen interest in Greek and Balkan affairs, Russian names turn up in Greek history. Bouboulina's father had been taking part in an incident involving the Orlov brothers. Her mother remarried in Spetes, a captain Lazarou-Orlov. Bouboulina married twice, both captains, the second being Dimitrios Bouboulis. Both her husbands were killed by pirates, leaving her wealthy. The Turks tried to confiscate her property, claiming that her husband had been in the pay of Russia. The Russian ambassador Stroganov helped her, she retrieved her property, and joined the *Filiki Etairia*, the secret society of Greek patriots. She financed and commanded her own ships during the War of Independence. In 1825 she retired from her naval career.

Bouboulina had six children. One of them eloped in 1825, and in the course of a family quarrel, a bullet struck down the heroine. The naval museum has many records of the struggle. The blowing up of Turkish ships is still celebrated in September with a spectacular firework display.

Visit Dappia Square which is the island's social centre, or take a walk and discover some of the secluded bays for a swim.

The tiny island to the south is Spetsopoula, owned by the fabulously wealthy Niarchos shipping family.

Salamis

SALAMIS (01)
Police: 4651100
Municipality: 4651138
Port: 4653252
OTE: 51199

Famed for the decisive sea battle which brought crushing defeat on the Persians, its long connection with ships continues to this day. On the north side lies a naval dockyard. Not a holiday island but of interest to shipping enthusiasts. A pleasant short trip by boat from Piraeus.

Sunset in Hydra: The magic of colours

MUSEUMS

Opening times are given on the 24 hour system, i.e. 10.00-15.00, indicating 10 a.m. to 3 p.m. Admission times are subject to change. Better call before visiting.

Archeological

Archeological Funds Department, Tossitsa 1, (part of the National Archeological Museum) Monday-Friday 11.00-13.00: Free passes are available for certain artists, archeologists, art historians/professors, guides, journalists.

Infotip. Any official document in Greece is likely to require two small photos and valid ID, (student card, union card, license as appropriate).

National Archeological Museum

44, Patission and Tossitsa St. Tel: 821-7724 (Information in English) Tues.-Fri. 08.00-16.00, Sun 08.00-15.00 Trolleys 2, 4, 7, 8, 9, 11, 12, 13 Buses 030, 031, 032, 034

The Archeological Museum is a superb collection of statuary, vases, jewels, wall paintings from prehistoric to Hellenistic times. Only after the War of Independence (1821) were educated Greeks able to found a national collection of Greek antiquities, and begin to halt the centuries-long souvenir-hunting that enriched the museums of other countries. The present Museum was begun in 1866.

The Museum Shop selling reproductions is down a corridor on your right just outside the main door: it closes at 13.00. Books and postcards are on sale in the entrance lobby, and so is a concession selling reproduction jewellery.

The collection is described in chronological order. But in the museum itself you have to backtrack to find the next sequence of halls. They are numbered, which helps you to find your way.

Prehistoric Rooms 4, 5, 6

Behind the entrance hall on the left is Room 5, housing the collection of Neolithic remains from northern Greece (Dimini, Sesklo, Thessaly), mostly vases and statuettes. Vases are remarkably long-lived objects - over 5,000 years in some cases. On the right (Room 6) are the charming figures from the Cycladic Islands where an island culture flourished in the Bronze Age.

In central Room 4 are the spectacular finds from the **tombs of Mycenae.** No one knows from where or how all the gold suddenly appeared from which the artisans of Mycenae created masks, novelty drinking cups in the shapes of animals, inlaid swords and jewellery. The upper classes were impressed by the merry Minoans and adapted their motifs, costumes, designs and even hair-dos to their somewhat grimmer world view. Among the dazzling body decorations and weapons there is an astonishing statuette in ivory showing two females and a child, in the topless outfit of ruffled trousers known to us from Crete - yet in pose and mood resembling the sinuous, sculptured ladies of India. Some of the most exquisite works are the small rings and seals in gold, amethyst and clay.

Sculpture-Archaic Period: Rooms 7-13 Left of Entrance Hall

Here begin examples of sculpture from Keramikos and lots of "Kouroi", naked young men stepping forward on one foot with long formally curled hair, expressions of blank good nature and clenched fists. These are memorial pieces from tombs, which explains why there are fewer "Korai" (girls) because having to provide her dowry is enough, never mind memorials. These daughters are always dressed in stiffly folded drapery. "Phrasikleia" in Room 9 looks like someone you might like to know - but they have unkindly moved her boyfriend (they were found together) into the next room.

In Room 12 is the **"Stele of the Hoplite"** which has been called a

Golden Death mask from Mycenae.

The stele of the "Hoplite".

running warrior - but if anybody ever ran like that he'd go flat on his face. Obviously, he's snapping his fingers and dancing: you can see similar poses in any taverna when the mood's right. Tombstones become more elaborate as we approach classical times, until they are whole family portraits, complete with mourning relatives. One of the carved bases of a kouros shows some bare youths playing a game suspiciously like hockey.

Classical Period: Rooms 14-20

These rooms contain the classical works of the fifth century BC, the period of the greatest achievements in philosophy, art, architecture - the Golden Age of Perikles. The major work in Room 15 is the (human) life-size bronze of **Poseidon,** arms outstretched as though aiming a spear or trident. His face is calm, as well it should be: this confident sea-god sank the ship carrying his statue off to Rome.

Stelae made a comeback: the next rooms are full of them.

No. 1419 in Room 18 is a fragment of a stone poster, publicizing some state decree. Rooms 19 and 20 look out on to the courtyard where the coffee bar is located, and contain various heads, statuettes and stelae. A clumpy Athena is supposed to resemble the great Parthenon statue, and since her helmet has become so complicated that it looks like a sinister growth, it's a depressing notion. However, a much smaller and more delicate version - in spite of the excrescences on the helmet - may be found at the other end of the room. Room 18 contains some very sophisticated stelae, with expressive draped figures. Among the pale marbles it's sometimes hard to remember that these were coloured brightly as icons, with gold jewellery, blue backgrounds and patterned draperies.

Late Classical Period: Rooms 21-28

Room 21 contains a life-size horse leaping forward in an incredible achievement of balanced metal. A very intense small jockey boy, found separately, has been placed on his back. A couple of marble matrons stand contemplating the crowds which gather around the **Jockey bronze.** Room 22 contains architectural sculpture from Epidaurus, and the sanctuary of Asklepios. Room 23 contains more stelae, which now become more like illustrations: Alkias (No. 751) is shown stomping on his fallen enemy in a wild dance, and there's quite a lot of dialogue among the figures of the stele of the Ilissos. Sphinxes have now been replaced by Sirens with sweet faces.

Room 24: No longer mere gravestones, now we find monumental sculptures: huge vases of stone; complex figures. Rooms 25-27 have more of those marble posters - decrees; public accounts. Once more, in 317 BC, an edict forbidding grave monuments was sternly spoken, er, carved: perhaps as a result of protest from persons who could not afford almost fully rounded portraits like the one from the shrine of Aristonautes, (No. 738). One wonders if there were demonstrations for funerary equality, with marble banners... The sculptor of the

Boy Jockey from Artemision.

horseman (No. 4464) might have carved this elaborate piece and sold it to an Athenian of Kolonos, where it was found in 1948.

Room 28 contains a lovely youth, with a hand raised and curved as if holding something small and round. His bronze face is embellished with real eyes and informally tumbled curls, and the roughness of semi-finished clay. His face is idealized, as are so many of the period. He is labelled variously as Paris with the golden apple; Perseus holding the Medusa's head (presumably by a very large round snake-head); or an athlete with a ball. Some nice ladies occupy this room as well, and two tripods from the Street of Tripods in Plaka. In Room 29 is a lovely and very drapey Themis from Rhamnous.

Hellenistic Period: Rooms 29-32

Room 30 contains portrait heads, no longer idealized. The philosopher of Antikythera looks like the work of a disillusioned pupil who considered his Master to be a lump with sharp eyes. His feet and a hand are displayed in a case nearby. The boxer looks more like a kindly chap who would have been good company in the taverna, while the Poet is brooding over his lost ideals, love, or patron.

At this time, the focus of power was in Macedonia with Alexander, and was soon to be lost to Greece altogether. Athens was already historical: hence portraits were to please patrons, rather than ideals to celebrate the glory of gods. A Poseidon from the same island as the Venus de Milo makes a rhetorical gesture, far away from the strong throw of the bronze of the earlier period. Stelae from the provinces a relief of Herakles relaxing, from Eleusis: heads, and more portraits show the characteristic flowing lines and curling forms of the Hellenistic Age, coincidental with the elaboration of the Corinthian column in architecture. The "Slipper Slapper", a slick, unconvincing cartoon of a Pan being rejected by Aphrodite gives evidence of some splendid smoothing tools. Room 34, the room of the Altar, holds various small reliefs and statuettes.

Graeco-Roman Period: Rooms 41-43

Greece was becoming a Roman colony, which meant constant "export" of her works of art, artists, sculptors. Greek marble statuary was in demand as Roman garden ornaments or home decorating novelties. The city of Athens retained her faded glory as the only place a Roman citizen could expect to find real culture (and bring some home with him, of course, for the garden: "If not an original, at least get a copy, Marcus, or bring the copyist home as a slave!"). Portrait heads from Rome are very serious and though blank-eyed, convey a great sense of Moral Superiority. Portrait heads from enslaved Roman Greece are melancholy and thoughtful. Portraits of the Roman Emperors - Augustus, Claudius, Hadrian,

left: The Marathon Boy. right: The Youth of Antikythera.

Verus, Marcus Aurelius, with Herod Atticus and a "philosopher" who looks like the conventional image of the chap from Galilee, and more funerary portraits in the outdated Archaic or Classical style include a number of philosophers. By now schools of philosophy were the only cultural attraction of Athens. Room 43 contains two busts of **Antinoos** (Nos 417 and 418), a young man whose suicide in the Nile caused Hadrian to cry himself to sleep.

Bronzes: All periods

Most of these are small statuettes, offerings to the gods as thanks or prayers. Portraying god, sacrificer or sacrifice, they vary from votive miniatures of great skill to the delectable Thessalian warrior (No. 12831) with his enormous neck, silly grin and wing-like shield. He wears a thick belt, a large masculinity and a little woolly hat knitted by his mum, and is identified as Achilles, the chap whose tantrums terrorized Troy.

There is a geometrically decorated General (No. 16727) considering the omens as he balances on chubby little bare feet. Room 37 contains Archaic works in bronze, with the familiar smile; stylized sphinxes in relief; brooches, and a small figurine with seven women dancers, from Olympia. Among these is the head of a very smug warrior.

This room also contains a number of works found on the Acropolis. When the Persians invaded, they threw down all the statuary from the temples. When the Athenians were able to return to their homes, they buried these bronzes in the rock where they were not found until the 1880's. These are the votive statues dedicated mostly to Athena, offered during the Archaic Period Winged Victories; Athenas; kouroi (youths) and horses; vase handles; mirrors - all much less formal and stiff than the contemporary marble carvings.

The major piece in this area is the elegant **"Marathon Boy"**, a Hermes who was probably used as a lampstand in Herod Atticus Villa. He seems to be considering something very seriously as he leans on a wall. Praxiteles, perhaps Greece's greatest sculptor, did not have to resort to extra bracing at the feet.

Mycenean and earlier pottery is shown in the prehistoric rooms Here are the delightful, restored frescoes and pottery found on the island of Santorini (Thera). These show trade with both Crete and Mycenae. From the very complete murals of ships and villages much has been clarified about warships of the period. **"Boxing Children"** and **"Antelopes"** are exquisite.

UPPER FLOOR: Room 48

Misleadingly called the "Vase Collection" this section contains all sorts of pottery besides vases - house models, heads, figurines, spoons, chariot models and paintings on wood. There are, indeed, a lot of vases, depicting mostly X-rated scenes of men and women, men and men, satyrs and people, animals and people in all sorts of unprintable positions.

Rooms 49-56

The Geometric period, which followed the decline of the Minoan and Mycenean, produced works in which naturalistic designs of flowers, plants and animals give way to formal patterning. Examples date from the 11th c. BC and came from Dipylon (Keramikos) and were used as tombstones. Often a hole was left in the bottom of the vase to drain offerings of milk and honey or wine to the dead. Urns were used as receptacles for the ashes after cremation. Vases were also used to commemorate other events like weddings, or for votive offerings.

By the 7th century, the painting of black figures on natural clay was becoming predominant, with some elements picked out in red. White also begins to be used for emphasis. Natural forms reappear.

Room 52 has finds from the Temple of Hera in Argos, with animal-shaped spoons, models and miniature horses. Tempera-on-wood paintings from the 6th century occupy the central table, a rare chance to compare painting on a flat surface with the curved vase paintings.

Room 52 holds further black figure vases and a charming wooden chariot with a horse, a bier, and mourners. Some of the best-known pieces are displayed here, many from the Acropolis. No. 606, a handsome battle composition on a tripod, shows chariots in use in Homeric times, a slight anachronism. The painters of many of these have been identified by manner or signature. By 480 BC the artists were painting the backgrounds black and the figures were left the clay colour, with a combination of brush addition and stylus removal of paint (red-figure). This room contains some pots made like heads, labelled "Plastic" which doesn't mean what you think.

In Room 55 we find the white lekythoi, called the "flowers of Death". Rows and rows of these funereal pots, all the same shape, with different paintings on the white background, and the same bases and border decorations, give the whole room a rather spooky effect. A few red-figure vases punctuate the gloom. In Case 99 are the two most famous of these, slightly charred from the fire in the tomb. Spooky.

To Room 56 with some relief, and some striking masterpieces: the Gigantomachy (Battle of Giants) *pelike*, No. 1333: the Panathenaic Amphoras, showing athletes freely drawn in the silhouette effect of traditional black figure approved in Athens; the "Attic Amphora" No. 15113; the elaborately coloured red and white figures of the 4th century - and the charming Tanagra figurines.

Eleni Stathatou Room

This room contains small treasures from a private collection, and treasures they are: gold; elaborate Byzantine jewels; tiny delicate carvings; Ancient Greek Easter Eggs in coloured marble; costumes and works from the least-known periods as well as the best.

Goulandris Cycladic Art Museum

4, Neofytou Douka St. Tel.: 7234931 Daily: 10.00-16.00 Sat.: 10.00-13.00 Closed: Thur.-Sun.

A spectacular collection of the strange sculptures of the prehistoric Cycladic islands, exhibited to maximum advantage in a new and beautifully designed setting. Labels are clear in Greek and English, as are poster commentaries. Don't miss the exhibit of comparison photos of modern art works by Picasso and Henry Moore, or the historical charts donated by the British Museum near the coffee bar downstairs. Fine gift shop with reasonable prices.

National Epigraphical Museum

1, Tossitsa St. (Nat. Arch. Mus.) Tel.: 821-7637 Daily: 08.30-13.30 Sun. 09.00-13.00 Closed: Tues. Adm.: Free

Eulogies to dead heroes, war memorials, temple dedications, building records and epigrams are all here laboriously carved on stone slabs for the populace to read. Among the more interesting items are the decrees published from time to time by the Athenian authorities. Perhaps then as now laws did not come into effect until published. The earliest known decree defines the status of Klerucks (foreigners) on Salamis. An edict of Diocletian found at Aigina published fixed price limits for wages, merchandise and foodstuffs in 301 AD. Perikles gets a mention in a decree concerning the water system of Athens, and the disposition of the revenue accruing from it. The laity also took a close interest in Temple finances and an account of the sacred fund of Nemesis was published around 450 BC.

There were close connections between Athens and Cyprus, and Cypriot merchants obtained a decreee granting permission to found a sanctuary in Attica to Aphrodite.

Military affairs featured in an important edict concerning the evacuation of Athens and preparations for naval defence before the battle of Salamis in 480 BC - all successfully executed when the time came. No wonder the Persians rushed around wrecking the place when they discovered how the Athenians had planned to lure them to leave their ships and cut their supply lines!

National Numismatic Collection

1, Tossitsa St. (Nat. Arch. Mus.), Tel.: 821-7769. Daily: 09.30-13.30 Sun: 09.00-14.00 Closed: Mon. Adm.: Free

This collection of coins and seals is fascinating in its variety. Seals are made from many materials including tiny precious stones, some only a quarter of an inch across with meticulously carved impressions, full of tiny detail. There are coins from many countries and eras, including those of Egina, where the first European coins were minted. They bore the picture of a tortoise. Appropriately, the modern mint on Egina produced the first coins after independence - this time carrying the impression of a phoenix.

There are several private collections on display and some treasure trove, hard-won savings buried for safety in times of danger and never recovered.

Impressive in size and weight are the copper talents, made in the shape of ox hides which were then the customary exchange medium. The huge metal talents represented the first step from barter to currency - a great new 'convenience' to buyers and sellers though not quite as handy as credit cards are today. No small change these - no wonder the great chunks of metal were hidden under a bushel!

Acropolis Museum

See Acropolis, page 52

Agora Museum (Stoa of Attalos)

See Agora, Page 59

Kanellopoulos Museum

Theorias/Panos St., Plaka (top road skirting Acropolis) Tel.: 321-2313 Daily 09.00-15.00 Sun. 09.30-14.30 Closed: Tues.

This fine mansion houses a private collection of artifacts from all periods of Greek history: stone axe-heads in mint condition, carved with precision to absolute symmetry to give the finest balance incredibly well preserved spear-heads of the Mycenaean period clay figures from the 4th c. BC crafted with exquisite detail. Every single item in the museum is beautifully displayed and lit but, sadly there is very little labelling, even in Greek.

Keramikos (Oberlaender) Museum

See Keramikos, page 62

Amphiaraion Museum

See Amphiaraion, page 94

VASES AND CONTAINERS

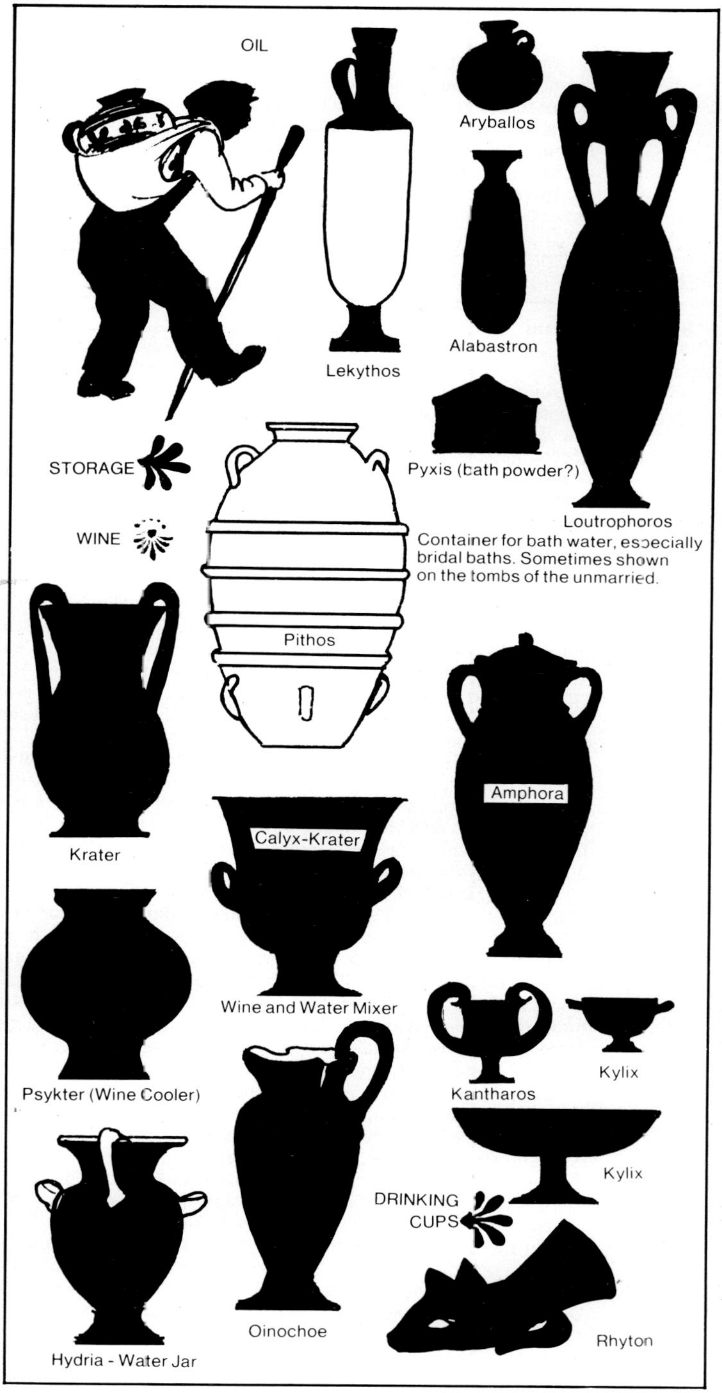

Piraeus Archeological Museum

31, Harilaou Trikoupi St. Tel.: 452-1598 Daily: 09.00-15.00 Sun: 09.30-14.30 Closed: Tue.

The famous bronze statues of Athena and Apollo have now been restored to Piraeus. The statues were discovered in Piraeus harbour where they had sunk in ancient times, probably en route to embellish some Roman gentleman's villa. What happened to the Roman? Perhaps Athena's friend Nemesis stepped in before he could carry out his intent.

There are some interesting pairs of reliefs showing battles between the Greeks and the Amazons.

Historical

Benaki Museum

Vas. Sofias Ave/Koumbari St. Tel: 361-1617 Daily: 08.30-14.00 Closed: Tues.

Anthony Benaki was an Alexandrian Greek, devoted to his country's culture, who persuaded his sisters to share in his offer of the family house to the cause of culture. He (and later others) contributed his personal collection of things that interested him. The result is a museum of decorative arts, history and costume, gathered together as a Museum of the Greek soul. On the right of the entrance are rooms in which books, gifts and cards may be purchased. There are three floors of exhibits.

Objects from Mycenaean, archaic and classical periods - tiny figures of clay, stone and gold. Room II is Alexandrian and Roman, with a case of very fluttery gold necklaces. Throughout the whole Museum are found an incredible number and variety of earrings; and many works are miniatures which bear close study. The early Christian (Coptic) culture which reached from Syria to Africa combined Greek, Roman and Byzantine elements in textiles, crafts and carvings. Byzantium is represented by gold, jewellery and some magnificent church relics, ivories, and of course, paintings.

Islamic art is shown on the ground and first floors. At one end of room V is a jazzy 17th century reception hall from Egypt, made of small tiles in contrasting colours, and including a fountain, a basin and tiled walls. Wall hangings of velvets with gold patterns; window frames; various ornaments; pottery; some pointed helmets and other metalwork covering the 7th to the 18th centuries are here.

Post-Byzantine church art is in Room VI, mostly relics from the 15th to 19th centuries which were brought from Asia Minor by the refugees of 1922. Among the Post-Byzantine paintings (15th cent. to 1669) are found two early works by El Greco (Domenico Theotokopoulos). Room VIII offers a chance to study the changes in icon painting over the centuries. Iconography is much more ritually formalized than Western Art - the Renaissance was almost irrelevant to this specialized image-making - yet there are subtle changes in style and approach with foreign influences seeping in.

With Room IX comes a sudden change of pace. It is a memorial to Eleftherios Venizelos, the statesman who worked to join Crete to Greece and whose diplomatic efforts molded the relationships between Greece and Europe in the early 20th century. The room shows photographs of important moments and treaties: a charming naïf painting of the gentleman in foustanella, standing on a tiger: letters and documents of historical importance.

On the stairs and landings, views of Greek history by foreign visitors - mostly dating from the exciting period of the 19th century War of Independence, and the monarchies of Otho and Amalia, and George I. These are fascinating records, sometimes made by sophisticated foreign witnesses, and more often by untrained patriots trying to record moments of vital importance. Paintings and artefacts, maps and charts of battles, weapons and mementoes of the War and the warriors; memorabilia of Lord Byron - a lock of hair, pistols, portraits... Intriguing item No. 8346, in a glass case of

Portrait from Fayum, 3d c.AD.

documents and snuffboxes, shows "Rings of members of a secret society formed in connection with the succession to the throne..." The rings are little Borgia boxes.

The Oriental collection from Egypt, Persia, Syria continues with carvings and textiles, weapons and jewellery. Suddenly, in Room XX, the Greek soul seems to have undergone an astonishing metamorphosis, producing T'ang Horses, jade and crystal Buddhas, pottery, Ching Dynasty embroidered robes and "famille rose" porcelain. Well, the porcelain elephant was a gift from the Mikado to King George. This Chinese pottery collection was a legacy from another Greek benefactor, G. Eumorphopoulos, expressing perhaps the Greek identity in its sea-going or world-traveller aspect.

The remainder of this floor consists of displays of traditional embroidery from the Greek islands and villages, suggesting an unbelievable amount of patience and spare time on the part of the women. There are acres of tiny stitches - bed covers, curtains, table cloths, pillows and clothing, mostly 17th and 18th century. An elaborate sedan chair looking like a stray Parisian occupies one end of the room..

Greek folk culture under Turkish domination. In the 18th century Greeks had considerable freedom of movement and a chance to get rich if they could. Arts flourished. Islamic influences overlay the Byzantine, producing a new synthesis of vision. This floor has a wonderful number and variety of costumes and jewellery displayed on models. Embroidery everywhere, mostly gold, and belt buckles approaching the size and shape of small spacecraft, the ever-present earrings and many examples of such folk arts as pottery, carvings, wooden chests, furniture.

Room XXVIII is a room almost entirely made of finely carved wood, with an awe-inspiring ceiling. It is a reception room, but has a churchly feel to it, possibly because of the arch motifs and the carved fireplace, which seems to cry out for a statue of the Virgin. There are several fine icons, as well as the wooden chests, chairs and panelling.

Reference rooms at the Benaki are open from 10 a.m. to 1:30, except Tuesday and Saturday. There are photo and historical archives, manuscripts as well as a library. Cassettes of liturgical and traditional music are on sale.

The top floor has a nice terrace and coffee bar.

Historical & Ethnological Museum

13, Stadiou, St. Tel.: 323-7617 Daily: 09.00-14.00 Sun: 09.00-13.00 Closed: Mon. Closed all August

Costumes, pictures - wondrous old prints and books - and documents relating to Greek history.

City of Athens Museum

7, Paparrigopoulou St. Klafthmonos Sq., Stadiou St. Tel.: 323-0168 Mon, Wed, Frid. only 09.00-13.00 Wed: Free Closed: July

King Otho and Queen Amalia made their home in this small mansion while their palace, now the Parliament building, was being constructed. A modest royal cottage with a simple throne-room - the sunny kitchen with its ceramic storage jars and brightly shining copper jelly moulds is a cheerful and happy place. One feels that it was probably a good deal pleasanter to be a cook than a king, especially in view of the large number of framed cartoons from French newspapers depicting the predicament of Greece, vis-a-vis the great powers. Many excellent pictures and architectural plans of the period are impeccably displayed and lit.

Jewish Museum

36, Amalias St. 3rd Floor Tel.: 323-1577 Daily: 09.00-13.00 Closed: Sat. Admission: Free

Art and artifacts from the centuries-old Jewish community in Greece.

Eleftherios Venizelos

Eleftherias Park, Vass. Sofias Ave. Daily 09.00-13.00
Closed: Sun. Admission: Free

Personal mementoes and documents of the patriot and his period.

Gennadios Library Museum

61, Souidias St. Tel.: 721-0536 Daily: 09.00-17.00 Tues/Thurs 09.00-20.00 Sat.: 09.00-14.00 Closed: Sun. Closed: August Admission: Free

Pictures of Makrigianni, watercolours, icons, engravings and personal mementoes of Lord Byron and others of the Revolutionary Period.

Maritime Museum of Greece

Akti Themistokleous Zea Marina - Piraeus Tel.: 451-6822 Daily: 09.00-12.30 plus Sunday afternoon Closed: Sun.-Mon.

Items from the navy, civil and merchant marine from 3,000 BC, displayed in a crescent of 12 rooms grouped according to period. There is a fine library and a lecture room and the central courtyard contains the complete bridge of the submarine *Papanikolis*, a great place for youngsters to climb up and play captains.

Ship enthusiasts may also enjoy visiting the Battleship Averof, launched in 1910 and veteran of two world wars. Temporary headquarters of the Greek navy during the war, the Averof escorted convoys through the Indian Ocean and finally returned the exiled Government to Greece in 1944. Her last duty was a joyous one as she took part in the celebrations held in Rodos on the return of the Dodecanese Islands to Greece.

This valiant veteran is now permanently berthed at Palio Faliro.

Cretan Icon, 17th c.

Art

Byzantine Museum

22, Vas. Sofias Ave. Tel.: 721-1027 Daily: 08.00-17.00 Closed: Mon.

The house was built for the wild Duchess of Plaisance in 1848, but its design around a central courtyard and the simple style suggest the monastic. As soon as you enter, the traffic of the busy avenue is forgotten in the peaceful garden. A fountain, mosaics, and samples of Byzantine capitals and doorways are arranged along the walls.

The wing on the left shows icons, illustrated books and manuscripts dating back to the 9th century, and a collection of iridescent glassware and jewels from a tomb in the Peloponnese. The prophet Elijah has inspired some striking paintings, the four wildscarlet horses drawing his chariot leading to some amazing effects, especially on gold leaf backgrounds.

The central building is devoted more to carvings and marbles, columns and altars. Fragments of capitals mounted in plain plaster give a cool impression, considering the ecclesiastical style of elaborate decoration.

A shelf over the door of the central room shows four pouting heads of the Frankish period: other sculpture samples include some mythological figures.

A replica of an 11c Byzantine small church, again in cool white, with cupola and very fine carvings from churches in Athens, and a floor mosaic from the Acropolis in its Christian period follows. A reproduction of a Post Byzantine flat-ceiling church, mostly 18th century with a heavy Oriental feel, a richly carved and gilded wooden iconostasis, wheel-chandelier of carved wood, and paintings, together with brass, gold, silver and inlaid sacred objects - reliquaries, croziers, chalices, monstrances are in a room without labels: on the walls are frescoes from demolished churches.

More frescoes are stored in the right wing, and in a separate building, beyond the garden is the Loverdos Collection. Here a superb icon collection is displayed to the best possible advantage. Most are 15th to 18th century. A charming family tree of Christ by Poulakis: a splendid carved iconostasis, carved candlesticks as tall as a man: and a chance to really study the variations permitted by Orthodox icon-painting traditions.

Nea Smyrni Middle Byzantine Icon Museum

Paleologou 1, Nea Smyrni Tel.: 933-3702 Thurs only 10.00-14.00 Admission: Free

About 40 Byzantine icons.

National Gallery & Alexandros Soutsos Museum

50, Vas. Konstandinou Ave. Tel.: 721-1010 Tus.-Sat.: 09.00-15.00 Sun.: 10.00-14.00 Closed: Mon.

Endowed by Soutsos, this large gallery occupies the corner opposite the Hilton. The gallery houses temporary exhibits of international modern art. The top floors show works by Greek artists of the 19th and 20th centuries. The naifs and iconists apart, Greek painters have clearly been well aware of European movements and schools since the Renaissance. (See chart p. 38).
A new sculpture gallery is being completed.
Coffee shop in basement.

Pieridi Collection

29, Vas. Georgiou B΄ Ave. Glyfada Tel.: 893-1496 Mon. and Wed. 17.00-21.00 Admission: Free Sat.-Sun.: 10.00-13.30

Permanent exhibition of works by modern Greek artists, sculptors and engravers. Selecting the work of many of the same artists as exhibited in the Vorres, the collector has chosen works with a different emphasis and the contrast is interesting.

Gounaropoulos Museum

Gounaropoulou 6, St. Ano Ilissia Tel.: 777-7601 Mon, Fri: 09.00-13.00 Tues, Thurs.: 17.00-20.00 Admission: Free

Art and memorabilia at the home of one of Greece's best known artists.

Vorres Museum of Contemporary Art

Paiania, Attika Tel.: 664-2520 Sat. and Sun only: 10.00-14.00 Or by appointment: 664-3713, 664-2639

Private collection housed in a specially built series of rooms and courtyards attached to a reconstructed cottage on the east side of Mount Hymettus. A diverse collection of paintings and sculptures by all the major Greek artists and many unknowns.

The Folk Museum contains Greek and foreign art and artifacts ranging from Byzantine icons to millwheels displayed in the house of the owner. The entrance is through the museum. Ask for times of admission to the house. Bus 303 from Thission.

Folk Art

Centre for Folk Art and Traditions

6, Angelikis Hadzimihali St. Plaka (near the top of Adrianou) Tel.: 324-398 Wed.Fri.Sat.: 09.00-13.00, 17.00-20.00 Tue. Thur.: 09.00-21.00 Closed: Mon. Sun Admission: Free

Hadzimihalis House (1924) is an elegant mansion which the cit has used to good advantage, keeping much of the built-in furniture, and using the original kitchens in which to display the appropriate articles. Old musical instruments, wooden pipes, flasks and combs and a hammock for carrying a baby are among the less common items which have been carefully collected to show a wide range of activity. One room is devoted to Angeliki Hadzimihali who won world-wide recognition in the art and dance world of the 1920's and 30's, including a Gold Medal at the Paris Exhibition of 1937.

Angeliki's interest in all Greek things included a study of the nomadic shepherds from the Pindus, and the upper floor contains photographs and a complete house built of withes and straw.

Greek Popular Art Museum

17, Kidathineon St., Plaka Tel.: 321-3018 Daily: 10.00-14.00 Closed: Mon. Admission: Free.

The national collection includes exhibits of spinning, weaving, dying and printing, and the types of equipment used. Also embroidery techniques using traced designs, counted stitches and corded work in gold or silver wire. The woodwork section features elaborately carved distaffs used in spinning, the favourite theme being St. George and the dragon surrounded by elaborately carved birds, flowers, snakes and lacy curlicues.

Traditional and Court costumes are displayed on the upper floor, with heavy, elaborate and ornate chains, stomachers and belts of silver often encrusted with precious stones.

A side room contains wall panels featuring historical and mythical events painted by the naif painter Theophilos Hadzimihail around the turn of the century in a lively and imaginative style and a personal concept of perspective.

Aharnon Folklore Museum

Agiou Valassiou, Sq. Menidi

About 500 items of local costume, embroidery, icons, ecclesiastical objects.

Science

Natural History Museum

13, Levidou St., Kifissia (beyond shopping centre) Tel.: 808-6405 Mon.-Thur.: 09.00-13.00, 17.00-20.00 Sat.-Sun : 10.00-16.00 Closed: Fri.

A charming mansion standing in its own garden contains a beautifully displayed collection. Lichens; butterflies; insects; shells; reptiles and animals, including the skeleton of 25 ft long Triceratops, a vegetarian with a wicked looking pair of tusks. Good labelling in Greek and English and excellent diagrams showing the evolution of both plants and animals.

The museum shop sells exquisite original silver jewellery set with semi-precious stones. Also shells, some packaged in little presentation baskets, at modest prices.

Museum of Experiments in Physics, Eugenides Institute

Leof. Syngrou Ave. Amfithea (Near race Course) Tel.: 941-1181 Daily: 09.30-13.30 Sun. 17.30-20.30 Sun. Admission: Free.

Demonstrations of principles of science, most of which are designed to be handled. Fun for children. This museum is connected to the Planetarium (programs are in Greek). In summer telephone first: closed August.

International Museum of Oceanography

14, Pindou St., Moschato Tel.: 941-2393 Sat/Sun only 09.00-13.00

The waters of the Mediterranean abound in exotic flowers, both plant and animal: those anemones that look like dahlias are wild creatures with a fascinating life. Here you find exhibits of fish, molluscs, shells and corals.

War Museum

Vas. Sofias Ave. and Rizari St. Tel.: 729-0543 Daily: 09.00-14.00 Closed: Mon. Admission: Free

This modern building with huge picture windows houses a collection which covers every aspect of man's ingenuity in battle, from Neolithic knives and axes to the warplanes of 1914-18 and 1939-45. Models and pictures of famous battles through the ages include a series of excellent paintings and some amusing cartoons from the last war.

The cafeteria at the Rizari street entrance is cool and restful. The Greek coffee is excellent - and cheap.

Miscellaneous

Postal Museum

5, Panathenaic Stadiou St. Pangrati Tel.: 751-9066, 751-9042 Daily: 09.00-14.00 Mon.Wed: 17.00-20.00 Closed: Sat. Sun. Admission: Free

The Philatelic service is at 100, Aiolou St.

Train Museum

301, Liossion St. (on the left side leaving Athens) over the level crossing. Fri. only 05.00-08.00 Admission: Free.

Period engines and carriages from 1884, including that of King George I of the Hellenes and a very ornate one formerly belonging to Abdul Aziz.

Many of the old steamers which have been rusting away are now being restored. Tickets, telegraph machines, models and a couple of trams in very good condition.

Note: Travellers on the electric line in Athens will see many wooden carriages in sidings. These date from the early 1900's and have only recently been taken out of service and replaced with carriages built in East Germany.

Train lovers see also page 95 for details of the rack and pinion railway from Diakofto to Kalavrita in the Peloponnese.

Theatre Museum

50, Acadimias St. (Lower Floor of Cultural Centre) Tel.: 362-9430 Daily: 09.00-13.00 Mon., Wed., Fri 09.00-13.00, 17.00-19.30 Closed: Sat, Sun.

By theatre-lovers for theatre lovers, the museum contains a delightful series of tiny dressing rooms containing memorabilia of many of the one-time leading actors and actresses of the Greek stage. There are photographs from 1905 of the first performance at Epidaurus for two thousand years; of a performance of Antigone at the Stadium in 1905 (pic. 14, room F); of the same play at the Herodion in 1926, and a model made in 1938 before restoration. There are many printed books of plays dating back to 1804, a delightful display of models for stage sets, a fearsome mask of Cyclops and a collection of wonderfully nostalgic posters of theatrical performances from theatres throughout Europe and America.

Theatre Museum of Piraeus

Civic Theatre 2, Ag. Konstandinou St. Piraeus Tel.: 412-6411, 412-2339 Daily: 16.00-20.00 Mon., 09.00-14.00 Thurs. Admission: Free.

Original drawings for sets and costumes by Panos Aravandinos, famous for his theatrical designs in Greece and Germany in the early of this century.

HOTELS - CAMPING SITES

General Notes

Listing-Classification

This third part is an up to date list of all the hotels in the first four categories and Camping sites in Athens and Attica. For handy and quick reference we have divided this part of the guide according to major geographical areas with sub-divisions for places within each area. Hotels have been listed alphabetically within each category. They are classified as: De Luxe (L), A, B, C, D, and E category. This classification roughly corresponds to the star classification system used in Great Britain and Europe.

Camping sites are listed alphabetically with full information about how to get there as well as about the facilities they offer.

Prices

Standard of Accommodation, classification and pricing structures are set by the Government (Greek National Tourist Organization). Actually the Government sets the minimum per category with no ceiling as to what the maximum could be. You are advised to check prices before hand.

Symbols

A list of symbols along with their explanation is given on page 199.

Contents

Notes on Hotels

1) Service charge (15%) is included in the prices.
2) V.A.T. stamp duty, city or community taxes are not usually included.
3) The legal charges for central heating / air conditioning are usually, though not always, included in room prices.
4) A single person occupying a double room is charged 80% of the double room rate.
5) An extra bed in a room - only at the client's request - will increase the room rate by 20%.
6) The room rates are applicable daily up to 12.00 noon of the following day. Stay till 6 p.m. is charged for an extra half-day. Beyond 6 p.m. the charge is as for a full day.
7) An increase of 10% may be added to room rates for a stay of two days or less, but this doesn't occur in De luxe Hotels.
8) The room rates of hotels located in summer holidays areas, may be increased by 15% during the period June 1st to September 15th.
9) In all rooms a price chart is displayed giving full details of applicable charges.
10) Many hotels grant special rates for groups upon request, particularly during the low season.
11) Most hotels will accept credit cards, as this is indicated in the relevant entry. Traveller's cheques issued by banks are accepted almost everywhere. In most, if not in all, of the hotels you can pay in foreign currency but be careful with the exchange rates that are used!

Example of a Hotel Entry

Classification → **A' RIVA HOTEL APARTMENTS**

Address → 114, Mihalakopoulou Str. 115 27 ATHENS

Tel. 01/7706611-5, 7709350 ← Telephone and Telex number

Tlx. 214736 RIVA GR

Open: Jan. - Dec.

Additional Information: Nice one or two-bedroom apts. Grill-room RIVA: one of the best French restaurants in Athens, member of "World famous restaurants international". Special terms for groups.

rm 82/**b**180

C.C.: American Express

Accomodation and Facilities Symbols (Key to Symbols and Abbreviations page 199).

ATHENS

*** L´ ACROPOLE PALACE HOTEL**
51, Patission Str. **Tel.** 01/5223851-3,
104 33 ATHENS **Tlx.** 215909 ACRO GR
rm 107/**b** 173 **Open:** Jan. - Dec.

L´ AMALIA HOTEL
10, Amalias Ave. **Tel.** 01/3237301-9
105 57 ATHENS **Tlx.** 215161 AMAL GR.
Open: Jan. - Dec.

The hotel is across the street from the National Gardens, not 100 yards from Syntagma Sq. and the airlines offices. Offers comfortable air-conditioned rooms, the balconies of several overlooking the Gardens, restaurant, bar, tea-room, an attractive shop, extensive lounge etc.

rm 100/**b** 188 S24h

C.C. American Express, Diners, Visa, Eurocard, Master Charge, Access

L´ ASTIR PALACE ATHENS HOTEL
2, Panepistimiou Str. **Tel.** 01/3643112-9
106 71 ATHENS **Tlx.** 222380 APAT GR
Open: Jan. - Dec.

Centrally located, fully air-conditioned, deluxe rooms and suites. Coffee shop "ASTERIA", gourmet restaurant "APOCALYPSIS", "ATHOS" bar, convention facilities (160 person room), 250 person banquet hall. Radio, colour T.V. with in-house movies and mini-bar in all rooms. Special prices for travel agents and senior air-company cadres.

rm 77/**b** 149

C.C: Visa, American Express, Diners, Eurocard, Master Charge, Access, J.C.B., Carte Blanche.

L´ ATHENAEUM INTERCONTINENTAL HOTEL
89-93, Syngrou Str. **Tel.** 01/9023666
117 45 ATHENS **Tlx.** 221553-4 ATHI GR
Open: Jan. - Dec.

A city in itself in the heart of the business district, with it's many dazzling shops and entertainment facilities, the hotel offers unparalleled services to the guest: a fine selection of restaurants, bars, clubs and lounges. T.V. - video, multi-channel music and mini-bar in all rooms and a complete health club with sauna, steam bath, swimming pool and many other facilities. Also many function rooms and a main bathroom for conventions - meetings - banquets, of up to 1700 with audio/visual control booths, simultaneous translation, closed circuit T.V., telex, telefax, and photostat facilities. Secretarial, translation and interpreter services are available on request.

rm 620/**b** 1200 S24h

C.C.: American Express, Diners, Eurocard, Master Charge, Access, Visa, Grand Metropolitan, En Route

L´ ATHENEE PALACE HOTEL
1, Kolokotroni Str. **Tel.** 01/3230791
105 62 ATHENS **Tlx.** 216188 DAMI GR
Open: Jan. - Dec.

Convention rooms, banquet halls etc.

rm 109/**b** 176 S24

C.C.: American Express, Diners

L´ ATHENS CHANDRIS HOTEL
385, Syngrou Ave. **Tel.** 01/9414824-6
175 64 ATHENS 4520715
Tlx. 218112 ATCH GR
Open: Jan. - Dec.

Whether you are travelling on business or for pleasure, this hotel is an ideal base, being but 10 min. away from Athens center on our bus service, within easy reach of Apollo Coast beaches and the port and airport. We have conference rooms for up to 400, and a choice of bars and restaurants to match your every mood, as well as a roof garden and a pool-side snack-bar with a magical view. Superbly equipped and elegantly furnished the hotel offers a unique blend of hospitality and comfort.

rm 386/**b** 720 S24h

C.C.: American Express, Diners, MasterCharge, Access, Eurocard, Visa

***L´ ATHENS HILTON HOTEL**
46, Vas. Sophias Ave. Tel. 01/7220201-10
106 76 ATHENS **Tlx.** 215808 HILT GR
Open: Jan. - Dec.

rm 480/**b** 1000 S24h

C.C.: American Express, Diners, Master Charge, Access, Eurocard, J.C.B., Visa, Hilton International, En Route, Lufthansa Credit Card

L´ CARAVEL HOTEL
2, Vas. Alexandrou Ave. **Tel.** 01/7290721,60 lin
116 10 ATHENS **Tlx.** 214401 CH GR

Located near the town-centre, giving easy access to business areas and historical sites, CARAVEL is the best place for Conferences, Exhibitions, Meetings and Holidays. Our 11 halls, earthquake and fire proof, recently renovated and fitted with static-free woolen carpets, can accommodate up to 2,000 persons. Also available are a health studio, jogging track, and ample parking space.

rm 471/**b** 841 S24h

C.C.: Diners, Visa, Master Charge, Access, J.C.B., American Express, Eurocard

L´ GRANDE BRETAGNE HOTEL
Syntagma Sq. **Tel.** 01/3230251-10,
105 63 ATHENS 3238361-10
Tlx. 215346 HBRT GR
Open: Jan. - Dec.

Starting in 1862 as a guest house for royalty, Grande Bretagne was turned into a grand class hotel in 1872 and has undergone intensive expansion since, which has left untouched its old-world character and ambience. Famous for the splendour and elegance of the decor and furnished with rare antiques, the public rooms are sought after for banquets and receptions and frequented by international celebrities. Everything that is important in Athens, both Ancient and modern is around G.B., within a ride from the main entrance.

n 372/b 668

24h C.C.: American Express, Din-
s, Master Charge, Access, Eurocard,
isa, J.C.B

´HOLIDAY INN ATHENS

), Mihalakopoulou Str. **Tel.** 01/7248322-9, 7248182-8
15 28 ATHENS **Tlx.** 218870
Open: Jan. - Dec.

Gracefully designed, modern, not 2 miles om city center and the main archaeologi- al/historical sites, HOLIDAY INN is ready enchant the guest, businessman and urist alike. Special arrangements for con- rences, conventions, shows, receptions, eminars, for up to 700. Also special rates r groups on request.

n 190/b 338

24h C.C.: Diners, merican Express, Visa, Master Charge, ccess

´KING GEORGE HOTEL

Georgiou A´ Str. **Tel.** 01/3230651-70
)5 63 ATHENS **Tlx.** 215296 KING GR
Open: Jan. - Dec.

A notable establishment, in the most ivileged site of the city, that for over 4 de- des has built a well deserved world-wide putation. Good taste and love of fine arts e immediately felt upon entering the ajestic marble-floored lobby. The roof ter- ce restaurant enjoys a breathtaking view the city and the memorable spectacle of oodlit Acropolis at night. Individually and stefully furnished rooms and all the up- -date amenities are offered to the discri- inating clientele.

n 150/b 25

24h C.C. Master Charge, Access, urocard, Diners, Visa, American Express

´LEDRA MARRIOTT HOTEL (5 star)

13-115, Syngrou Ave. **Tel.** 01/9525211
17 45 ATHENS **Tlx.** 221833
Open: Jan. - Dec.

20th Century elegance in the Capital of e ancient world. The Marriott tradition of ervice is continued in the newest five-star xury hotel in Athens. Has restaurants in- uding a polynesian one. All rooms quipped with mini fridge and T.V. - video. very detail planned to make you feel wel- ome.

n 265/b 500

S 24h C.C.: Amex, Visa, laster Charge, Eurocard, Diners

´N.J.V. MERIDIEN HOTEL

, Vas. Georgiou Str. **Tel.** 01/3255301
05 64 ATHENS **Tlx.** 210568 MJVM GR
Open: Jan. - Dec.

Deluxe hotel located at Syntagma quare. Elegant spacious rooms Ideal for usinessmen, right in the heat of the At- ens business center.

n 182/b 320

24h C.C.: American Express, Diners, Access, Master Charge, Eurccard, Carte Blanche, J.C.B. Visa,

L´PARK HOTEL

10, Alexandras Ave. **Tel.** 01/8832711-9
106 82 ATHENS **Tlx.** 214748 PARK GR
Open: Jan. - Dec.

Park Hotel is centrally located, facing one of the biggest parks of Athens and within walking distance of the Athens National Museum. All rooms with private facilities, conference rooms, restaurant, bar, roof-garden with swimming pool, and prvate garage.

rm 147/**b** 279

S 24h C.C.: Diners, Visa, Carte Blanche, Master Charge, Eurocard, Ac cess, American Express

L´ROYAL OLYMPIC HOTEL

28-43, Diakou Str. **Tel.** 01/9226411
117 43 ATHENS **Tlx.** 215753
Open: Jan. - Dec.

Royal Olympic is the ultra-modern in con- trast with the classic. You'll be struck by the breathtaking view from the private ter- race of your room. You will enjoy two exqui- site restaurants, 2 bars, a swimming-pool and a sauna. Also book-jewel-souvenir shops and convention, banquet, meeting etc. facilities for up to 800.

rm 305/**b** 600 S

C.C.: American Express, Diners, Visa, J.C.B., Master Charge, Access, Eurocard

L´SAINT GEORGE LYCABETTUS HOTEL

2, Kleomenous Str. **Tel.** 01/7297110-19
106 75 ATHENS **Tlx.** 214253 HEAN GR
Open: Jan. - Dec.

Located at the foot of Likavitos hill, the hotel offers pleasant environment, magnifi- cent view, ideal service. The guest can find: warm hospitable living rooms and lounges, excellent cuisine, cocktail bar, snack bar, a charming swimming-pool and grill room on the roof garden, boutiques, beauty parlour, and meeting hall.

rm 149/**b** 276

S 24h C.C.: Diners, American Express, Visa, Master Charge, Access

A´ARIANE HOTEL APARTMENTS

22, Tim. Vassou Str. **Tel.** 01/6437302, 6466361
115 21 ATHENS **Open:** Jan. - Dec.

First Class hotel apartments, of one, two, or three rooms. Centrally air-conditioned, full amenities, excellent service, T.V. on re- quest, direct dial telephone. Located in the fashionable quiet residential and business area near the USA embassy.

r 42/**b** 52

C.C.: American Express, Diners

A´ASTOR HOTEL

16, Kar. Servias Str. **Tel.** 01/3255555,3255111
105 62 ATHENS **Tlx.** 214018 ATEX GR.
Open: Jan. - Dec.

Splendid view of the Acropolis and the old town (Plaka) from the commercial and cosmopolitan centre of the city. High standard facilities, friendly atmosphere, first class service. Beautifully furnished air-conditioned rooms with telephone, radio and central heating.

rm 131/**b** 234 S

C.C.: American Express, Diners

*A´ATTICA PALACE HOTEL

6, Kar. Servias Str. **Tel.** 01/3223006-8
105 62 ATHENS **Tlx.** 215909 ACRO GR.
Open: Jan. - Dec.

rm 78/**b** 147

A´AVA HOTEL APARTMENTS

9-11, Lyssikratous Str. **Tel.** 01/3236618, 3237478
105 58 ATHENS
Open: Jan. - Dec.

Spacious, comfortable apts/rooms with kitchenette and refrigerator, in a quiet street of Plaka (old town), under the shadow of the Acropolis.

rm 18/**b** 40 S P
C.C.: American Express, Visa, Master Charge, Access

A´BLUE HOUSE HOTEL

19, Voukourestiou Str. **Tel.** 01/3620341, 3626831
106 71 ATHENS
Open: Jan. - Dec.

Family atmosphere, tidiness, eager service.

rm 18/**b** 29 S24h

A´DELICE HOTEL APARTMENTS

3, Vas. Alexandrou Str. **Tel.** 01/7238311-3
115 28 ATHENS **Open:** Jan. - Dec.

Located in one of the most exclusive area of Athens, next to the Athens Hilton. Has a T.V. lounge, bar and cafeteria. All apartments and rooms are fully air-conditioned, with fully equipped kitchen and bathroom, private balconies with sun shades, telephone and hi.fi. music.

rm 44/**b** 77 S P
C.C.: Diners, American Express

A´DIVANI ZAFOLIA ALEXANDRAS HOTEL

87-89 Alexandras Ave. **Tel.** 01/6469200, 6438086
114 74 ATHENS **Tlx.** 214468

Situated in the heart of Athens within walking distance from the National Museum, and one of the most beautiful Parks of Athens. Elegant and comfortable rooms, the balconies of most commanding a view of the well-known Likavitos hill. Roof garden with a swimming pool and a panoramic view of Athens. Reduced prices during off-season (1/11-15/3).

rm 192/**b** 350 S24h

P **C.C.:** Visa, J.C.B., Diners, American Express, Master Charge, Access, Eurocard

A´DIVANI ZAFOLIA PALACE HOTEL

19-25, Parthenonos Str. **Tel.** 01/6438086, 9229153-4
117 42 ATHENS

Tlx. 2138
Open: Jan. - De

Under the shadow of the Acropolis, a fe minutes from Plaka where one can go sho ping or enjoy the fantastic night life. A rooms are air-conditioned, have a direc dial telephone, combine comfort with goc taste, and most of them have a view of th Acropolis and Philopappou hill.

rm 193/**b** 361 S24h

C.C.: Visa, J.C.B., Diners, Amer can Express, Master Charge, Access, Eu ocard

A´ELECTRA HOTEL

5, Ermou Str. **Tel.** 01/3223222-8, 32269
105 63 ATHENS **Tlx.** 216896 ELEC G
Open: Jan. - De

Whether you are in Athens for busines or relaxation Electra is your ideal choice. S tuated in the heart of Athens, Syntagm Sq., the hotel offers the quick and punctu service your schedule demands. Also, yo are in the shopping centre of Athens and stone's throw from Plaka, the Athenia Village.

rm 120/**b** 200

S24h **C.C.:** Diners, Visa, American E press, Master Charge, Access

A´ELECTRA PALACE HOTEL

18, Nikodimou Str. **Tel.** 01/3241401-
104 42 ATHENS **Tlx.** 216896 ELEC G
Open: Jan. - De

Tastefully furnished rooms with nice ve andas facing the Acropolis or Likavitos hi Taste Greek and international specialitie or have a banquet arranged for your busi ess meetings, in the restaurants. Mak your rendez-vous in our nice lounge or on of our bars. Be refreshed in our swimmin pool on the top floor. Whether on busines or holiday the ELECTRA PALACE is ideal.

rm 120/**b** 200

S24h P **C.C.:** Diners, Visa Master Charge, American Express

A´EMBASSY HOTEL APTS

15, Tim. Vassou Str. **Tel.** 01/6421152-
115 21 ATHENS **Tlx.** 22102
Open: Jan. - De

apts 12/**b** 42 S24h

P **C.C.:** American Express, Maste Charge, Eurocard, Visa, Arabian Express

A´ESPERIA PALACE HOTEL

22, Stadiou Str. **Tel.** 01/3238001-9, 3238106-
105 64 ATHENS **Tlx.** 215773 ESPE G
215067 KING G
Open: Jan. - De

Located in the center of the city, a rooms with verandas, the upper floor one with a view of the Acropolis and Likavito T.V. - VIDEO on request. Personal safe an telex available. Four convention/confer ence rooms (15-300 person capacity) a your disposal. A well-trained staff promise an unforgettable stay.

rm 185/**b** 338 S24

C.C.: American Express, Diner J.C.B., Visa

´GOLDEN AGE HOTEL
7, Mihalakopoulou Str. **Tel.** 01/7240861-9, 7240860
15 28 ATHENS
Tlx. 2·9292 GAH GR
Open: Jan. - Dec.

At your disposal 110 rooms and 10 uites, with 3-channel music, T.V. on reuest, telephone, and air conditioning. Also ano-bar, gift shop, conference hall and taerna with Greek specialities.

n 122/b 230 C.C.: American Express, iners, Visa, Master Charge, Access, Eurcard

´HERODION HOTEL
Rovertou Galli Str. **Tel.** 01/9236832-6
17 42 ATHENS **Tlx.** 219423
Open: Jan. - Dec.

Fully air-conditioned, decorated with Karstos hand-hewn stone in an effort to eate a Greek atmosphere. A few blocks om Hadrian's Arch, the Acropolis, Herod tticus theatre and Plaka (old town). Direct al phone in all rooms.

n 90/b 171 C.C.: American Express, iners, Visa, Master Charge

´KING MINOS HOTEL
Pireos Str. **Tel.** 01/5231111-18, 5231365
)5 52 ATHENS **Tlx.** 215339 HOMI GR
Open: Jan. - Dec.

n 175/b 287 C.C.: Diners, Visa, American Express

´KOLONAKI HOTEL APARTMENTS
3, Kapsali Str. **Tel.** 01/7213759, 7228412
)6 74 ATHENS **Open:** Jan. - Dec.

ots 10/b 19

´LION HOTEL APARTMENTS
Evzonon Str. **Tel.** 01/7248722-4
15 21 ATHENS **Open:** Jan. - Dec.

n 17/b 34

´OLYMPIC PALACE HOTEL
3, Filelinon Str. **Tel.** 01/3237611-5
)5 57 ATHENS **Tlx.** 215178 OPH GR
Open: Jan. - Dec.

In the fashionable center of Athens, near yntagma Sq. and the old city (Plaka). Luxrious but cozy atmosphere, beautifully deorated rooms, air-conditioning, conference and entertainment facilities all contriute to an ideal stay.

n 90/b 180 C.C.: American Express, Diners, Visa, arte Blanche, Master Charge, Access, urocard

´PARTHENON HOTEL
Makri Str. **Tel.** 01/9234594-8, 9250786
17 42 ATHENS **Tlx.** 221579 EOEX GR
Open: Jan. - Dec.

A modern, new building situated in a uiet location close to Syntagma Sq. and ven closer to the Acropolis. The guest can njoy luxurious lounges, a small garden, bar nd restaurant offering Greek and international specialities.

rm 79/**b** 152 C.C.: American Express, Visa

A´PERLI HOTEL APARTMENTS
4, Arnis Str. **Tel.** 01/7248794-8
115 28 ATHENS **Tlx.** 215444
Open: May - Oct.

Built in 1977 in the center of Athens, close to HILTON and HOLIDAY INN. All apts, fully air-conditioned, have a bedroom for two, a living room with sofa convertible to a double bed, private bathroom, fully equipped kitchen, and direct dial telephone. T.V. on request.

rm 30/**b** 60 C.C.: Diners, American Express Access, Visa, Master Charge

A´PRESIDENT HOTEL
43, Kifissias Ave. **Tel.** 01/6924600
115 23 ATHENS **Tlx.** 218585
Open: Jan. - Dec.

Situated near the city center, the hotel offers deluxe accommodation at moderate prices. Apart from the 530 air-conditioned rooms, all with balconies, one can enjoy: a roof-garden, heated swimming-pool, discoclub, 2 restaurants, 2 bars, 2 lounges, conference hall, shopping center and beauty parlour.

rm 529/**b** 1017 C.C.: American Express, Diners, Visa, Master Charge, Access, Eurocard

A´RIVA HOTEL APARTMENTS
114, Mihalakopoulou Str. **Tel.** 01/7706611-5, 7709350
115 27 ATHENS
Tlx. 214736 RIVA GR
Open: Jan. - Dec.

Nice one or two-bedroom apts. Grill-room RIVA: one of the best French restaurants in Athens, member of "World famous restaurants international". Special terms for groups.

rm 82/**b** 180 C.C.: American Express, Diners

B´ACADIMOS HOTEL
58, Akadimias Str. **Tel.** 01/3629220-9
106 79 ATHENS **Open:** Jan. - Dec.

Built next to Athens University and the National Library, the hotel provides every modern amenity. Excellent cuisine, impeccable service, efficient courteous staff, spacious lounges, provide a quiet retreat. Within easy reach of museums, archaeological sites, theatres and cinemas, shopping centers, travel agencies, bus and trolley terminals.

rm 116/**b** 220
C.C.: Diners, American Express

B´ACROPOLIS HOUSE (Pension)
6-8, Kodrou Str. **Tel.** 01/3222344,3226241
105 58 ATHENS **Open:** Jan. - Dec.

Beautifully preserved example of last century's architecture, on a pedestrian street at the edge of Plaka. Family-run since 1965. Offers breakfast and T.V.

lounge, single, double or bigger rooms with central heating and hot water 24 hours a day.

rm 20/b 40

B΄ ADAM'S HOTEL
6, Herefondos Str. **Tel.** 01/3225381, 3246482, 3238553
105 58 ATHENS
Open: Jan. - Dec.

ADAM'S hotel is located at the heart of the old town (Plaka) far from the noise of the traffic.

rm 14/b 27 S

B΄ADONIS HOTEL (Pension)
3, Voulis Str. **Tel.** 01/3249737-8, 3249741
105 58 ATHENS **Open:** Jan. - Dec.

The hotel is proud of its clean and comfortable centrally heated rooms. Single, double, or bigger, all with a balcony, telephone and private bathroom. There is a roof-garden with a view of the Parthenon and Likavitos Hill, where breakfast and cocktails are served. Built in 1975 in a quiet pedestrian street of Plaka.

rm 26/b 50

*B΄ ADRIAN HOTEL
74, Adrianou Str. Tel. 01/3221553, 3250454
105 56 ATHENS **Open:** Mar. - Oct.

rm 22/b 44

B΄AKRON HOTEL (Pension)
16, Thiras Str. **Tel.** 01/8626220, 8626228
112 57 ATHENS **Open:** Jan. - Dec.

Tideness - eager service - family environment. Reduced prices long-staying students.

rm 22/b 39 S24h
C.C.: Visa

B΄ALEXANDROS HOTEL
8, Tim. Vassou Str. **Tel.** 01/6430510, 6430464,
115 21 ATHENS **Tlx.** 216013 ALEX GR
Open: Jan. - Dec.

Situated in a quiet street within easy reach of embassies, museums and the shops and boutiques of the Athens Tower, the hotel offers efficient service and a fine Greek and Continental cuisine. The roof-garden and grill-room offer a panoramic view of pine-covered Likavitos. The restaurant and hall also afford convention facilities.

rm 96/b 174
S C.C.: American Express, Diners, Visa

B΄ANASTASIA HOTEL
7, Victorias Sq. **Tel.** 01/8834511-5
104 34 ATHENS **Tlx.** 216774 TOB GR.
Open: Jan. - Dec.

rm 61/b 116
S

B΄ANGELA HOTEL
38, Stournari Str. **Tel.** 01/5233262-3
104 32 ATHENS **Open:** Jan. - Dec.

Renovated and modernized the hotel combines comfort with luxury.

rm 14/b 24 S24h

B΄ARCADIA HOTEL
46, Marni Str. **Tel.** 01/5226571-2-5, 523385
104 38 ATHENS **Open:** Jan. - De

rm 98/b 154
C.C.: American Express

B΄ARETOUSSA HOTEL
6-8, Mitropoleos Str. **Tel.** 01/3229431-8
105 63 ATHENS **Tlx.** 216882 AH G
Open: Jan. - De

A new building situated in the heart of Athens, Syntagma Sq. with the best view the Acropolis. 87 air-conditioned room each with its own hall, private-facilitie phone and radio. Also lounges, restauran bar, roof-garden and a modern cafeteria.

rm 87/b 158
S C.C.: American Express, Diner Visa, Access, Master Charge

B΄ARISTOFANIS HOTEL
38, Aristofanous Str. **Tel.** 01/325087
105 53 ATHENS **Open:** Jan. - De

rm 9/b 20

B΄ATHENIAN INN HOTEL
22, Haritos Str. **Tel.** 01/7238097, 72187
106 75 ATHENS **Tlx.** 2240
Open: Jan. - De

rm 28/b 53
C.C.: American Express, Diners

B΄ATHENS CENTER
26, Sofokleous Str. **Tel.** 01/5248511
105 52 ATHENS **Tlx.** 2217
Open: Jan. - De

Modern hotel in the business center Athens: right next to the Town Hall an Omonia Sq. Fully air-conditioned room with 3-channel music and veranda. Delux restaurant and bar, roof-garden with a pa oramic view and spacious reception hal for up to 150.

rm 136/b 259
S C.C.: American Express, Din

B΄ATHENS CITY HOTEL
232, Patission Str. **Tel.** 01/8629115
112 53 ATHENS **Open:** Jan. - De

Friendly atmosphere in a quiet hotel, min. from the center of Athens. Service of big hotel at reasonable prices. 10% di count to groups of over 6.

rm 40/b 80 S24h

B΄ATHENS GATE HOTEL
10, Syngrou Ave. **Tel.** 01/9238302-9, 9238781
117 43 ATHENS **Tlx.** 219660 GATE G
Open: Jan. - De

A distinguished hotel facing Hadrian Arch and the temple of Zeus, with a panor mic view of the Acropolis. In the heart business and entertainment, 5 min. wa from Syntagma Sq. Rooms with balconie direct dial phone, radio and music. Comfo table lounge and restaurant offering Gree and international dishes and good wine.

rm 106/b 202
C.C.: American Express, Diners, Mast Charge, Visa

B´ ATHENS HOUSE HOTEL (Hostel)
4, Aristotelous Str. **Tel.** 01/5240539
104 32 ATHENS **Open:** Jan. Dec.

Centrally located, with sunny verandas, friendly atmosphere, information/assistance about tours, tickets, etc.

rm 15/**b** 30
C.C.: Diners

B´ ATHINAIS HOTEL
99, Vas. Sophias Ave. **Tel.** 01/6431133, 6461682
115 21 ATHENS **Tlx.** 219336 ATIN GR
Open: Jan. - Dec.

A new hotel idealy located in the Embassies area, near the Athens Tower shopping center. Spacious modern rooms with private balconies, direct dial phone, radio, and stereo music. Air-conditioning, snack-bar, roof-garden, comfortable lounges and irreproachable service. Recommended for a pleasant, restful stay.

rm 84/**b** 162
C.C.: Diners, Visa, Master Charge, American Express, Access

B´ ATLANTIC HOTEL
60, Solomou Str. **Tel.** 01/5235361-7, 5235087
104 32 ATHENS **Tlx.** 215723 ATLA GR
Open: Jan. - Dec.

Reduced prices for groups.

rm 158/**b** 275
C.C.: American Express, Diners

* B´ ATTIKON HOTEL
1, Kalirois Str. **Tel.** 01/9227425-7
117 43 ATHENS **Tlx.** 211507 AKTN GR
Open: Jan. - Dec.

rm 20/**b** 38

B´ BALASKA HOTEL
45, Liossion Str. **Tel.** 01/8835211-15
104 39 ATHENS **Tlx.** 210618 HBAL GR.
Open: Jan. - Dec.

A modern comfortable hotel in the centre of Athens, with up-to-date facilities and eager to serve staff. Near the R.R. station and the museums, it has fully air-conditioned rooms with 2-channel music and balcony, and a roof garden with a view extending as far as the sea.

rm 83/**b** 152
C.C.: American Express

B´ BYRON PENSION
19, Vironos Str. **Tel.** 01/3253554, 3230327
105 58 ATHENS **Open:** Jan. - Dec.

A modern small hotel located in Plaka, the most picturesque spot in Athens, with an excellent view of the Acropolis. Beautiful, comfortably furnished single, double and triple rooms.

rm 14/**b** 35

B´ CAÏRO CITY HOTEL
42, Marni Str. **Tel.** 01/5233361-3
104 38 ATHENS **Tlx.** 215556 IBER GR
Open: Jan. - Dec.

Recently renovated, near Omonia Sq., National Museum, R.R. station, and park, the hotel offers every possible comfort.

rm 86/**b** 144

B´ CANDIA HOTEL
40, Deliyiani Str. **Tel.** 01/5246112-7
104 38 ATHENS **Tlx.** 214171
Open: Jan. - Dec.

rm 142/**b** 254
C.C: American Express, Diners

B´ CHRISTINA HOTEL
15, Petmeza Str. **Tel.** 01/9215342, 9215353-7
117 43 ATHENS **Tlx.** 219304
Open: Jan. - Dec.

Located in the center of Athens near the Acropolis, has comfortable air-conditioned rooms with private bath, telephone and radio. Restaurant, bar, T.V. room, perfect service.

rm 93/**b** 173
C.C.: American Express

B´ DAMON HOTEL
142, Syngrou Ave. **Tel.** 01/9232171-4
176 71 ATHENS **Tlx.** 215775 DAM. GR
Open: Jan. - Dec.

Air-conditioned rooms and suites, with private bathroom, music, direct dial phone, music. T.V. and fridge on request. Facilities include living room, restaurant, bar, open-air bar, kiosk, roof-garden, garage and conference/banquet facilities.

rm 97/**b** 177
C.C.: American Express, Diners, Visa

B´ DIMITRIOS HOTEL
37-39, Falirou Str. **Tel.** 01/9227449
117 42 ATHENS **Open:** Jan. - Dec.

The hotel's cafeteria, restaurant and garden are also accessible from Syngrou Ave. (No 60).

rm 72/**b** 137
C.C.: American Express

B´ DIOMIA HOTEL
5, Diomias Str. **Tel.** 01/3233034-8
105 63 ATHENS **Tlx.** 214265 ELTE GR
Open: Jan - Dec.

Unrivaled hospitality combined with up-to-date comfort, in the heart of the city. Pleasantly designed and furnished, with an efficient, courteous staff anxious to satisfy the most exacting guest, the hotel ensures a restfull, happy never - to - be - forgotten stay.

rm 71/**b** 130
C.C.: American Express, Diners, Visa, Eurocheques

B´ DORIAN INN HOTEL
17, Pireos Str. **Tel.** 01/5239782-5
105 52 ATHENS **Tlx.** 214779 DORI GR
Open: Jan. - Dec.

Built in 1974 by Omonia Sq., modern, fully air-conditioned, ideal for tourists and businessmen. Rooftop swimming pool and bar with a panoramic view of Athens and beyond. All rooms are sound-proofed with wall to wall carpeting, direct dial phone and 3-channel music. 24-hour attendance, for information/assistance; also telex service.

rm 146/**b** 287 **C.C.**: Dinners, American Express, Visa, Carte Blanche

B´ DRYADES HOTEL
4, Driadon Str. **Tel.** 01/3602961,3622881
114 73 ATHENS **Open:** Jan. - Dec.

The hotel is in an advantageous location on Strefi hill with a nice view, surrounded by greenery. Pleasantly decorated rooms with private balcony.

rm 15/**b** 31 S24h

B´ EGNATIA HOTEL APARTMENTS
64, 3 Septemvriou Str. **Tel.** 01/8227807, 8210834
104 33 ATHENS **Open:** Jan. - Dec.

Kitchen and fridge available.

apts 11/**b** 33

B´ EL GRECO HOTEL
65, Athinas Str. **Tel.** 01/3244553-7
105 52 ATHENS **Tlx.** 219682 APRI GR
Open: Jan. - Dec.

rm 92/**b** 167 S24h

B´ ELLI HOTEL
29, Heiden Str. **Tel.** 01/8815876,8823487
104 34 ATHENS **Open:** Jan. - Dec.

rm 14/**b** 27 S

B´ ERETRIA HOTEL
12, Halkokondili Str. **Tel.** 01/3635310-19
106 77 ATHENS **Tlx.** 215474 TEAC GR
Open: Jan. - Dec.

rm 63/**b** 126 S24h
C.C.: American Express, Diners

B´ FERON HOTEL
15, Rodou Str. **Tel.** 01/8232083, 8823207
112 52 ATHENS **Open:** Jan. - Dec.

rm 15/**b** 27 S24h
C.C.: Diners

B´ GEKAS HOTEL
21, Okeanidon Str. **Tel.** 01/9345562, 9321594
117 45 ATHENS **Tlx.** 210708 ESAV GR
Open: Jan. - Dec.

rm 110/**b** 74 S

B´ ILISSOS POTAMOS
72, Kalirois Str. **Tel.** 01/9215371, 9223523-9
117 41 ATHENS **Tlx.** 210537 ILIS GR
Open: Jan. - Dec.

A new comfortable hotel with experienced personnel, fluent in several languages. 3-programme music and direct dial phone in all rooms, elegant dining-room offering Greek and international specialities, relaxing cocktail lounge and a panoramic roof garden. Also a conference room for up to 40, telex service and personal safes.

rm 96/**b** 176 TV S
C.C.: American Express, Diners, Access, Master Charge, Eurocard, J.C.B.

B´ GEORGE HOTEL (Hostel)
46, Nikis Str. **Tel.** 01/3226474
105 58 ATHENS **Open:** Jan. - Dec.

rm 7/**b** 18

B´ GRAND HOTEL
10, Veranzerou Str. **Tel.** 01/5243156-9
104 32 ATHENS **Open:** Jan. - Dec.

Located in the commercial center of the city, 0,5 km from the National Museum, 20 min. walk from the Acropolis. Reduced prices for groups (over 20 persons) up to 30%.

rm 99/**b** 190 S
C.C.: Master Charge, Eurocard, Access, American Express

B´ ILION HOTEL
7, Ag. Konstandinou Str. **Tel.** 01/5237411-5
104 31 ATHENS **Open:** Jan. - Dec.

rm 105/**b** 166 S24h

* B´ ILISSIA HOTEL
25, Mihalakopoulou Str. **Tel.** 01/7244051-5
115 28 ATHENS **Tlx.** 214924 ILIS GR
Open: Jan. - Dec.

rm 69/**b** 131

B´ IOKASTI'S HOUSE HOTEL (Hostel)
65, Aristotelous Str. **Tel.** 01/8226647, 8234011
104 34 ATHENS **Open:** Jan. - Dec.

Close to the National Museum, the subway station and the beaches-and-Sounio bus terminals. Special terms during low season for students and groups.

rm 16/**b** 36 **C.C.**: Visa

B´ IONIS HOTEL
4, Halkokondili Str. **Tel.** 01/5232311-3
104 32 ATHENS **Tlx.** 218425 IONI GR
Open: Jan. - Dec.

Located in the town-center close to Omonia Sq., IONIS was built in 1977. Fully air conditioned, it has 102 B´ superior class rooms, all with a private bath. There is also a pleasant living room area, a bar and a restaurant.

rm 102/**b** 200 S
C.C.: American Express, Diners, Visa, Eurocard, Master Charge, Access

* B´ IRIS HOTEL
8, Sorovits Str. **Tel.** 01/8647442, 8653222,
112 52 ATHENS **Open:** Jan. - Dec.

rm 19/**b** 36

* B´ JOY HOTEL
38, Feron Str. **Tel.** 01/8231012
104 34 ATHENS **Open:** Jan. - Dec.

rm 20/**b** 45

* B´ KYPSELI HOTEL
7, Skyrou Str. **Tel.** 01/8216236, 8213116, 8219898
113 61 ATHENS **Open:** Jan. - Dec.

rm 10/**b** 18

B´ LYCABETTE HOTEL
6, Valaoritou Str. **Tel.** 01/3633514-8

106 71 ATHENS **Tlx.** 221147 GTSA GR
Open: Jan. - Dec.

Built in 1964 in the most fashionable part of Athens, renovated in 198‸, the hotel has 40 luxurious rooms with spacious balconies. A beautifully furnished T.V. lounge, cocktail bar, travel-information desk and an experienced staff make for a perfectly comfortable stay.

rm 39/**b** 63 S
C.C.: American Express, Diners, Eurocard

B´ LYDIA HOTEL

121, Liossion Str. **Tel.** 01/8219980, 8237952
104 45 ATHENS **Tlx.** 219786
Open: Jan. - Dec.

Most comfortable B´ class hotel very near Omonia Sq. and the R.R. station. All rooms have telephone and hot water, most of them with private shower and W.C. Free parking space available. Snack bar, hospitable and friendly atmosphere.

rm 38/**b** 71 S
C.C.: American Express, Visa

B´ MARATHON HOTEL

‸3, Karolou Str. **Tel.** 01/5231865-8
‸04 37 ATHENS **Open:** Jan. - Dec.

94 modern rooms with air-conditioning and stereo music. Restaurant, bar, snack-bar, roof garden and underground garage for 120 cars.

rm 94/**b** 176 S
C.C.: Diners, American Express

B´ MINERVA HOTEL

‸, Stadiou Str. **Tel.** 01/3230915-7
‸05 62 ATHENS **Tlx.** 215838 STAD GR
Open: Jan. - Dec.

In the heart of the city and next to all air-terminals. Superb view of Likavitos hill.

rm 50/**b** 86 S
C.C.: American Express

B´ MINOA HOTEL

‸2, Karolou Str. **Tel.** 01/5234622-4
‸04 37 ATHENS **Open:** Jan. - Dec.

Half way between Omonia Sq. and the RR station, the hotel has spacious modern sunny rooms, with private bathroom and hot water around the clock.

rm 50/**b** 84 S 24h
C.C.: American Express, Diners, Master Charge, Visa

B´ MYRTO HOTEL

‸, Nikis Str. **Tel.** 01/3227237, 3234560
‸05 58 ATHENS **Open** Jan. - Dec.

rm 12/**b** 21

B´ NANA HOTEL

‸, Neofytou Metaxa Str. **Tel.** 01/3842211-5
‸04 39 ATHENS **Open:** Jan. - Dec.

Newly-built, family-run hotel near the RR station with 3-channel music, direct dial phone, T.V. (on request) and balcony in every room. Breakfast 7-10 a.m., 24 hour bar, daily tours & cruises, car rental and ticket booking service.

rm 47/**b** 88 T.V.
24h

B´ ODEON HOTEL

42, Pireos Str. **Tel.** 01/5239206-9
104 37 ATHENS **Open:** Jan. - Dec.

rm 60/**b** 98 P

B´ OMIROS HOTEL

15, Apollonos Str. **Tel.** 01/3235486-7
105 57 ATHENS **Open:** Jan. - Dec.

rm 37/**b** 60 S
C.C.: American Express, Diners, Visa

B´ ORION II HOTEL

105a, Emm. Benaki Str. **Tel** 01/3605193, 3627362, 3628441
114 73 ATHENS
Open: Mar. - Nov.

rm 23/**b** 30 P **C.C.:** Visa

B´ OSCAR HOTEL

25, Filadelfias Str. **Tel.** 01/8834215-9
104 38 ATHENS **Tlx.** 221256 BRAZ GR
Open: Jan. - Dec.

A new hotel opposite the RR station, with balcony. T.V. (on request) and stereo music in every room, roof-garden with a panoramic view, snack-bar, restaurant, swimming-pool and conference hall.

rm 164/**b** 279 T.V.
S 24h **C.C.:** American Express

B´ PALLADION HOTEL

54, Panepistimiou Str. **Tel.** 01/3623291-5
106 78 ATHENS **Open:** Jan. - Dec.

rm 58/**b** 115 S 24h

B´ PAN HOTEL

11, Mitropoleos Str. **Tel.** 01/3237816-9, 3237810
105 57 ATHENS
Tlx. 221911 PANH GR
Open: Jan. - Dec.

Modern 10-storey hotel with every amenity, ideally situated in the heart of Athens, next to airline terminals and shopping center. Prompt service, air-conditioning and constant hot water in every room.

rm 56/**b** 92 S 24h
P **C.C.:** American Express, Diners, Master Charge, Access, Eurocard, Visa, J.C.B.

B´ PATISSIA HOTEL

221, Patission Str. **Tel.** 01/8627511-2
112 53 ATHENS **Open:** Jan. - Dec.

Private shower, hot water, music, phone and balcony in every room.

rm 29/**b** 44 S 24h

B´ PLAKA HOTEL

7, Kapnikareas Str. **Tel.** 01/3222096, 3222098
105 56 ATHENS **Tlx.** 221020 PLAH GR
Open: Jan. - Dec.

3 Minutes from Syntagma Sq. and all airline offices. Restaurant, bar, roof-garden restaurant, greek taverna on the top floor, with a magnificent view of the Acropolis, Agora, Thission, Attalus arcade etc. Spoken: English, French, German, Italian, Arabian. Airlines and travel agencies employees are given a 10% discount.

rm 67/**b** 123 S
P **C.C.:** American Express, Visa.

Diners, Master Charge, Access

* B´ PLAZA HOTEL
78, Aharnon Str. **Tel.** 01/8225111-7
104 40 ATHENS **Tlx.** 214686
Open: Jan. - Dec.

rm 126/**b** 239

B´ PNYX HOTEL (Pension)
51, Apostolou Pavlou Str. **Tel.** 01/3468859
118 51 ATHENS **Open:** Jan. - Dec.

rm 14/**b** 24

B´ PRIAMOS HOTEL APARTMENTS
26, Fokianou Str. **Tel.** 01/7291134-9
116 35 ATHENS **Open:** Jan. - Dec.

The hotel is situated in a quiet street near the Stadium and the National Garden, within walking distance from many famous archaelogical sites. Warm and friendly atmosphere, 30 single or double rooms, 14 fully equipped apts, restaurant, taverna, bar, roof-solarium, conference facilities for up to 100.

rm 42/**b** 84 S
C.C.: American Express, Diners

B´ PROTEA HOTEL
9, Lambrou Katsoni Str. **Tel.** 01/6430735-6
114 72 ATHENS **Open:** Jan. - Dec.

A modern hotel conveniently located, 5 min. walk from the center of Athens, in a quiet street under Likavitos hill.

rm 22/**b** 30 S

* B´ REMVI HOTEL
284, Patission Str. **Tel.** 01/2024124, 2231405
112 55 ATHENS **Open:** Jan. - Dec.

rm 15/**b** 26

B´ ROY HOTEL
15, Rodou Str. **Tel.** 01/8615765, 8610843
112 52 ATHENS **Open:** Jan. - Dec.

rm 28/**b** 45 S24h
C.C.: Diners, Eurocard

* B´ SOUDAN HOTEL
47, Mavromihali Str. **Tel.** 01/3605037
106 80 ATHENS **Open:** Jan. - Dec.

rm 15/**b** 29

B´ STADION HOTEL
38, Vas. Konstandinou Str. **Tel.** 01/7291619, 7226054-6
116 35 ATHENS **Tlx.** 215838 STAD GR
Open: Jan. - Dec.

In the most aristocratic area of Athens. Superb view of the Acropolis and Likavitos hill.

rm 70/**b** 126 S
C.C.: American Express, Diners

B´ STANLEY HOTEL
1-3, Odisseos Str. **Tel.** 01/5241611-8, 5240142-45
104 37 ATHENS **Tlx.** 216550 STAN GR
Open: Jan. - Dec.

Roof-garden with open-air swimming pool, overlooking the Acropolis.

rm 396/**b** 714 S **C.C.:** American Express

B´ TITANIA HOTEL
52, Panepistimiou Str. **Tel.** 01/3609611-9
106 78 ATHENS **Tlx.** 214673 IFEL GR
Open: Jan. - Dec.

Superior B´ class hotel situated between Omonia and Syntagma Sq., offering services and facilities like 24 hour telex, private safes, bank, baby-sitting, secretarial service etc. A restaurant presents Greek and international cuisine, and the bar/solarium on the roof garden gives a unique view of the city, clear out to the sea.

rm 398/**b** 754 S24h **C.C.:** American Express, Diners, Visa

B´ VOLCAN HOTEL
10A, Ithakis Str. **Tel.** 01/8815385
113 61 ATHENS **Open:** Jan. - Dec.

rm 14/**b** 24

B´ XENOPHON HOTEL
340, Aharnon Str. **Tel.** 01/2020310-14
111 45 ATHENS **Tlx.** 215294
Open: Jan. - Dec

rm 168/**b** 340 **C.C.:** Diners, American Express

C´ ACHILLEAS HOTEL
21, Leka Str. **Tel.** 01/3225826, 3233197, 322853
105 62 ATHENS **Tlx.** 21645
Open: Jan. - Dec

T.V. and fridge available upon request.

rm 34/**b** 65 S24h
C.C.: American Express, Visa

C´ ACHILLION HOTEL
32, Ag. Konstandinou Str. **Tel.** 01/522561, 5230971, 522191
104 37 ATHENS **Open:** Jan. - Dec

rm 56/**b** 98 S24h
C.C.: American Express

C´ ACROPOLIS VIEW HOTEL
8, Robertou Galli Str. **Tel.** 01/9217303
117 42 ATHENS **Tlx.** 21993
Open: Jan. - De

A quiet hotel in the center of Athen 100m from the Acropolis.

rm 25/**b** 47
C.C.: American Express, Visa, Eurocard, Access, Master Charge

C´ ALBYON HOTEL
20, Akominatou Str. **Tel.** 01/5223058, 522202, 52311
104 37 ATHENS **Open:** Jan. - De

Family environment, excellent service.

rm 22/**b** 38 S24h

C´ ALCESTIS HOTEL
18, Theatrou Sq. **Tel.** 01/321981
105 52 ATHENS **Tlx.** 222450 SELE C
Open: Jan. - De

Spacious modern rooms and apts mo with private veranda, a roof-garden faci the Acropolis, air-conditioned T.V. loung deluxe restaurant and snack-bar, a fe steps from Omonia Sq. Recommended f a restful enjoyable stay.

rm 128/**b** 232
C.C.: American Express, Visa, Master Charge

C´ ALMA HOTEL
5, Dorou Str. **Tel.** 01/5240858-9
104 32 ATHENS **Open:** Jan. - Dec.
rm 64/**b** 114

C´ AMARYLLIS HOTEL
45, Veranzerou Str. **Tel.** 01/5238738-9
104 32 ATHENS 5238539
Open: Jan. - Dec.
Built in 1964 and completely renovated in 1978, situated in the center of Athens near Omonia Sq. All rooms, furnished with elegance and good taste have private bathroom, hot water, phone, and balcony or veranda, thus offering the most up-to-date comfort to the guest.
rm 57/**b** 100

C´ AMAZON HOTEL
19, Metropoleos Str. **Tel.** 01/3234002-5
105 57 ATHENS **Tlx.** 218673
Open: Jan. - Dec.
Amazon Hotel is located in the heart of Athens (Syntagma Sq.) 3 minutes away from the old town (Plaka). All rooms have a private bath and most of them are air conditioned. There is also a roof garden having a magnificent view of the Acropolis and a T.V.-lounge on the 1st floor.
rm 46/**b** 77

C´ AMI HOTEL
10, Iras Str. **Tel.** 01/9220820, 9234177
117 43 ATHENS **Open:** Jan. - Dec.
Quiet and tidy hotel not far from the center, with big balconies facing the Acropolis.
rm 18/**b** 29

C´ ANNABEL HOTEL
28, Koumoundourou Str. **Tel.** 01/5243454, 5245834
104 37 ATHENS
Open: Jan. - Dec.
Clean tidy rooms, warm friendly hospitality, youthful student environment around the bar.
rm 14/**b** 29

* C´ APHRODITE HOTEL
21, Apollonos Str. **Tel.** 01/3234357-9, 3226047
105 57 ATHENS **Open:** Jan. - Dec.
rm 84/**b** 162

C´ APOLLON HOTEL
14, Deligeorgi Str. **Tel.** 01/5245211-4
104 37 ATHENS **Open:** Jan. - Dec.
In a quiet street not far from Omonia Sq. Well-stocked cafe-bar, restaurant, T.V. lounge, helpful staff, roomy Parking.
rm 70/**b** 136

C´ APOLLONION HOTEL
1, Leonidou Str. **Tel.** 01/5224298, 5227787
104 37 ATHENS **Open:** Jan. - Dec.
rm 29/**b** 43

C´ ARES HOTEL
7, Pireos Str. **Tel.** 01/5234347-9, 5242446
105 52 ATHENS **Open:** Jan. - Dec.
rm 39/**b** 71

C´ ARGO PENSION
25, Vict. Hugo Str. **Tel.** 01/5225939
104 37 ATHENS **Open:** Jan. - Dec.
Laundry facilities, money exchange, travel information, island tickets, baggage storage, low off-season prices.
rm 16/**b** 31

* C´ ARIAS HOTEL
20, Karolou Str. **Tel.** 01/5228527-9
104 37 ATHENS **Open:** Jan. - Dec.
rm 53/**b** 79

C´ ARISTIDES HOTEL
50, Socratous Str. **Tel.** 01/5223881, 5223940
104 31 ATHENS **Open:** Jan. - Dec.
Renovated and fire-proofed in 1983. ARISTIDES Hotel offers a warm, family hospitality. All rooms have private bathroom, phone and central heating. The air-conditioned bar is open day and night. Conveniently located in the centre of Athens near Omonia Sq. the hotel gives easy access to the subway, bus and RR stations, air terminals, shopping centers and business areas of the city.
rm 90/**b** 158
C.C.: Diners

C´ ARISTOTELES HOTEL
15, Aharnon Str. **Tel.** 5228126-7, 5228706-7
104 38 ATHENS **Tlx.** 221305 NIC GR
Open: Jan. - Dec.
rm 60/**b** 102

C´ ARTEMISSION HOTEL
20, Veranzerou Str. **Tel.** 01/5230036, 5230524
104 32 ATHENS **Open:** Jan. - Dec.
rm 42/**b** 79

C´ ASPASIA HOTEL
26, Satovriandou Str. **Tel.** 01/5243211-3
104 32 ATHENS **Open:** Jan - Dec.
Rooms with private bathroom and telephone. Family atmosphere, plentyful breakfast, central heating, near Omonia Sq. Reduced prices for extended stay.
rm 35/**b** 65

C´ ASTY HOTEL
2, Pireos Str. **Tel.** 01/5230424-8
104 31 ATHENS **Open:** Jan. - Dec.
In the very centre of Athens, close to business and entertainment areas. Cooperation with all kinds of travel and entertainment agencies. Coaches stop right in front of the hotel entrance.
rm 128/**b** 224
C.C.: American Express, Diners, Premium Visa, Access, Eurocard, Master Charge

C´ ATHENS CONNECTION HOTEL
20, Ioulianou Str. **Tel.** 01/8213940, 8224592
106 82 ATHENS **Open:** Jan. - Dec.
Our location and experience allows us to

offer the best accommodation. Very popular in Europe and the States among young people, we are highly recommended by the "LET'S GO: EUROPE" and "EUROPE ON $20 A DAY", plus many European guide books.

rm 26/**b** 59 S24h
C.C.: Traveller's Cheque

C´ ATHINEA HOTEL
9, Vilara Str. **Tel.** 01/5243884-5
104 37 ATHENS **Tlx.** 22212 HOTA
Open: Jan. - Dec.

Built in 1983, ATHINEA is situated in the center of Athens by Omonia Sq. All its rooms, furnished with good taste, have a balcony or veranda, hot water, air conditioning, 2-channel music, radio, and a fully automatic fire protection system. The bar and caffeteria are open day and night.

rm 42/**b** 80 S24h

* C´ ATLAS HOTEL
30, Sophocleous Str. **Tel.** 01/5235309, 5227204
105 52 ATHENS **Open:** Jan. - Dec.

rm 23/**b** 33

C´ ATTALOS HOTEL
29, Athinas Str. **Tel.** 01/3212801-3
105 54 ATHENS **Tlx.** 218829
Open: Jan. - Dec.

Newly decorated clean and comfortable rooms with private balcony. Roof garden giving a panoramic view of Athens. Efficient service by a courteous English speaking staff.

rm 80/**b** 155 S

* C´ BANGHION HOTEL
18B, Omonia Sq. **Tel.** 01/3242259
104 31 ATHENS **Open:** Jan. - Dec.

rm 54/**b** 93 P

C´ BILL HOTEL
33, Kerameon Str. **Tel.** 01/5239617-9
104 36 ATHENS **Open:** Jan. - Dec.

Close to the city-center and even closer to the RR station.

rm 33/**b** 61 T.V. S

C´ CAPITOL HOTEL
11, M.Kotopouli Str. **Tel.** 01/5249111
104 32 ATHENS **Open:** Jan. - Dec.

Our location in Omonia Sq. (city centre) enables our patrons to deal with their business in a record-time, to move in any direction, and/or to have memorable holidays at reasonable prices.

rm 88/**b** 168 S

C´ CAPRI HOTEL
6, Psaromilingou Str. **Tel.** 01/3252085, 3252091
105 53 ATHENS **Tlx.** 210800 ACT GR.
Open: Jan. - Dec.

Superior C´ class hotel a few minutes from Plaka, Syntagma Sq., Omonia Sq. and subway station. Roof-garden with an excellent view of the Acropolis.

rm 44/**b** 78 S

C´ CARLTON YOUTH HOTEL
7, Omonia Sq. **Tel.** 01/5223201, 5222812
104 31 ATHENS **Open:** Jan. - Dec.

Located in the town center (Omonia Sq.).

rm 40/**b** 60 S

C´ CAROLINA HOTEL
55, Kolokotroni Str. **Tel.** 01/3220837-8
105 60 ATHENS **Open:** Jan. - Dec.

A comfortable hotel in the city-center near all airline terminals. Laundry facilities, left luggage storage. The manager Mr. Papagianoulas lived in Sidney for 10 years.

rm 31/**b** 57 S24h

C´ CLARIDGE HOTEL
4, Dorou Str. **Tel.** 01/5223013, 5221561
104 31 ATHENS **Open:** Jan. - Dec.

Reduced prices for groups.

rm 48/**b** 93 S

C´ CRYSTAL HOTEL
68, Kolonou Str. **Tel.** 01/5231083-6, 5229363
104 37 ATHENS **Tlx.** 216566
Open: Jan. - Dec.

rm 84/**b** 162
P

C´ DELOS HOTEL
12, Makri Str. **Tel.** 01/9220287, 9220106
117 42 ATHENS **Open:** Jan. - Dec.

Very quiet and tidy hotel 5 min. from the Acropolis and Plaka. Many bus lines are easily accessible.

rm 14/**b** 27

C´ DELPHI HOTEL
1, Ag. Konstandinou Sq. **Tel.** 01/5222751
104 37 ATHENS **Open:** Jan. - Dec.

rm 51/**b** 74 P

C´ DELTA HOTEL
27, Kerameon Str. **Tel.** 01/5247522-3
104 37 ATHENS **Open:** Jan. - Dec.

Friendly family environment.

rm 32/**b** 60 S24h
C.C.: Diners

* C´ DIOSCOURI HOTEL
6, Pitakou Str. **Tel.** 01/3248165, 3246582
105 58 ATHENS **Open:** Jan. - Dec.

rm 11/**b** 24

C´ DIROS HOTEL
21, Ag. Konstandinou Str. **Tel.** 01/5248112-4
104 31 ATHENS **Open:** Jan. - Dec.

Tidy, family-run hotel. Eager service. Special terms for groups upon agreement.

rm 45/**b** 84 S24h

C´ ECONOMY HOTEL
5, Klisthenous Str. **Tel.** 01/5220520-2, 5226146
105 52 ATHENS
Tlx. 221529 KANA GR
Open: Jan. - Dec.

The ECONOMY hotel offers the comforts of a big hotel at nice prices, in 56 comfortable air-conditioned rooms. Also quietness, family atmosphere and friendly service.

rm 56/**b** 105 S P

C´ ELENA HOTEL
2, Psiloriti Str. **Tel.** 01/8813211-3
104 39 ATHENS **Open:** Jan. - Dec.
rm 75/**b** 136

C´ ELITE HOTEL
23, Pireos Str. **Tel.** 01/5221523, 5235020
105 52 ATHENS **Open:** Jan. - Dec.
rm 44/**b** 80

C´ EPIDAVROS HOTEL
14, Koumoundourou Str. **Tel.** 01/5230421-2, 5244920
104 37 ATHENS **Open:** Jan. - Dec.
10% discount to groups of over 7.
rm 50/**b** 89
C.C.: American Express, Visa, Diners

C´ ERATO HOTEL
72, Hiraklidon Str. **Tel.** 01/3459996-8
118 51 ATHENS **Open:** Jan. - Dec.
rm 20/**b** 38
C.C.: Travellers Cheques

C´ ERECHTHION HOTEL
8, Flamarion Str. **Tel.** 01/3459606
118 51 ATHENS **Open:** Jan. - Dec.
A delightfull small hotel just across the street from Ancient Agora with a beautifull view of the Acropolis. A short walk to Plaka. Listening to the "Sound and Light" show from one's balcony is a delight!
rm 22/**b** 38

C´ EUROPE HOTEL
7, Satovriandou Str. **Tel.** 01/5223081, 5229931
104 30 ATHENS **Open:** Jan. - Dec.
rm 37/**b** 67

C´ EVRIPIDES HOTEL
79, Evripidou Str. **Tel.** 01/3212301-3
105 53 ATHENS **Tlx.** 222518 HEKI GR
Open: Jan. - Dec.
Modern hotel, centrally located. Spacious beautifully furnished rooms with bathroom, hot water 24 hours a day, phone and radio. Roof garden, American bar, snacks, panoramic view of Athens.
rm 62/**b** 119

C´ EXARCHION HOTEL
55, Themistokleous Str. **Tel.** 01/3601256, 3603296
106 83 ATHENS **Open:** Jan. - Dec.
Famous for its cleanliness and efficient friendly service, the hotel has spacious rooms with balconies and a roof garden.
rm 49/**b** 93
C.C.: American Express, Diners, Visa

C´ FILO-XENIA HOTEL
50, Aharnon Str. **Tel.** 01/8828611-3
104 33 ATHENS **Open:** Jan. - Dec.
Centrally located, fully air-conditioned, international bar, restaurant with a panoramic view, private bathroom, telephone, veranda in all rooms. 1 mile from the center of Athens. 5 minutes walk to the National museum.
rm 51/**b** 97
C.C.: Access, Eurocard, Master Charge

C´ FLORIDA HOTEL
25, Menandrou Str. **Tel.** 01/5223214, 5239712
105 52 ATHENS **Open:** Jan. - Dec.
Very near Omonia Sq., comfortable lounge and bar, breakfast room, high standard service.
rm 69/**b** 127

C´ FRIDA HOTEL
2, Zossimou Str. **Tel.** 01/6443324, 6443297
114 72 ATHENS **Open:** Jan. - Dec.
Family atmosphere - friendly service.
rm 15/**b** 26

C´ GRECA PENSION
48, Syngrou Ave. **Tel.** 01/9215262
117 42 ATHENS **Open:** Jan. - Dec.
rm 21/**b** 48

C´ HELICON HOTEL
3, Dorou Str. **Tel.** 01/5221695, 5228428
104 31 ATHENS **Open:** Jan. - Dec.
rm 24/**b** 51

C´ HELLINIS-MILANO HOTEL
177, Syngrou Ave. **Tel.** 01/9349611-5
117 55 ATHENS **Open:** Jan. - Dec.
Elegant, airy, spacious rooms, all with private balcony.
rm 80/**b** 180
C.C.: American Express, Diners

*** C´ HERA HOTEL**
9, Falirou Str. **Tel.** 01/9236682
117 42 ATHENS **Open:** Jan. - Dec.
rm 49/**b** 92

*** C´ HERMES HOTEL**
19, Apollonos Str. **Tel.** 01/3235514-6
105 57 ATHENS **Open:** Jan. - Dec.
rm 45/**b** 85

C´ IMPERIAL HOTEL
46, Mitropoleos Str. **Tel.** 01/3227617-8, 3227780
105 63 ATHENS **Open:** Jan. - Dec.
In the center of the city, 2 minutes walk to Syntagma Sq. and all airline offices. New modern building, private bathroom, hot water and veranda in all rooms, giving a magnificent view of the Acropolis and Athens.
rm 21/**b** 33

C´ INIOHOS HOTEL
26, Veranzerou Str. **Tel.** 01/5230811-8
104 32 ATHENS **Open:** Jan. - Dec.
A new modern hotel in the heart of Athens. In the hotel's restaurant one can enjoy Greek and international specialities. Pleasantly set bar and cafeteria. Spacious conference rooms for every social event and business meetings.
rm 134/**b** 250

C´ INN STUDENT HOTEL
16, Kidathineon Str. **Tel.** 01/3244808
105 58 ATHENS **Open:** Jan. - Dec.
Modest but comfortable. Balconies overlook Plaka's main square or the Acropolis.

Private breakfast bar and snacks in a vine covered courtyard. In-house washing machine.

rm 33/**b** 70

C´JASON HOTEL
3-5, Nikiforou Str. **Tel.** 01/5248031-3
104 37 ATHENS **Open:** Mar. - Oct.

rm 82/**b** 152 **S** **P**

C´JOHN'S PLACE HOTEL
5, Patroou Str. **Tel.** 01/3229719
105 57 ATHENS **Open:** Jan. - Dec.
Nice and clean rooms, friendly service.

rm 15/**b** 31

C´KARAYANNIS HOTEL
94, Syngrou Ave. **Tel.** 01/9215903, 9217150
117 41 ATHENS **Open:** Jan. - Dec.

rm 30/**b** 55

C´KERAMIKOS HOTEL
30, Keramikou Str. **Tel.** 01/5247631, 5247443
104 36 ATHENS **Tlx.** 221602 MARI GR
Open: Jan. - Dec.
Situated just off Omonia Sq., KERAMIKOS is an ideal spot to spend a few days in a big city. Clean, neat, quiet, with a cosy bar-cafeteria, lounge and roof-garden boasting a full view of Athens. All rooms have private balconies, private bath/W.C. English-speaking staff. Continental breakfast served.

rm 30/**b** 54 **S**24h **P**

C.C.: Visa, American Express, Eurocard, Diners

C´KING JASON HOTEL
26, Kolonou Str. **Tel.** 01/5234721-4
104 37 ATHENS **Open:** Jan. - Dec.

rm 114/**b** 216 **S** **P**

C´KISSOS HOTEL
6, Mezonos Str. **Tel.** 01/5243011-3
104 38 ATHENS **Open:** Jan. - Dec
Located in an area five minutes walk from the center of Athens. All rooms with private bathroom, air-conditioning and music. Garage open 24 hours a day. 20% discount to students and young people (under 26). Also for groups of over 10, 10-30% discount depending on the season.

rm 28/**b** 54 **S**24h
P

C´KOSMOS HOTEL
16, Psaron Str. **Tel.** 01/5239201-4, 5220125
104 38 ATHENS **Tlx.** 225965 TAGA GR
Open: Jan. - Dec.
Centrally located, out of the traffic noise. Solar heating - hot water around the clock. Pizzeria.

rm 124/**b** 236
C.C.: American Express

C´KOUROS HOTEL
11, Kodrou Str. **Tel.** 01/3227431
105 58 ATHENS **Open:** Mar. - Dec.

rm 10/**b** 17 **S**24h

C´KRONOS HOTEL
18, Ag. Dimitriou Str. **Tel.** 01/3211601-3
105 54 ATHENS **Open:** Jan. - Dec.
The ideal C´ class hotel right in the heart of Athens. Modernly furnished rooms, all with hot water, most with private bathroom. Bar, snack-bar, roof garden, excellent service and friendly atmosphere.

rm 57/**b** 100

C´LA MIRAGE HOTEL
3, M. Kotopouli Str. **Tel.** 01/5234071, 5234755
104 31 ATHENS **Tlx.** 222598 SASA GR
Open: Jan. - Dec.
Wall to wall carpeting. Sound proofing. Available are: Restaurant, snack-bar, main bar with T.V. - video, roof-garden and conference rooms

rm 208/**b** 400 **S**24h

* C´LETO HOTEL
15, Missaraliotou Str. **Tel.** 01/9231768, 9230743
117 42 ATHENS
Open: Jan. - Dec.

rm 20/**b** 32

C´LIDO HOTEL
2, Nikoforou Str. **Tel.** 01/5248211, 5225040
104 37 ATHENS **Open:** Jan. - Dec.
All rooms have a balcony. Colour T.V. and Video in the bar. Family environment.

rm 82/**b** 175 **S**24h **P**

C.C.: Diners, American Express, Visa

C´MARBLE HOUSE PENSION
35, An. Zini Str. **Tel.** 01/9215577, 9234058
117 41 ATHENS **Open:** 15th Mar. - 30th Oct.
A pension close to Olympic Airways terminal and within walking distance from the Acropolis. Comfortable clean rooms, family environment. Best service ever. From 15/3 to 15/5 and 1/10 to 30/10, 20-30% discount, depending on the number of persons. Also during low season (1/11 to 15/3) rooms are let by the month at half price.

rm 17/**b** 39 **S** **P**

C´MARIE HOTEL
100, Zoodohou Pighis Str. **Tel.** 01/3605564, 3605632
114 73 ATHENS
Open: Jan. - Dec.

rm 17/**b** 19 **S**24h

C´MARINA HOTEL
13, Voulgari Str. **Tel.** 01/5229109, 5237832
104 37 ATHENS **Open:** Jan. - Dec.
Completly renovated in 1984, the hotel operates under a new management. It is in the city centre and has a snack-bar and breakfast-room.

rm 81/**b** 144 **S**

C´MEDITERRANEAN HOTEL
28, Veranzerou Str. **Tel.** 01/5222631, 5222679
104 32 ATHENS **Open:** Jan. - Dec.

rm 42/**b** 84

C´MEDOUSA HOTEL
4, Evripidou Str. **Tel.** 01/9426216, 9426254
176 74 ATHENS **Open:** Jan. - Dec.
Colour T.V. in every room, video in some.

rm 27/**b** 50 TV **S**24h **P**

C´ MELIS HOTEL
22, Tenedou Str. **Tel.** 01/8655755, 8655745-7
112 57 ATHENS **Open:** Jan. - Dec.
rm 52/**b** 99

C´ MINION HOTEL
3, Mezonos Str. **Tel.** 01/5234222-3, 5225959
104 38 ATHENS **Open:** Jan. - Dec.
rm 35/**b** 60

C´ MORPHEUS HOTEL
3, Aristotelous Str. **Tel.** 01/5234601
104 32 ATHENS **Open:** Jan. - Dec.
rm 19/**b** 35

C´ MUSEUM HOTEL
16, Bouboulinas Str. **Tel.** 01/3605611-3
106 82 ATHENS **Open:** Jan. - Dec.
All rooms with private facilities, most with balcony.
rm 59/**b** 109 S
C.C.: American Express, Diners, Master Charge, Access

C´ MYSTRAS HOTEL
26, Kerameon Str. **Tel.** 01/5227737, 5221807
104 37 ATHENS **Open:** Jan. - Dec.
Next to the R.R. station, very close to the city center.
rm 32/**b** 61 S24h

C´ NAUSIKA HOTEL
21, Karolou Str. **Tel.** 01/5239381-3
104 37 ATHENS **Open:** Jan. - Dec.
Situated between Omonia Sq. and the R.R. station, the hotel has modern, spacious, sunny rooms with hot water day and night. Civilized family environment.
rm 41/**b** 70 S24h
C.C.: American Express, Visa, Master Charge, Diners

C´ NEFELI HOTEL
16, Iperidou Str. **Tel.** 01/3228044-5
105 58 ATHENS **Open:** Jan. - Dec.
Warm friendly atmosphere, pleasant unforgettable stay in our family-run hotel. Built in a quiet street in Plaka, out of the traffic noise, 10 minutes from the Acropolis or Syntagma Sq.Reduced prices from November to February.
rm 18/**b** 32 S24h

C´ NEON KRONOS HOTEL
12-14, Ag. Assomaton Str. **Tel.** 01/3251106-8
105 53 ATHENS **Open:** Jan. - Dec.
Located near the Ancient Agora, Thission, Keramikos, and bazaar area, modernly furnished, each room with a veranda overlooking the Acropolis, the hotel offers excellent service and a most enjoyable stay.
rm 54/**b** 102
C.C.: Visa

C´ NESTOR HOTEL
58, Ag. Konstandinou Str. **Tel.** 01/5235576-8
104 37 ATHENS **Open:** Jan. - Dec.
rm 50/**b** 95 S

C´ NICOLA HOTEL
4, Olenou Str. **Tel.** 01/8837911
113 62 ATHENS **Open:** Jan. - Dec.
The hotel is a new one (open since 1980). It is located by "Pedion tou Areos" park.
rm 29/**b** 53 S24h
C.C.: Visa

*** C´ NIKI HOTEL**
27, Nikis Str. **Tel.** 01/3220913-5, 3220886
105 57 ATHENS **Open:** Jan. - Dec.
rm 24/**b** 45

*** C´ OLYMPIA HOTEL**
25, Pireos Str. **Tel.** 01/5222429
105 52 ATHENS **Open:** Jan. - Dec.
rm 40/**b** 70

C´ OMEGA HOTEL
15, Aristogitonos Str. **Tel.** 01/3212421-3
105 52 ATHENS **Open:** Jan. - Dec.
rm 54/**b** 108 S24h

C´ OMONIA HOTEL
4, Omonia Sq. **Tel.** 01/5237321-9
104 31 ATHENS **Open:** Jan. - Dec.
A tourist-class hotel in Omonia Sq. a few minutes from air and bus terminals, metrò and R.R. station. The hotel has comfortably furnished rooms all with balcony. There are 9 floors, 4 lifts and 2 escalators.
rm 252/**b** 486 S

C´ ONIRO HOTEL
57, Sp. Tricoupi Str. **Tel.** 01/8832731-3
114 73 ATHENS **Open:** Jan. - Dec.
rm 24/**b** 43 S

C´ ORPHEUS HOTEL
58, Halkokondili Str. **Tel.** 01/5224996
104 32 ATHENS **Open:** Jan. - Dec.
rm 40/**b** 75

*** C´ PARADISE HOTEL**
28, Mezonos Str. **Tel.** 01/5220084
104 38 ATHENS **Open:** Jan. - Dec.
rm 11/**b** 23

C´ PARIS HOTEL
49, Geraniou Str. **Tel.** 01/5239955-7, 5243537
104 31 ATHENS **Open:** Jan. - Dec.
rm 57/**b** 106 S24h

*** C´ PARNON HOTEL**
20, Tritis Septemvriou Str. **Tel.** 01/5235196, 5230013-4, 5230131
104 32 ATHENS **Open:** Jan. - Dec.
rm 48/**b** 88

*** C´ PELLA INN HOTEL**
104, Hermou Str. **Tel.** 01/3250598
105 54 ATHENS **Open:** Jan. - Dec.
rm 21/**b** 28

C´ PERGAMOS HOTEL
14, Aharnon Str. **Tel.** 01/5231991-3
104 33 ATHENS **Open:** Jan. - Dec.
rm 33/**b** 61 S

C´ PHIDIAS HOTEL
39, Apostolou Pavlou Str. **Tel.** 01/3459511-2
118 51 ATHENS **Open:** Jan. - Dec.

rm 15/**b** 30
C.C.: American Express, Diners, Visa, Master Charge, Access, Eurocard

C´ PHILIPPOS HOTEL
3, Mitseon Str. **Tel.** 01/9223611-5
117 42 ATHENS **Tlx.** 241527 KAGE GR
Open: Jan. - Dec.
A modern hotel for tourists and businessmen at the foot of the Acropolis. Tastefully furnished rooms, comfortable lounge, panoramic roof garden, pleasant and friendly atmosphere.
rm 48/**b** 84
C.C.: Traveller's Cheques

C´ PHOEBUS HOTEL
12, Peta Str. **Tel.** 01/3220142-3
105 58 ATHENS **Open:** Jan. - Dec.
The budget hotel in the famous area of Plaka, a short walk to the centre and the Acropolis. Personal care of guests guarantees a very pleasant stay.
rm 23/**b** 43

* C´ PRINGHIPIKON HOTEL
27, Veranzerou Str. **Tel.** 01/5232397, 5248490
104 32 ATHENS **Open:** Jan. - Dec.
rm 30/**b** 48

C´ PYTHAGORION HOTEL
28, Ag. Konstantinou Str. **Tel.** 01/5242811-4
104 37 ATHENS **Open:** Jan. - Dec.
PYTHAGORION Hotel is located in the centre of the city not far from the central railway station and close to the metrò stop as well. We provide a lot of facilities at the lowest prices possible.
rm 56/**b** 106
C.C.: Diners

C´ RHEA HOTEL
31, Neofytou Metaxa Str. **Tel.** 01/8213760
104 39 ATHENS **Open:** Jan. - Dec.
rm 36/**b** 69

C´ RIO YOUTH HOSTEL
13, Odisseos Str. **Tel.** 01/5233943, 5222081, 5223672
104 36 ATHENS
Open: Jan. - Dec.
Travel and tours service - tickets.
rm 35/**b** 70
C.C.: Diners, Visa, Access, Master Charge, American Express

C´ RIVOLI HOTEL
10, Ahileos Str. **Tel.** 01/5239714-5, 3248175
104 36 ATHENS **Open:** Jan. - Dec.
Most modern up-to-date hotel. Spacious rooms with private balcony.
rm 51/**b** 96

C´ ROOSEVELT HOTEL
5, Favierou Str. **Tel.** 01/5247793, 5223413
104 38 ATHENS **Open:** Jan. - Dec.
3 min. walk to Omonia Sq. All rooms have telephone, most have balcony. Free left-luggage storage, money exchange. 30% discount given to groups of over 10. Also 20% discount to students and young people under 26.
rm 34/**b** 55

C ROYAL HOTEL
44, Mitropoleos Str. **Tel.** 01/3234220, 3238596
105 63 ATHENS **Tlx.** 216128
Open: Jan. - Dec.
Situated within walking distance from the Acropolis, Plaka, the Flea Market, metrò, and Syntagma Sq. Rooms can be converted to 3 or 4-bedded ones suitable for families. Some have large balconies giving a view of the Acropolis.
rm 20/**b** 35

* C´ SANS RIVAL HOTEL
2, K.Paleologou Str. **Tel.** 01/5248675, 5249443
104 38 ATHENS **Open:** Jan. - Dec.
rm 47/**b** 83

C´ SOFOS HOTEL
18-20, Hormovitou Str. **Tel.** 01/8226402-5
104 40 ATHENS **Open:** Jan. - Dec.
Special terms for groups.
rm 37/**b** 70
C.C.: Eurocard, Master Charge, Access

C´ SOLOMOS HOTEL
72, Solomou Str. **Tel.** 01/5231435
104 32 ATHENS **Open:** Jan. - Dec.
rm 45/**b** 85

C´ STALIS HOTEL
10, Akominatou Str. **Tel.** 01/5241411-2
104 37 ATHENS 5241433
Open: Jan. - Dec.
rm 34/**b** 68

C´ TEGEA HOTEL
44, Halkokondili Str. **Tel.** 01/5242211-5
104 32 ATHENS 5233167
Open: Jan. - Dec.
In the center of Athens near Omonia Sq. Comfortable rooms with hot water continually. Staff at your service all the time.
rm 100/**b** 150

C´ THEOXENIA HOTEL
6, Gladstonos Str. **Tel.** 01/3600250, 3600268
106 77 ATHENS **Tlx.** 221579 EOEX GR
Open: Jan. - Dec.
Located in one of the finest pedestrian streets of Omonia Sq. the hotel combines quietness, comfort and perfect service. Breakfast and T.V. room. Two parkings close by.
rm 59/**b** 113
C.C.: Visa, American Express

C´ THESEUS INN
10, Thisseos Str. **Tel.** 01/3245960
105 62 ATHENS **Open:** Jan. - Dec.
Located in Syntagma Sq. within walking distance from the Acropolis, Museum and public services. Recommended to students and young travellers.
rm 14/**b** 32

C´ TONY'S PENSION
26, Zaharitsa Str. **Tel.** 01/9230561, 9236370
117 41 ATHENS **Open:** Jan. - Dec.
Quiet and clean pension located in fron

of the Acropolis (5 min. walk). Roof giving a view of the Acropolis. Rooms with private bathroom, hot water any time.

rm 13/b 26 S24h P

C´ TROIKON HOTEL
20, Trias Str. **Tel.** 01/8217319, 8816695
112 57 ATHENS **Open:** Jan. - Dec.
Quiet, tidy, family-run hotel, very close to the city-centre, giving easy access to the metrò station and many bus lines. A short walk to the biggest park in Athens.

rm 33/b 62 S24h

C´ VETO HOTEL
7, Lykourgou Str. **Tel.** 01/3247369
105 51 ATHENS **Open:** Jan. - Dec.
Warm family atmosphere in a quiet street in the city centre.

rm 52/b 104 S

C´ VICTOR HUGO HOTEL
16, Victoros Hugo Str. **Tel.** 01/5241708, 5241747, 5241721
104 38 ATHENS **Open:** Jan. - Dec.

rm 40/b 75 P
C.C.: Visa

*** C´ VICTORY HOTEL**
12, Monis Prodromou Str., **Tel.** 01/8839811-3
104 34 ATHENS **Open:** Jan. - Dec.

rm 19/b 33

C´ VIENNA HOTEL
20, Pireos Str. **Tel.** 01/5249143, 5225605
104 31 ATHENS **Open:** Jan. -Dec.
Centrally located, tidy, offering excellent service.

rm 62/b 114 S24h P

C´ ZINON HOTEL
3, Keramikou Str. **Tel.** 01/5239206-9, 5239200
104 37 ATHENS **Open:** Jan. - Dec.

rm 60/b 110 S24h P

D´ DIETHNES HOTEL
52, Peoniou Str. **Tel.** 01/8832878
104 40 ATHENS **Open:** Jan. - Dec.
Comfortable, clean and friendly hotel for young travellers, near the R.R. and metrò stations. 1, 2, 3, and 4-bed rooms, hot showers 24 hours a day, luggage storage, pub, breakfast, drinks, music.

rm 22/b 44 S

D´ EVA HOTEL
31, Viktoros Hugo Str. **Tel.** 01/5225226, 5223079
104 37 ATHENS **Open:** Jan. - Dec.
Newly-built hotel near the R.R. stations. Rooms with balcony, bar with a friendly, civilized environment.

rm 18/b 31 S24h P
C.C.: Visa

D´ HERMION HOTEL
66C, Ermou Str. **Tel.** 01/3212753
105 51 ATHENS **Open:** Jan. - Dec.

rm 29/b 41

D´ ILION HOTEL
17th km Athens-Lamia National Road
145 65 ATHENS **Tel.** 01/8071305
Open: Jan. - Dec.
The hotel lies in a green countryside with a view of Parnitha and Pendeli mts.

rm 27/b 52 S24h P

D´ OREA THESSALIA HOTEL
23, Mayer Str. **Tel.** 01/5234686
104 38 ATHENS **Open:** Jan. - Dec.
Inexpensive, nicely decorated family-run.

rm 25/b 56

D´ ORION I HOTEL
105, Emm. Benaki Str. **Tel.** 01/3627362, 3628441, 3605193
114 73 ATHENS **Open:** Jan. - Dec.

rm 20/b 27 C.C.: Visa

ATHENS SUBURBS

Aghia Paraskevi

*** C´ PARK HOTEL**
9, Efkalipton Str. **Tel.** 01/6596040-2
153 42 AG. PARASKEVI **Open:** Jan. - Dec.

rm 40/b 75 P

Aharne

*** C´ ACHARNIS HOTEL**
20th klm Parnitha Ave. **Tel.** 01/2467961
136 71 A HARNE **Open:** Jan. - Dec.

rm 41/b 77 P

Drossia

C´ ANIXIS HOTEL
P.O. Box 15 **Tel.** 01/8135014, 8135747
145 65 DROSIA **Open:** Jun. - Oct.
This hotel combines a quiet comfortable stay with excellent service. We serve breakfast, lunch and dinner, offering Greek cuisine specialities.

rm 22/b 42 TV S24h P C.C.: Diners, American Express, Access

Halandri

B´ OLYMPIC HOTEL
1, Souri Str. **Tel.** 01/6813430, 6813757
152 32 HALANDRI **Open:** Jan. - Dec.
The hotel is in a quiet area just off the main square. Friendly, restfull atmosphere, beautiful garden. Less than 2 km from the Olympic Stadium.

rm 22/b 33 S24h P
C.C.: Traveller's Cheques, American Express

C´ ACROPOLE HOTEL
71, Pendelis Ave. **Tel.** 01/6826650, 6826221,
152 33 HALANDRI **Tlx.** 222880 HOAC GR.

Open: Jan. - Dec.

Built in 1976 in the green residential suburb of Halandri, 2 km from the Olympic Stadium and less than 1 km from the shopping area and main sq., with a bus-stop just outside, ACROPOLE offers A´ class accommodation at C´ class prices. Free transportation to and from airport and R.R. stations for 5-15 persons.

rm 55/**b** 105 S

*** C´ EGYPTOS HOTEL**
6, Gini Str. **Tel.** 01/6829300
152 33 HALANDRI **Open:** Jan. - Dec.

rm 30/**b** 57

Iraklio

*** C´ GREEN HILL HOTEL**
36, Amaroussiou Str. **Tel.** 01/2812316
141 22 IRAKLIO **Open:** Jan. - Dec.

rm 16/**b** 30

Kifissia

L´ PENDELIKON HOTEL
66, Deliyiani Str. **Tel.** 01/8012837-8, 8019477
145 62 KIFISSIA **Open:** Jan. - Dec.

Convention and banquet facilities. Garden parties in the summer.

rm 48/**b** 110 S24h
C.C.: American Express, Visa, Diners, Master Charge, Access, Eurocard, Carte Blanche

A´ CECIL HOTEL
7, Xenias Str. **Tel.** 01/8013836-9
145 62 KIFISSIA **Open:** June - Sept.

Just 15 km from Athens, the hotel is situated in the most beautifull spot of Kifissia, amidst green gardens. Large halls, tastefully decorated, along with wonderful natural surroundings create a charming atmosphere. You will appreciate the exquisite French cuisine. Relax in the comfortable T.V. lounges and flowery verandas, and enjoy the friendly atmosphere of the bar.

rm 100/**b**153 S24h
C.C.: Access, Master Charge, Eurocard

A´ COSTIS DIMITRACOPOULOS HOTEL
65, Deliyianni Str. **Tel.** 01/8012546
145 62 KIFISSIA **Open:** Jan. - Dec.

rm 27/**b** 54 S

A´ GRAND CHALET HOTEL
38, Kokinara Str. **Tel.** 01/8084837-9
145 62 KIFISSIA **Tlx.** 223818 GRAN GR
Open: Jan. - Dec.

Personalized service in a warm friendly atmosphere. A 50-person convention room and catering for professional meals. Garden parties by the pool in the summer.

rm 30/**b** 58 S24h
C.C.: American Express, Diners

A´ SEMIRAMIS HOTEL
36, Har. Trikoupi Str. **Tel.** 01/8012930, 8017231, 8013396
145 62 KIFISSIA **Tlx.** 219093

Open: Jan. - Dec.

Spacious rooms all with veranda. Deluxe restaurant, snack-bar, night club, beautiful garden and a large swimming pool. Ideally located 12 km out of Athens, in Kifissia, the most beautiful suburb, this hotel is recommended for a restful and enjoyable stay.

rm 42/**b** 73 S
C.C.: Diners, American Express

A´ THEOXENIA HOTEL
2, Filadelfeos Str. **Tel.** 01/8012751-65, 8016736-42
145 62 KIFISSIA
Open: Apr. - Oct.

The hotel lies in front of a pine-tree park, in an area full of entertainment centres, bars, restaurants, discos, cafeterias etc.

rm 65/**b** 120 S

B´ NAFSIKA HOTEL
6, Pelis Str. **Tel.** 01/8013255, 8013495
145 61 KIFISSIA **Open:** Jan. - Dec.

The quietest hotel in Kifissia, 250 m away from the subway terminal. Two bus lines have stops in front of the hotel.

rm 18/**b** 32 S
C.C.: Visa

*** C´ ACROPOLIS HOTEL**
32, Kolokotroni Str. **Tel.** 8012221, 8017366
145 62 KIFISSIA **Open:** Jun. - Sep.

rm 25/**b** 53

C´ AEGLI HOTEL
Platanos Sq. **Tel.** 01/8012591
145 62 KIFISSIA **Open:** Jan. - Dec.

rm 22/**b** 45

C´ DES ROSES HOTEL
4, Miltiadou Str. **Tel.** 01/8019952-3, 8018025
145 62 KIFISSIA **Open:** Jan. - Dec.

rm 37/**b** 71 S24h

C´ KATERINA HOTEL
3, Mikonou Str. **Tel.** 01/8018495, 8019826
145 62 KIFISSIA **Open:** Jan. - Dec.

rm 48/**b** 88 S

C´ ROUSSOS HOTEL
18, P. Tsaldari Str. **Tel.** 01/8012660, 8012551
145 61 KIFISSIA **Open:** Apr. - Oct.

Once the house of princess Aspasia Manou, ROUSSOS Hotel is situated in the Pyrna district of Kifissia, 300 m from the subway terminal and the shopping center, 15 km from Athens. Far from the noise and pollution of the city, the hotel is surounded by 3,750 sq. m of pine-trees. We assure you of a quiet, comfortable stay.

rm 39/**b** 77 S

Melissia

*** C´ AKRAEON HOTEL**
143, Pendelis Ave. **Tel.** 01/8041084
151 27 MELISSIA **Open:** Jan. - Dec.

rm 23/**b** 44

Metamorfossi

C΄ ANESSIS HOTEL
227, Tatoiou Ave. **Tel.** 01/2814827, 2811814
144 52 METAMORFOSSI **Open:** Jan. - Dec.

The hotel is near the Athens-Lamia national road, half an hour's ride to "Mont Parnès" casino. Comfortable rooms with a nice view. Reduced prices to groups from 1/7 to 31/8.

rm 44/**b** 88
C.C.: American Express, Diners

∗ C΄ IBISCOS HOTEL
144, Tatoiou Ave. **Tel.** 01/2796316, 2777997
144 52 METAMORFOSSI **Open:** Jan. - Dec.
rm 32/**b** 62

Nea Kifissia

∗ C΄ LIDA HOTEL
103, Tatoiou Ave. **Tel.** 01/8038802, 8071580
145 64 NEA KIFISSIA **Open:** Jan. - Dec.
rm 20/**b** 38

Parnitha

∗ A΄ CASINO MONT PARNES
136 71 PARNITHA **Tel.** 01/2469111-5
Open: Jan. - Dec.
rm 106/**b** 212

∗ B΄ XENIA HOTEL
136 71 PARNITHA **Tel.** 01/2469101-3
Open: June - Sept.
rm 161/**b** 300

Pefki

∗ B΄ CYBELE HOTEL
7, Kolokotroni Str. **Tel.** 01/8028052, 8023049
151 21 PEFKI **Open:** Jan. - Dec.
rm 24/**b** 44

APOLLO COAST

Anavissos

B΄ HELIOS HOTEL
45th klm Sounion Ave. **Tel.** 0299/36998, 37017
190 13 ANAVISSOS **Tlx.** 222891 STEK GR
Open: June - Sep. 20th

A new modern hotel in a quiet location with a direct approach to the sea. All rooms have a private balcony overlooking the seashore. Conference facilities available.

rm 103/**b** 206

C΄ SILVER BEACH HOTEL
Smirnis 1, Sounion Ave. **Tel.** 0299/36203, 37746
190 13 ANAVISSOS
Open: 15th Apr. - 15th Oct.

An ideal family-run hotel 50 m. off the beach, next to the famous sea-food tavernas of Anavissos. 28 rooms all with private bathrooms.

rm 28/**b** 54
C.C.: Eurocard

Ano Voula

A΄ AFRODITE HOTEL APTS.
16, Dafnis Str. **Tel.** 01/8952009, 8958250, 8954158
166 73 ANO VOULA
Open: May - Oct.

Furnished apts. for 1-6 persons (bedroom, living-room, fully equipped kitchen, bathroom-shower, 2 big balconies) overlooking Saronikos gulf. Garden with swimming-pool, T.V. lounge, bar. Daily service, cleaning-linen etc. Shopping area nearby. Prices 20% reduced during low season (1/5 to 30/6 & 16/9 to 31/10).

apts 12/**b** 24
C.C.: American Express, Diners

B΄ AKTAEON HOTEL
49, Alkionidon Ave. **Tel.** 01/8958600, 8958900
166 73 ANO VOULA **Open:** Apr. - Oct.
rm 16/**b** 31

B΄ GALINI HOTEL
95, Alkionidon Ave. **Tel.** 01/8959093, 8959175
166 73 ANO VOULA
Open: Jan. - Dec.
rm 40/**b** 78
C.C.: American Express, Diners

Glyfada

L΄ ASTIR BUNGALOWS
58, Vas. Georgiou Ave. **Tel.** 01/8944293, 8946461-5
166 74 GLYFADA
Tlx. 215925 AGAG GR
Open: 15th Apr. - 15th Oct.

Suites and superior rooms, communicating bungalows for families. Fridge and mini-bar in every room. Snack-bar, refreshment bars, car rental, sightseeing tours. Accommodation for functions and groups, special prices for groups. M.D. available at all times. Mini golf next door, 1 km to the 18-hole Glyfada golf course, 3 km to the airport, a short walk to Glydada Sq. and shopping center.

bung 128/**b** 256
C.C.: American Express, Diners, Access, Master Charge, Eurocard, Visa

A΄ ATRIUM HOTEL
10, Vas. Georgiou Ave. **Tel.** 01/8940971
166 74 GLYFADA **Tlx.** 218373 ATRM GR
Open: Jan. - Dec.

On the Glyfada beach, near the airport, sound-proof building.

rm 60/**b** 104
C.C.: American Express, Visa, Master Charge, Access, Eurocard

A΄ BRASIL APARTMENTS HOTEL
4, Eleftherias Str. **Tel.** 01/8942124-6, 8942886
166 74 GLYFADA **Open:** Jan. - Dec.
rm 15/**b** 30

A΄ CONGO PALACE HOTEL
75, Vas.Georgiou B΄ Ave. **Tel.** 01/8946711-2,

166 74 55 GLYFADA 8946717-9
Open: Jan. - Dec.

The hotel is located 250 m off the main Sq. and shopping centre. Completely renovated in 1984, all rooms with phone, music, air-conditioning and a sea-view. Special prices for members of organisations and clubs.

rm 96/**b** 200

A´ EKAVI HOTEL APTS.
10, Iras Str. **Tel.** 01/8951550, 8954625
166 74 GLYFADA **Open:** Jan. - Dec.

1 & 2-bedroom air-conditioned apts. in a magically peacefull area, 700 m from "ASTERIA" beach. Laundry facilities and garden available. In EKAVI you will find friendly service, family atmosphere and the unforgettable Greek hospitality. Once here you'll wish to come back.

Apts 10/**b** 26

A´ EMMANTINA HOTEL
33, Vas. Georgiou Ave. **Tel.** 01/8932110-1
166 75 GLYFADA **Tlx.** 210615 EMMA GR
Open: Jan. - Dec.

Built in 1980, fully air-conditioned, with modern facilities.Luxurious rooms with private bathroom, phone, radio and balcony facing the Saronikos gulf. Elegant restaurant, roof-garden, swimming-pool, two bars, ballroom and disco.

rm 80/**b** 144 **C.C.:** Diners, Master Charge, Visa, Eurocard, J.C.B., American Express

A´ FILISSIA HOTEL APARTMENTS
45, I. Metaxa Ave. **Tel.** 01/8941539, 8941552
166 74 GLYFADA **Open:** Jan. - Dec.

In the most exclusive residential area of Athens, 2 blocks away from the beach, 5 min. walk to the local shopping and entertainment center. 15 air-conditioned, fully equipped apts receiving the personal attention of the propriators. 7-day cleaning service.

apts 15/**b** 70

A´ FIVI HOTEL APARTMENTS
6, Fivis Str. **Tel.** 01/8943276-8
166 74 GLYFADA **Open:** Jan. - Dec.

A new building of independent luxurious furnished apts of one or two bedrooms, large living room, hall, and well equipped kitchen with fridge. Surrounded by beautiful garden.

rm 10/**b** 22

A´ OASIS HOTEL APARTMENTS
27, Vas. Georgiou Ave. **Tel.** 01/8940495, 8940901, 8941555
166 74 GLYFADA **Tlx.** 219407 OHA GR
Open: Jan. - Dec.

Newly-built hotel, 150 m. from a sandy beach and a yacht marina with many seasport facilities, within walking distance from the Glyfada Golf Club. Apts for 1-4 persons with american kitchen and fridge, air-conditioning, radio and private balcony overlooking Saronikos gulf. In the large, flowery landscape garden, you can find a cocktail lounge and snack-bar, as well as two swimming-pools (one of them for children).

apts 70/**b** 134

A´ OLIVIA HOUSE HOTEL APTS
86, Kyrpou Str. **Tel.** 01/8932294, 8932292
166 74 GLYFADA **Open:** Jan. - Dec

Beautifully situated on the Saronikos coast, only minutes away from the beach. Excellent local shops and restaurants. A warmly welcoming hotel personally supervised by the owners. Fully equipped air-conditioned apts cleaned dayly. Reduced prices for long-staying guests.

apt 18/**b** 80

A´ REGINA MARIS HOTEL
11, Diadochou Pavlou Str. **Tel.** 01/8940468, 8931241, 8945050
166 75 GLYFADA **Tlx.** 219420 REMA GR
Open: Jan. - Dec.

Conveniently close to sandy beaches, yacht marina, restaurants, coffee shops, night clubs shops, and the famous 18-hole Golf Club the hotel offers 70 air-conditioned rooms, with wall-to-wall carpeting, 3 channel music and balcony, swimming pool, indoors and outdoors bar, conference room, and a cozy fireplace lounge, meeting place for golfers, tennis players, divers, and yachtsmen.

rm 70/**b** 154 **C.C.:** American Express, Diners

A´ VILLA SOPHIE HOTEL APTS
7, Pallados Str. **Tel.** 01/8932027, 8932852
166 74 GLYFADA **Open:** Jan. - Dec.

16 fully furnished apts. centrally heated. Tennis court - big garden - 250 m off "ASTERIA" beach.

apts 16/**b** 32

B´ ANTONOPOULOS HOTEL
1, Lambraki Str. **Tel.** 01/8945636, 8946242
166 75 GLYFADA **Open:** Jun. - Sep.

rm 44/**b** 85

* B´ DELFINI HOTEL
5, Xanthou Str. **Tel.** 01/8942692
166 74 GLYFADA **Open:** Jan. - Dec.

rm 42/**b** 73

B´ FENIX HOTEL
1, Artemidos Str. **Tel.** 01/8947229, 8945812,
166 75 GLYFADA **Tlx.** 221784 EFE GR
Open: Jan. - Dec.

Only 9 miles from the centre of Athens and 1 mile from the Glyfada Golf Club. Luxurious rooms and suites with private veranda. International restaurant, cocktail lounge, conference rooms and swimming pool surrounded by green lawn.

rm 139/**b** 265

B´ FOUR SEASONS HOTEL
76, Vas. Georgiou Ave. **Tel.** 01/8942211-3
166 74 GLYFADA **Open:** Jan. - Dec.

Modern, newly-built hotel near "Asteria" beach, ideal for tourists and businessmen. Tastefully furnished rooms, comfortable air-conditioned lounge, restaurant and bar with music, creating a pleasant friendly atmosphere. Guests and visitors can enjoy a panoramic view from the hotels roof-garden.

rm 78/**b** 150 S 24h P **C.C.:** American Express, Diners

B´ GOLDEN SUN HOTEL
72, I. Metaxa Ave. **Tel.** 01/8955218-9, 8955810-1, 8953974
166 74 GLYFADA **Open:** Jan. - Dec.

A brand new ultra-modern hotel offering A´ class luxury at B´ class prices. Comfortable rooms with a sea view from the balcony, a tastefull lounge, a dining room and an international bar. A stone's throw from the sea, surrounded by tavernas, discos, night-clubs, cinemas, tennis courts, a Golf Club and the Palais des Sports.

rm 60/**b** 112 TV S P **C.C.:** Diners, Visa, American Express, Eurocard, Access, Master Charge

✱ B´ GRIPSHOLM HOTEL
4, Karapanou Str. **Tel.** 01/8944911-4
166 75 GLYFADA **Tlx.** 212426 YARD GR
Open: Jan. - Dec.

rm 67/**b** 107 P

✱ B´ IDEAL HOTEL
47, Lazaraki Str. **Tel.** 01/8944937, 8932041
166 74 GLYFADA **Open:** Apr. - Nov.

rm 40/**b** 74 P

B´ JOHN'S HOTEL
3, Pandoras Str. **Tel.** 01/8946837-9
166 74 GLYFADA **Tlx.** 210778 PETH GR
Open: Jan. - Dec.

Two-channel music, T.V. room, two sun terraces.

rm 68/**b** 140 S 24h P **C.C.:** American Express, Visa, Traveller's Cheques

B´ KREOLI HOTEL
17, Vas. Georgiou Ave. **Tel.** 01/8944301-2
166 74 GLYFADA **Open:** Jan. - Dec.

The hotel lies 15 km from Athens, by the sea where you can swim and sunbathe in wide sandy beaches or little rocky bays. You also have a wide choice of sports and amusements, like golf, tennis, sea sports, yachting, night clubs, tavernas etc. Each room has a nice view from the balcony, and the restaurant serves the best Greek specialities as well as excellent French cuisine.

rm 52/**b** 92 S P

B´ LETO HOTEL
2, Menippis & Veli Str. **Tel.** 01/8940365
166 75 GLYFADA **Open:** Jan. - Dec.

rm 8/**b** 12 P

B´ MIRANDA HOTEL
11, Meropis Str. **Tel.** 01/8946561, 8946689
166 75 GLYFADA **Open:** Jan. - Dec.

rm 34/**b** 64 S P

✱ B´ NIKI HOTEL
47, Diadohou Pavlou Str. **Tel.** 01/8932106
166 75 GLYFADA **Open:** Jan. - Dec.

rm 61/**b** 113 P

✱ B´ RIVIERA HOTEL
2, Fivis Str. **Tel.** 01/8944743
166 74 GLYFADA **Open:** Jan. - Dec.

rm 81/**b** 151 P

B´ SEA VIEW HOTEL
4, Xanthou Str. **Tel.** 01/8951311-4
166 74 GLYFADA **Open:** Jan. - Dec.

A modern, up-to-date, family-run seaside hotel, near the luxurious recreation centers, sports and marine sports installations. A short drive to the center of Athens.

rm 74/**b** 148 S P **C.C.:** American Express, Diners

✱ B´ SIVYLLA HOTEL
7, Evlimenis Str. **Tel.** 01/8946258, 8945954
166 75 GLYFADA **Open:** Jan. - Dec.

rm 39/**b** 71 P

B´ STERGIOS HOTEL
31, Ilias Str. **Tel.** 01/8943723, 8932011-2
166 75 GLYFADA **Tlx.** 215136 SHAC GR
Open: Jan. - Dec.

A friendly hotel of 44 rooms and suites with many modern amenities. Deluxe restaurant, snack-bar, swimming pool, convention and banquet facilities, open-air cocktail bar-cafeteria. Baby-sitting available. Very near the airport, transportation to and from provided. First class accommodation at second class prices.

rm 44/**b** 90 TV S 24h P **C.C.:** Diners, American Express

B´ VILLA KATERINA HOTEL
6, Panagouli Str. **Tel.** 01/8947281, 8947069
166 75 FLYFADA **Open:** Jan. - Dec.

rm 28/**b**47 S P **C.C.:** Traveller's Cheques

B´ VILLA VALERIA APARTMENTS
49, Lambraki Ave. **Tel.** 01/8942715, 8932632
166 75 GLYFADA **Open:** Jan. - Dec.

apts 12/**b** 22 S

B´ ZINA HOTEL APARTMENTS
6, Evangelistrias Str. **Tel.** 010/8945767, 8944926
166 74 GLYFADA **Open:** Jan. - Dec.

We are located out of range of the airport noise, within walking distance from local shops, restaurants, cinemas, beaches, basketball, volleyball and tennis courts. Spacious lobby, T.V.-room, open verandas, barbeque-parties upon request.

apt. 18/**b** 36 S 24h P

C´ ADONIS HOTEL
2C, Nikiforou Str. **Tel.** 01/8943216-7
166 75 GLYFADA **Open:** Jan. - Dec.

rm 44/**b** 85

∗ C´ ARION HOTEL
13 Lazaraki Str. **Tel.** 01/8945851, 8945082
166 75 GLYFADA **Open:** Jan. - Dec.

rm 30/**b** 57 P

C´ AVRA HOTEL
5, Lambraki Str. **Tel.** 01/8947185, 8946264
166 75 GLYFADA **Tlx.** 219440 AVRA GR.
Open: Jan. - Dec.

A modern hotel surrounded by shops, bars, tavernas, discos and the "Asteria" beach near the famous Glyfada Golf Club. Comfortable rooms with sea-view balconies, T.V.-video lounge. Continental and English breakfast. Light snacks served on the terrace, in the dining room, or by the swimming pool. Personal service, friendly atmosphere.

rm 37/**b** 81 S P
C.C.: Visa, Access, Master Charge

C´ BLUE SKY HOTEL
26, Eleftherias Str. **Tel.** 01/8959918, 8954666
166 74 GLYFADA **Tlx.** 225050
Open: Jan. - Dec.

Quiet family-run hotel, near "Asteria" beach.

rm 20/**b** 40 S

∗ C´ GLYFADA HOTEL
40, Vas. Georgiou B´ Ave. **Tel.** 01/8946833, 8941137
166 75 GLYFADA **Open:** Apr. - Oct.

rm 52/**b** 100 P

C´ ILION HOTEL
4, G. Kondili Str. **Tel.** 01/8946175
166 75 GLYFADA **Open:** Jan. - Dec.

Live music from a group every evening at the bar.

rm 41/**b** 80

C´ OCEANIS HOTEL
23, Gr. Lambraki Str. **Tel.** 01/8944038, 8944058
166 75 GLYFADA **Open:** Apr. - Oct.

A modern hotel in Glyfada, just 100 m. from the famous "Asteria" beach, and 200 m. from the main square. Comfortable rooms with verandas, garden, swimming pool. Special prices for groups of over 20.

rm 73/**b** 135 TV P

C´ PERLA HOTEL
7, Chrisidos Str. **Tel.** 01/8944212-4, 9237662
166 75 GLYFADA **Tlx.** 215812
Open: Mar. - Nov.

Greek party every week in the garden. Beautiful sandy beach just across the street.

rm 58/**b** 118 S P
C.C.: American Express, Diners, Visa

C´ RIAL HOTEL
7, Vas. Georgiou Str. **Tel.** 01/8940023, 8944209
166 74 GLYFADA

Open: Jan. - Dec.

rm 35/**b** 67 P

∗ C´ THEMIS HOTEL
5, Vas. Georgiou B´ Ave. **Tel.** 01/8944666, 8948666
166 75 GLYFADA **Open:** Jan. - Dec.

rm 45/**b** 84 P

Kalamaki

A´ MARINA ALIMOS HOTEL APARTMENTS
15, Posidonos Ave. **Tel.** 01/9828911-18
174 55 KALAMAKI **Tlx.** 210919 XENE GR.
Open: Jan. - Dec.

Elegantly furnished apts. of one or two twin-bedrooms, sitting-room, fully equipped kitchen with fridge, bathroom and a large balcony with a view to the sea. 4-6 persons can be accommodated with additional beds on request, (baby-cots too). The phones are direct dialling, there's a chambermaid 7 days a week, dishwashing and baby-sitting service at a small charge, 24-hour reception service, currency exchange and booking-ticket arrangements.

apts 29/**b** 82 TV S P
C.C.: American Express, Diners

A´ SARONIS HOTEL
13, Vas. Georgiou B´ Ave. **Tel.** 01/9810365, 9825035
174 55 KALAMAKI **Open:** Jan. - Dec.

Situated at an ideal seaside spot, this newly built hotel has comfortable, elegantly furnished rooms with balcony, lounges and bar with a splendid sea-view and a spacious terrace. 24-hour service, laundry and valet facilities, courteous and efficient staff create a wonderfull sense of friendliness and hospitality.

rm 38/**b** 74 S 24h P

B´ ALBATROS HOTEL
77, Posidonos Str. **Tel.** 01/9824981-3, 9832807
174 55 KALAMAKI **Open:** Jan. - Dec.

Newly built hotel 10 km from Athens, 3 km from the airport. Comfortable rooms with 3-channel music and private verandas. Spacious lounge, cocktail bar, and roof-garden with a superb view of the blue Saronikos gulf. Many sport facilities, including an 18-hole golf course are within 5 miles.

rm 80/**b** 151 S P **C.C.:** American Express, Diners, Visa, J.C.B., Master Charge

∗ B´ DALIA HOTEL
14, Vas. Konstandinou Str. **Tel.** 01/9824259, 9820606
174 55 KALAMAKI **Open:** Jan. - Dec.

rm 15/**b** 22 P

B´ IMPERIAL HOTEL (Hostel)
87, Thoukididou Str. **Tel.** 01/9813572, 9817453
174 55 KALAMAKI **Open:** Jan. - Dec.

rm 16/**b** 31 P

B´ REX HOTEL
40, Vas. Georgiou B´ Str. **Tel.** 01/9810762, 9828144
174 55 KALAMAKI

Open: Jan. - Dec.
Dinner is served in "CANTON HOUSE" the hotel's chinese restaurant from 19.00´ to 01.00´

rm 34/**b** 63
C.C.: Visa, Master Charge, Access, Eurocard, Diners

B´ VENUS HOTEL
9, Megistis Str. **Tel.** 01/9810806, 9813404
174 55 KALAMAKI **Open:** Jan. - Dec.
Situated in Kalamaki, 50 m. from a sandy beach, within walking distance from a yacht marina. Near the airport and the well known Glyfada Golf Club. Spacious rooms with private balcony.

rm 28/**b** 54 S24h
C.C.: American Express

*** C´ ALKYON HOTEL**
2, Kotzia Str. **Tel.** 01/9825190
174 55 KALAMAKI **Open:** Jan. - Dec.

rm 14/**b** 26 P

C´ ATTICA HOTEL
18, P. Tsaldari Str. **Tel.** 01/9810576-9
174 55 KALAMAKI **Open:** Jan. - Dec.
Transportation available to our guests (coach). Also roof garden.

rm 40/**b** 75 S24h P

C´ BLUE SEA HOTEL
49-53, Themistokleous Str. **Tel.** 01/9815707-9
174 55 KALAMAKI **Open:** Jan. - Dec.

rm 73/**b** 138 S24h

C´ GALAXY HOTEL
39, Vas. Georgiou B´ Str. **Tel.** 01/9818603-4
174 55 KALAMAKI **Open:** Jan. - Dec.
Built in 1969, the hotel faces the picturesque Saronikos gulf and the sandy beach of Kalamaki. It has 54 luxurious rooms with private balcony, two comfortable lounges, a restaurant serving Greek and foreign specialities and a cosy roof-bar with a magnificent view.

rm 54/**b** 112
S24h P **C.C.:** American Express

C´ HELLINIKON HOTEL
76, Vas. Georgiou B´ Str. **Tel.** 01/9817227, 9817802
174 55 KALAMAKI
Open: Jan. - Dec.
Located very close to the airport at the seaside, this newly built hotel has 52 rooms, all with private balcony, giving a magnificent view of Saronikos gulf. Just across the street from two sandy beaches the hotel is connected with Athens and Piraeus by means of a frequent bus service.

rm 52/**b** 96 S24h P
C.C.: American Express

C´ NEFELI HOTEL
5, Fan Vaik Str. **Tel.** 01/9827049-51-53
174 55 KALAMAKI **Open:** Jan. - Dec.
Most elegant and comfortable hotel overlooking Saronikos gulf. All rooms with private balcony, radio, telephone, and air-conditioning.

rm 39/**b** 70 P

C´ TROPICAL HOTEL
74, Posidonos Str. **Tel.** 01/9813993-4, 9822217
174 55 KALAMAKI **Open:** Jan. - Dec.
Situated on the lovely Saronikos shore. All rooms are air-conditioned, with private balconies facing the sea. Lovely garden all around. Very close to the airport, free transportation to and from. Convenient for passengers staying overnight.

rm 44/**b** 88 S24h
C.C.: American Express, Eurocard, Master Charge, Diners, Access

*** D´ ALIMOS HOTEL**
8, Kotzia Str. **Tel.** 01/9811365
174 55 KALAMAKI **Open:** Jan. - Dec.

rm 15/**b** 23 P

*** D´ GRACE HOTEL**
67, Vas. Georgiou B´ Str. **Tel.** 01/9811372
174 55 KALAMAKI **Open:** Jan. - Dec.

rm 14/**b** 30 P

*** D´ VILLA MINOS HOTEL**
3, Vas. Konstandinou Str. **Tel.** 01/9819444, 9820743
174 55 KALAMAKI
Open: Jan. - Dec.

rm 10/**b** 19 P

Kavouri

*** B´ PINE HILL HOTEL**
22, Kronou Str. **Tel.** 01/8960871-2-6, 3621780
166 71 KAVOURI **Open:** Apr. - Oct.

rm 83/**b** 158 P

B´ SUNRISE HOTEL
11, Ag. Nicolaou Str. **Tel.** 01/8954709
166 71 KAVOURI **Tlx.** 223379 AMHL GR
Open: June - Sept.
Only 225 m. back from the sandy Kavouri beach, 22 km from Athens. Fully air-conditioned. Bar, lounge, breakfast room, snack-bar, conference room for up to 50. All rooms with private bathroom, music, phone and private balcony.

rm 60/**b** 170 P
C.C.: American Express, Visa, Master Charge, Diners, Access, Eurocard

C´ MARO HOTEL
2, Kyvelis Str. **Tel.** 01/8958503
166 71 KAVOURI **Open:** Apr. - Oct.
In our small family-run hotel, we offer a warm personal welcome to our guests.

rm 9/**b** 15 P

Lagonissi

B´ VAR HOTEL
40th km Athens-Sounion Ave.
190 13 LAGONISSI **Tel.** 0299/83512, 83534
Open: Apr. - Oct.
An ideal family hotel 300 m from the beach, 40 km from Athens. All rooms have private bathroom, telephone, music, private veranda with a panoramic view of Saronikos gulf.

rm 20/**b** 38 P
C.C.: Eurocard

Legrena

B´ MINOS HOTEL
195 00 LEGRENA Tel. 0292/39321-3
Open: May - Sep.

All rooms have big sun-balconies and face the sea. Beautiful uncrowded sandy beach, tasty meals, moderate rates. 10-20% discount for guests staying over 10 days.

rm 38/b 72

Paleo Faliro

B´ CORAL HOTEL
35, Posidonos Ave. Tel. 01/9816441-3, 9816447
175 61 PALEO FALIRO
Tlx. 210879 CORA GR
Open: Jan. - Dec.

Most elegant and comfortable hotel, 5 miles from Athens, with a panoramic view of Saronikos gulf. All rooms with veranda. International cuisine restaurant, roof garden and swimming pool. Frequent bus service close to shops, banks, cafeterias and a big park.

rm 89/b 160 C.C.: Diners, American Express, Eurocard

B´ POSIDON HOTEL
72, Posidonos Ave. Tel. 01/9822086, 9822041, 9822469
175 62 PALEO FALIRO
Open: Jan. - Dec.

Newly built hotel, 8 km from the centre of Athens, 3 km from the airport, on the Athens-Sounio seaside road. The comfortable, sunny rooms, all with verandas give an excellent view of the Saronikos gulf. In the luxurious dining room the best Greek and international dishes are served. For refreshment on hot summer days there is a swimming pool on the roof garden. The attendance and care of the highly trained staff ensures an unforgettable stay.

rm 90/b 168 C.C.: Visa, Diners, American Express, Master Charge, Access

C´ AVRA HOTEL
3, Nireos Str. Tel. 01/9814064-5
175 61 PALEO FALIRO Open: Jan. - Dec.
rm 39/b 70

∗ C´ EFI HOTEL
76, Tritonos Str. Tel. 01/9824219, 9824229
175 62 PALEO FALIRO Open: Jan. - Dec.
rm 18/b 35

C´ NESTORION HOTEL
8, Pendelis Str. Tel. 01/9425010, 9420820
175 64 PALEO FALIRO Tlx. 221427 NEST GR.
Open: Jan. - Dec.

Recently completed, the hotel overlooks the Saronikos gulf. 15 minutes from Athens, 10 min. from the airport, a short walk to the sea. Within easy reach from the horse-race track and a yachting marina.

em 29/b 54

D´ ARMA HOTEL
9, Sirinon Str. Tel. 01/9816319, 9831223
175 61 PALEON FALIRO Open: Jan. - Dec.
rm 30/b 54

Saronis

∗ B´ DELFINIA HOTEL APTS
44th km Athens-Sounion Ave.
190 13 SARONIS Tel. 0299/52449-51
Open: Jan. - Dec.
rm 18/b 36

Sounion

∗ A´ BELVEDERE PARK HOTEL
Athens - Sounion Ave. Tel. 0292/39102, 39143
195 00 SOUNION Open: Apr. - Oct.
rm 90/b 180

∗ A´ CAPE SOUNION BEACH HOTEL
Plakes Tel. 0292/39391-4
195 00 SOUNION Tlx. 214909 ACRO GR
Open: Apr. - Oct.
rm 152/b 304

∗ B´ SURF BEACH CLUB HOTEL
Pounda Zeza Tel. 0292/22363-4, 25778
195 00 SOUNION Tlx. 214155
Open: Apr. - Sept.
rm 266/b 521

C´ SARON HOTEL
60th km Athens-Sounio Ave.
SOUNION Tel. 0292/39045, 39144
Open: Jan. - Dec.

Beautiful locality by the sea, surrounded by pine trees. Piano, guitars, bouzouki and banjo available for the entertainment of our guests.

rm 28/b 52

Varkiza

∗ A´ APOLLONIA HOTEL
9, Naxou Str. Tel. 01/8970501, 8973796-8
166 72 VARKIZA Open: Apr. - Dec.
rm 38/b 68

∗ A´ GLAROS HOTEL
1, Xeniou Dios Str. Tel. 01/8971217-8
166 72 VARKIZA Open: May - Oct.
rm 48/b 81

∗ A´ HARIS HOUSE
21, Thassou Str. Tel. 01/8971986, 8971053
166 72 VARKIZA Open: Apr. - Oct.
rm 19/b 38

∗ B´ VARKIZA HOTEL
13-15, Rodou Str. Tel. 01/8970927-9
166 72 VARKIZA Open: Apr. - Oct.
rm 30/b 57

Voula

∗ A´ VOULA BEACH HOTEL
103, Alkionidon Str. Tel. 01/8953851-4
166 73 VOULA Open: Jan. - Dec.
rm 54/b 106

*** B´ATLANTIS HOTEL**
6, Afroditis Str. **Tel.** 01/8958443
166 73 VOULA **Open:** Jan. - Dec.
rm 15/**b** 27

*** B´CASTELLO BEACH HOTEL**
8, Kerkiras Str. **Tel.** 01/3958985, 8951571,
166 73 VOULA **Open:** Jan. - Dec.
rm 34/**b** 64

*** B´PLAZA HOTEL**
17, Alkionidon Ave. **Tel.** 01/8956057-9, 8953480
166 73 VOULA **Open:** Jan. - Dec.
rm 18/**b** 31

C´NOUFARA HOTEL
2, Metaxa Str. **Tel.** 01/8953186
166 73 VOULA **Open:** Jan. - Dec.

Spoken: English, French, German, Italian, Spanish, Arabic and Yugoslavian. Cabin cruiser available -accommodation 10- for 13-day cruises to Kithnos - Serifos - Sifnos - Kea - Makronisos - Sounior, or 25 for one-day cruises. Weekly parties organized, with guitar - bouzouki - accordion.

rm 23/**b** 42

*** C´PALMA HOTEL**
7, Alkionidon Ave. **Tel.** 01/8951020, 8955231-2
166 73 VOULA **Tlx.** 219691
Open: Mar. - Nov.
rm 34/**b** 65

C´PARTHENIS HOTEL
21, Alkionidon Ave. **Tel.** 01/8956072, 8952289
166 73 VOULA **Open:** Jan. - Dec.

Family-run hotel, personal care.

rm 16/**b** 31

C´RONDO HOTEL
6, Dodecanissou Str. **Tel.** 01/8958605, 8958710, 8951752
166 73 VOULA **Open:** Apr. - Oct.
rm 44/**b** 84

Vouliagmeni

L´ASTIR PALACE HOTELS
P.O. BOX 1226 ATHENS **Tel.** 01/8960211-9, 8960311-20
166 71 VOULIAGMENI **Tlx.** 215013 ASPA GR
Open: Jan. - Dec.

Luxury hotel and bungalows complex of 3 buildings: ARION, NAFSIKA, APHRODITE.

rm 165/**b** 330, **rm** 165/**b** 325, **rm** 239/**b** 462
C.C.: American Express, Visa, Diners, Master Charge, Access, Eurocard

A´ARMONIA HOTEL
1, Armonias Str. **Tel.** 01/8960105, 8960030, 8963308
166 71 VOULIAGMENI **Tlx.** 223379 AMHL GR.
Open: Apr. - Oct.

Most exclusive resort, located in Vouliagmeni. Swimming pool, air-conditioned bar, lounge and restaurant, conference facilities. All rooms have balcony with magnificent sea view.

rm 95/**b** 250
C.C.: American Express, Visa, Diners, Master Charge, Access, Eurocard

A´ELECTRA HOTEL APTS
28, Panos Str. **Tel.** 01/8960537, 8962329
166 71 VOULIAGMENI **Tlx.** 216283 LILI GR.

Reduced prices during low season (Oct. - May).

apt 17/**b** 31

B´IRA HOUSE HOTEL
1, Iasonos Str. **Tel.** 01/8960321, 8960661
166 71 VOULIAGMENI
Open: 15th Mar. - 15th Oct.

The hotel is near the Vouliagmeni lake, and the sandy beach. Meticulous cleannes, civilized environemnt.

rm 38/**b** 73
C.C.: American Express, Visa, Eurocard

B´PARADISE HOTEL
7, Danais Str. **Tel.** 01/8963304-7, 8962298
166 71 VOULIAGMENI **Tlx.** 223379 AMHL GR
Open: Apr. - Oct.

Located in a quiet area, 150 m. from the sandy Vouliagmeni beach. Fully air-conditioned bar, lounge, breakfast room. All rooms have balcony.

rm 60/**b** 120
C.C.: American Express, Visa, Diners, Master Charge, Access

NORTH-EAST COAST

Marathonas

*** B´GOLDEN COAST HOTEL**
Marathon Coast **Tel.** 0294/92102, 92917
190 07 MARATHONAS **Open:** Apr. - Oct.
rm 241/**b** 455

*** C´MARATHON HOTEL**
Marathonos Sq. Tymvos **Tel.** 0294/55122, 55222
190 07 MARATHONAS **Open:** Jan. - Dec.
rm 24/**b** 46

*** C´PANTHEON HOTEL**
31st km Athens-Sounio Ave.
190 03 MARCOPOULO **Tel.** 0299/25364
rm 10/**b** 19 **Open:** Jan. - Dec.

Mati

A´MATI HOUSE
33, Possidonos Str **Tel.** 0294/71511-5
109 09 MATI **Open:** Jan. - Dec.

Hotel MATI is located on the coast of the cool and sunny district of Mati, Attica, 28 kms from the centre of Athens. The hotel has a reserved beach, a swimming-pool in an idyllic environment, luxurious lounges, a restaurant, a discotheque, and a spacious garden that surrounds it.

rm 70/**b** 130

*** B´ ATTICA BEACH**
32, Possidonos Str. **Tel.** 0294/71711-3
109 09 MATI **Open:** Apr. - Oct.
rm 94/**b** 178

C´ MYRTO HOTEL
34, Marathon Ave. **Tel.** 0294/71431-3
190 09 MATI **Open:** Jan. - Dec.

MYRTO Hotel is located in the cool and sunny district of Mati, Attica, 28 kms from the centre of Athens, within a superb pine-wood. It is about 690 m fom the sea. Every room has its private bathroom or shower and is provided with every modern comfort. There is also a grand garden and a bar.

rm 31/**b** 60

Nea Makri

*** B´ MARATHON BEACH HOTEL**
190 05 NEA MAKRI **Tel.** 0294/91255, 91292
Open: Mar. - Oct.
rm 166/**b** 296

*** B´ THOMAS BEACH HOTEL**
3, Posidonos Ave. **Tel.** 0294/92790, 94440
109 05 NEA MAKRI **Open:** Jan. - Dec.
rm 30/**b** 57

B´ ZOUBERI HOTEL
Posidonos Ave. **Tel.** 0294/71920-4
190 05 NEA MAKRI **Open:** Mar. - Oct.
rm 128/**b** 238

C´ AFRODITI HOTEL
33rd km Athens-Marathonas Ave.
190 05 NEA MAKRI **Tel.** 0294/95095, 92534
Open: Apr. - Oct.
rm 29/**b** 56 S24h

*** C´ ASTORIA HOTEL APTS**
5, El. Venizelou Str **Tel.** 0294/93661
190 05 NEA MAKRI **Open:** Jan. - Dec.
apt. 8/**b** 16

*** C´ NIREFS HOTEL**
190 05 NEA MAKRI **Tel.** 0294/91214
Open: May - Dec.
rm 127/**b** 245

E´ BILL'S HOTEL
116, Marathonas Ave. **Tel.** 0294/91288, 93157
190 05 NEA MAKRI **Open:** Jan. - Dec.

There is a lounge, a kitchen and two big fridges available to our guests.

rm 12/**b** 21

Oropos

C´ ALKYONIS HOTEL
Nea Palatia **Tel.** 0295/32490-4
190 15 OROPOS **Open:** Apr. - Oct.

The hotel is built on the shore before a beach as clean as a swimming pool. There's a frequent bus service to Athens and a ferry boat to Evia. A couple of kms away from the little town of Oropos where shops and entertainment are available. Special prices for groups or long-staying guests, especially during the off-season.

rm 91/**b** 175 S24h

C´ DESPO HOTEL
Markopoulo Coast **Tel.** 0295/32324-5
190 15 OROPOS **Open:** June - Sept.

A seashore hotel 2 km from the village Markopoulo. There is a ferry-boat connecting the place with the "Dream Island" of Evia just across, and within eyesight from the hotel.

rm 17/**b** 32 S

*** C´ FLISVOS HOTEL**
Markopoulo Coast **Tel.** 0295/32480-3
190 15 OROPOS **Open:** Jan. - Dec.
rm 60/**b** 113

Pikermi

C´ PIKERMI HOTEL
21st km Marathonos Ave. **Tel.** 01/6677231,
190 09 PIKERMI 6677349, 6677497-500
Open: Jan. - Dec.
rm 14/**b** 28 S24h

Porto Rafti

A´ ARTEMIS HOTEL APARTMENTS
Porto Rafti **Tel.** 0299/72000, 74400-4
190 03 PORTO RAFTI **Tlx.** 215877
Open: Apr. - Oct.

A newly built complex of luxurious air-conditioned apts, all with veranda, radio and telephone. Also bar, restaurant, swimming pool, children's playground, sports facilities. Located in the holiday resort of Porto Rafti, near Athens, Sounio and Vravron.

apt. 24/**b** 64 S C.C.: Diners

*** C´ KORALI HOTEL**
Grezou Ave. **Tel.** 0299/72602-4,
190 03 PORTO RAFTI **Open:** Mar. - Sep.
rm 16/**b** 28

*** C´ KYANI AKTI HOTEL**
Ziki Str. Avlaki **Tel.** 0299/72241-2
190 03 PORTO RAFTI **Open:** May - Sep.
rm 25/**b** 47

Rafina

*** C´ AVRA HOTEL**
Rafina Coast **Tel.** 0294/22781-3, 23320
190 09 RAFINA **Open:** Apr. - Nov
rm 96/**b** 184

C´ BRAVO HOTEL
Kokkino Limanaki **Tel.** 0294/31488-9
190 09 RAFINA **Open:** Apr. - Sep.
rm 18/**b** 35

∗ C΄ INA MARINA HOTEL
Christou Mandika Str. Tel. 0294/22215
190 09 RAFINA Open: Apr. - Nov
rm 79/b 150

∗ D΄ AKTI HOTEL
4, Vithinias Str. Tel. 0294/23410, 24776
190 09 RAFINA Open: Apr. - Sep.
rm 21/b 43 P

D΄ CORALI HOTEL
1, N.Plastira Sq. Tel. 0294/22477
190 09 RAFINA Open: Jan. - Dec.
rm 17/b 35 S24h

∗ D΄ KYMATA HOTEL
1.Plastira Sq. Tel. 0294/23406
190 09 RAFINA Open: Jan. - Dec.
rm 18/b 29 P

∗ E΄ RAFINA HOTEL
2, Plastira Sq. Tel. 0294/23460
190 09 RAFINA Open: Jun. - Aug.
rm 10/b 22

Vravrona

∗ A΄ VRAONA BAY
109 03 VRAVRONA Tel. 0294/82591-5
Open: Apr. - Oct.
rm 352/b 670

PIRAEUS

΄CAVO D'ORO HOTEL
19, Vas. Pavlou Str. Tel. 01/4113742, 4113744-5
185 33 PIRAEUS Tlx. 212933 CADO GR
Open: Jan. - Dec.

Situated in Castella with an incredible view of Saronikos gulf, Cavo D'Oro is more than just a hotel. There is also an exclusive restaurant overlooking the sea, serving sea-food specialities, Greek and international dishes, in a background of soothing piano music, as well as a luxurious discotheque where a good time is guaranteed. So whether you desire a holiday or just a good night out, Cavo D'Oro will not let you down.

rm 74/b 134 TV 24h P C.C.: Diners, Visa, American Express, Arabian Express, Access, Master Charge, Eurocard

΄DIOGENIS HOTEL
27, Vas. Georgiou A΄ Str. Tel. 01/4125471-5
185 32 PIRAEUS Tlx. 213218
Open: Jan. - Dec.

Roof Garden, swimming pool, snack bar - restaurant, excellent French cuisine and delicious Greek dishes. Soothing and charming atmosphere, enchanting panorama.

rm 78/b 146 TV S C.C: Diners, American Express, Visa, Master Charge, Access

B΄ HOMERIDION HOTEL
2, Harilaou Tricoupi Str. Tel. 01/4519811-5
185 36 PIRAEUS Tlx. 214582 KIM GR
Open: Jan. - Dec.
rm 59/b 112 P

΄NOUFARA HOTEL
5, Iroon Politehniou Str. Tel. 01/4115541-3
185 35 PIRAEUS Tlx. 211296
Open: Jan. - Dec.
rm 48/b 84 S C.C.: American Express, Visa, Master Charge, Access, Eurocard

΄PARK HOTEL
103, Kolokotroni Str. Tel. 01/4524611-5
185 35 PIRAEUS Tlx. 212228 HPSA GR
Open: Jan. - Dec.

Roof-garden, conference facilities.

rm 80/b 152 C.C.: American Express, Visa, Master Charge, Access, Eurocard

B΄ SAVOY HOTEL
93, Iroon Politehniou Tel. 01/4131102-8
185 36 PIRAEUS Tlx. 211267 SIAHO GR
Open: Jan. - Dec.

A luxurious new building in the centre of Piraeus. Central air-conditioning. Three hi-fi music programs. Meeting and conference rooms. Telex. Restaurant. Bar. Cafeteria. Roof-garden.

rm 71/b 136 S C.C.: American Express, Diners, Visa, Access, Master Charge, Eurocard, J.C.B.

B΄ TRITON HOTEL
8, Tsamadou Str. Tel. 01/4173457-9
185 31 PIRAEUS Open: Jan. - Dec.

Situated in the heart of the commercial district, by the main port, close to the metrò, bus services R.R. station.

rm 57/b 104 S C.C.: Diners

∗ C΄ ACROPOLE HOTEL
7, D. Gounari Str. Tel. 01/4174190
185 31 PIRAEUS Open: Jan. - Dec.
rm 21/b 42

C΄ ANEMONI HOTEL
65-67, Evripidou Str. Tel. 01/4111768, 4130091
185 32 PIRAEUS Open: Jan. - Dec.

A new hotel (built in 1978) in the centre of Piraeus, just 5 min. walk to the central port. 24-hours room-service, T.V.-room bar, coffee shop, parking, garage. Rooms with private bathroom, phone, balcony.

rm 45/b 87 S24h P

C΄ ANITA HOTEL
25, Notara Str. Tel. 01/4121024
185 31 PIRAEUS Open: Jan. - Dec.
rm 26/b 47

C´ARGO HOTEL
23, Notara Str. **Tel.** 01/4121795-6, 4121918
185 31 PIRAEUS **Open:** Jan. - Dec.

Built in the heart of Piraeus, the hotel offers all modern facilities, central heating, telephone, bath and hot water at all times in every room. The spotless tidiness, prompt service and quietness make the hotel ideal for all visitors.

rm 32/**b** 47

C´ARION HOTEL
109, Vas. Pavlou Str. **Tel.** 01/4121425, 4125489
185 33 PIRAEUS **Open:** Jan. - Dec.

rm 36/**b** 69

C´ATLANTIS HOTEL
138, Notara Str. **Tel.** 01/4526871-4
185 36 PIRAEUS **Open:** Jan. - Dec.

Built in 1973 in the heart of Piraeus, the hotel is spotlessly clean, quiet and offers prompt service.

rm 54/**b** 93

C´CAPITOL HOTEL
147, Filonos Str. **Tel.** 01/4524911-4, 4524915
185 36 PIRAEUS **Open:** Jan. - Dec.

Built, in 1970 with all modern conveniences, near the customs building in the port, the hotel has a pleasant snack-bar as well as a comfortable T.V. lounge.

rm 56/**b** 84

C´CAROL HOTEL
31, Diovounioti Str. **Tel.** 01/4122933, 4134753-4
185 33 PIRAEUS **Open:** Jan. - Dec.

rm 35/**b** 67

C´CAVO HOTEL
79-81, Filonos Str. **Tel.** 01/4116134-5, 4175290
185 36 PIRAEUS **Open:** Jan. - Dec.

rm 47/**b** 89

C´DELFINI HOTEL
7, Leoharous Str. **Tel.** 01/4123512, 4123579
185 31 PIRAEUS **Open:** Jan. - Dec.

rm 52/**b** 78

* C´DIANA HOTEL
11, Filelinon Str. **Tel.** 01/4525020, 4525036
185 36 PIRAEUS **Open:** Jan. - Dec.

rm 41/**b** 79

C´GLAROS HOTEL
4, Harilaou Trikoupi Str. **Tel.** 01/4527887, 4517169, 4515421
185 36 PIRAEUS **Open:** Jan. - Dec.

rm 45/**b** 80

C´IDEAL HOTEL
142, Notara Str. **Tel.** 01/4511727, 4515931
185 36 PIRAEUS **Tlx.** 213113 SIDE GR
Open: Jan. - Dec.

Hotel ideal for a short or a long stay. Specialized service for every kind of guests: tourists, businessmen, sailors, families.

rm 30/**b** 56

C.C.: American Express

C´IONION HOTEL
10, Kapodistriou Str. **Tel.** 01/417099 41775
185 31 PIRAEUS **Open:** Jan. - De

rm 19/**b** 41

C´LERIOTIS HOTEL
294, Themistokleous Coast **Tel.** 01/451664 45166
185 39 PIRAEUS **Open:** Jan. - De

A hotel built on the seashore, overlookir Saronikos gulf. We promise a cool and con fortable stay one km. off the town-center.

rm 45/**b** 85

C´LILIA HOTEL
131, Zeas Str. **Tel.** 01/4179108, 41793
185 34 PIRAEUS **Open:** Jan. - De

Small elegant hotel located in Passa mani, just 10 min. walk to the central po All rooms with private bathroom, telephor and stereo music.

rm 17/**b** 31

C.C.: American Express, Traveller's Cheques

C´NIKI HOTEL
5, Yanakou Dzelepi Str. **Tel.** 01/41167 4116
185 31 PIRAEUS Open: Jan. - De

Large rooms with phone and two pr grammes of stereo-music. Excellent se vice.

rm 20/**b** 32

C´PHIDIAS HOTEL
189, Koundourioti Str. **Tel.** 01/4125942
185 35 PIRAEUS **Open:** Jan. - De

In this hotel the guest will find a friend family atmosphere and enjoy a drink watc ing a Video programme in the bar. Just minutes away from the central port the h tel is suitable for an excursion base to th islands.

rm 26/**b** 44

C´SANTORINI HOTEL
6, Harilaou Trikoupi Str. **Tel.** 01/4522147 45132
185 36 PIRAEUS **Open:** Jan. - De

rm 35/**b** 63

C´SCORPIOS HOTEL
156, Themistokleous Str.
185 39 PIRAEUS **Tel.** 01/4512172, 45247
Open: Jan. - De

rm 26/**b** 52

C´SERIFOS HOTEL
5, Harilaou Trikoupi Str. **Tel.** 01/452507 4525003, 45249
185 36 PIRAEUS **Open:** Jan. - De

Just across the street to the customs o fice building, by the main port, 100 m. awa from the boarding ramps of the local sea li ers.

rm 34/**b** 59

PIRAEUS SUBURBS

Dzidzifies

C´ SANDRA HOTEL
336, El. Venizelou Ave. **Tel.** 01/9423854, 9423931, 9424507
176 75 DZIDZIFIES **Open:** Jan. - Dec.
Located between Athens and Piraeus, with easy access to the port and airport. A short walk to the Faliro yacht marina. Has snack-bar, lounge and garden, also balcony with a nice view in every room.
rm 45/**b** 85

C´ SARONICOS HOTEL
33, Praxitelous Str. **Tel.** 01/9423358, 9423601
176 75 DZIDZIFIES **Open:** Jan. - Dec.
Pleasant and comfortable stay by the sea with many entertainment centers close at hand.
rm 42/**b** 69

Koridalos

C´ ALEXIADIS HOTEL
5, Filikis Eterias Str. **Tel.** 01/4957926
181 20 KORIDALOS **Open:** Jan. - Dec.
rm 32/**b** 60

Moschato

C´ ALMA HOTEL
0, Vas. Konstandinou Str. **Tel.** 01/4814888, 4812336
183 44 MOSCHATO **Open:** Jan. - Dec.
rm 42/**b** 78

C´ DELFINI HOTEL
2, Chrys. Smyrnis Str. **Tel.** 01/9415373, 9415380
183 44 MOSCHATO **Open:** Jan. - Dec.
rm 33/**b** 61

C´ KRITON HOTEL
, Platonos Str. **Tel.** 01/9423339, 9423380
183 44 MOSCHATO **Open:** Jan. - Dec.
rm 55/**b** 100

C´ LETO HOTEL
47, Possidonos Str. **Tel.** 01/9415763
183 44 MOSCHATO **Open:** Jan. - Dec.
rm 45/**b** 87

C´ MARY HOTEL
31, Posidonos Ave. **Tel.** 01/9411845-6
175 61 MOSCHATO **Open:** Jan. - Dec.
rm 33/**b** 61

C´ MIAMI HOTEL
, Ath. Diakou Str. **Tel.** 01/9410825, 9414298
183 44 MOSCHATO **Open:** Jan. - Dec.
rm 32/**b** 56

C´ MILANO HOTEL
, Vas. Georgiou Str. **Tel.** 01/9412056, 9411776
183 44 MOSCHATO **Open:** Jan. - Dec.
24-hour hot water in all rooms.
rm 37/**b** 70

C´ PLATON HOTEL
3, Platonos Str. **Tel.** 01/9423460, 9423363
183 44 MOSCHATO **Open:** Jan. - Dec.
rm 39/**b** 71

Neo Faliro

C´ ANGELA HOTEL
30, Filipou Str. **Tel.** 01/4122310, 4122409
185 33 NEO FALIRO **Open:** Jan. - Dec.
rm 28/**b** 50

C´ BIANCA BEACH HOTEL
2, El. Venizelou Str. **Tel.** 01/4823065-6
185 47 NEO FALIRO **Tlx.** 212889
Open: Jan. - Dec.
rm 67/**b** 124

C´ DELOS HOTEL
3, Falireos Str. **Tel.** 01/4815961
185 47 NEO FALIRO **Open:** Jan. - Dec.
rm 16/**b** 29

C´ HERMION HOTEL
8, Falireos Str. **Tel.** 01/4812919, 4814570
185 47 NEO FALIRO **Open:** Jan. - Dec.
rm 42/**b** 78

C´ JERRY'S HOTEL
10, Karaiskaki Str. **Tel.** 01/4822037-8, 4822057
185 47 NEO FALIRO **Open:** Jan. - Dec.
The hotel is near the Athens and Piraeus bus lines, metrò and taxis, 100 m. from the sea. Plenty of greenery, unpolluted atmosphere and above all, quietness. Suitable for a nice and peacefull holiday.
rm 22/**b** 42

C´ OLYMPIC HOTEL
11, Giannopoulou Str. **Tel.** 01/4820800, 4821020, 4823240
NEO FALIRO **Open:** Jan. - Dec.
Conveniently located in a nice area near the sea, within easy reach of bus and metrò lines to Athens, Piraeus and airport, the hotel is designed for a comfortable stay, and the experienced staff offers perfect service. There is a restaurant, two bars, a cafeteria - pizzeria and a roof-garden. More than C´ class accommodation at C´ class prices.
rm 110/**b** 250

D´ ILIOS HOTEL
1, Kifissou Str. **Tel.** 01/4183815, 4814708
182 33 NEO FALIRO **Tlx.** 211495 THEO GR
Open: Jan. - Dec.
Special rates for long stay.
rm 16/**b** 19 **C.C.:** Visa, Master Charge

Nikea

✱ C´ ALFA HOTEL
11, Athinon Ave. **Tel.** 01/4952357
184 54 NIKEA **Open:** Jan. - Dec.
rm 20/**b** 35 P

C´ ERI HOTEL
54, Petrou Ralli Str. **Tel.** 01/4962644, 496430
184 54 NIKEA **Open:** Jan. - Dec
An ideal C´ class hotel 15 minutes from Athens or Piraeus. Modernly furnished rooms with private bathroom, hot water and telephone. Bar, cafeteria and parking.
rm 48/**b** 92 SP

TOWARDS CORINTHOS

Elefsis

C´ MELISSA HOTEL
21, Persofonis Str. **Tel.** 01/5546547, 5543283
192 00 ELEFSINA **Open:** Jan. - Dec.
Our hotel is a friendly one, situated in Elefsina, a quiet town of archaeological interest, 20 km from Athens and Piraeus and connected to them by a frequent bus service. Easy to visit: Dafni, Sounion, Korinthos, Mycenae, Epidavros, Nafplio.
rm 17/**b** 31 S
P **C.C.:** Diners, Visa, Eurocard

Kinetta

✱ A´ KINETTA BEACH CLUB HOTEL
57th km Athens-Korinthos Nat.Road
191 00 KINETTA **Tel.** 0296/62512, 62534
Open: Apr. - Oct.
rm 181/**b** 362 P

✱ B´ SUN HOTEL
54th km Athens - Korinthos Nat.Road
191 00 KINETTA **Tel.** 0296/62243, 62068
Open: Apr. - Oct.
rm 51/**b** 96 P

C´ BOUSOULAS HOTEL
56th km Athens-Korinthos Nat.Road
191 00 MEGARA **Tel.** 0296/62260, 62780
Open: Jan. - Dec.
Beautiful sea-viewing rooms, large open space by the seashore, friendly atmosphere. Excellent cooking, especially fresh sea-food.
rm 25/**b** 48 P

✱ C´ HOTEL 50
50th km Athens-Korinthos Nat.Road
191 00 KINETTA **Tel.** 0296/62444, 62250
Open: Jan. - Dec.
rm 20/**b** 38 P

Nea Peramos

✱ C´ MEGALO PEFKO HOTEL
15, 28th Octovriou Str. **Tel.** 0296/33205, 33417-8
109 06 NEA PERAMOS
Open: Jan. - Dec.
rm 70/**b** 136 P

Porto Germeno

✱ C´ EGOSTHENION HOTEL
190 12 PORTO GERMENO **Tel.** 0263/41226-7
Open: Apr. - Dec.
rm 80/**b** 154 P

Skaramangas

✱ C´ ALFA HOTEL
6, S. Palaska Str. **Tel.** 01/5575587-8, 557493
124 62 SKARAMANGAS **Open:** Jan. - Dec
rm 50/**b** 94 P

✱ C´ ARGO HOTEL
124 62 SKARAMANGAS **Tel.** 01/557408
Open: Jan. - Dec
rm 30/**b** 53 P

✱ C´ ERSI HOTEL
32, Spyrou Miliou Str. **Tel.** 01/5572942-
124 62 SKARAMANGAS **Open:** Jan. - Dec
rm 18/**b** 34 P

✱ C´ GLAROS HOTEL
4, Schisto Ave. **Tel.** 01/5573459, 5574871-
124 62 SKARAMANGAS **Open:** Jan. - Dec
rm 33/**b** 62 P

✱ C´ LETO HOTEL
30, Schistos Ave. **Tel.** 01/5573524, 557210
124 62 SKARAMANGAS **Open:** Jan.- Dec
rm 45/**b** 76

Vilia

✱ B´ AKTAEON HOTEL
3, Ath. Vappa Str. **Tel.** 0263/22560, 22226
190 12 VILIA **Open:** Apr. - Oct
rm 26/**b** 50 P

C´ ARION HOTEL
39, Sakelariou Str. **Tel.** 0263/22253
190 12 VILIA **Open:** Jan. - Dec
rm 16/**b** 30 P

✱ C´ IDYLLION HOTEL
2, Plateon Str. **Tel.** 0263/22262, 22302
190 12 VILIA **Open:** Apr. - Oct
rm 22/**b** 42 P

✱ C´ KITHAERON HOTEL
5, Grammou Str. **Tel.** 0263/22354, 22210
190 12 VILIA **Open:** Apr. - Oct
rm 25/**b** 50 P

✱ C´ KYKLAMINA HOTEL
3, Sminagou Katsarou Str. **Tel.** 0263/22205
190 12 VILIA **Open:** Jan. - Dec
rm 12/**b** 20 P

✱ C´ VERORI HOTEL
69, Sakela riou Str. **Tel.** 0263/22291-
190 12 VILIA **Open:** Jun. - Sep
rm 54/**b** 86

SARONIC GULF ISLANDS

Egina

*** B´ AEGINA MARIS HOTEL/BUNG.**
Perdika **Tel.** 0297/25130-2, 51374, 24579
180 10 EGINA **Open:** Apr. - Oct.
rm 164/**b** 310

B´ APOLLO HOTEL
Aghia Marina **Tel.** 0297/32271-4, 32281
180 10 EGINA **Tlx.** 216661
Open: Apr. - Oct.
The hotel has all the latest facilities and a view of special interest and beauty. Most rooms have a balcony. Apart from other sport facilities there are speed boats available, and we have a wild green garden. Greek and Continental specialities in our restaurant. Besides our activities, the area offers a variety of night clubs and Greek style tavernas.
rm 107/**b** 203

B´ ARGO HOTEL
Aghia Marina **Tel.** 0297/32471-3
180 10 EGINA **Open:** Apr. - Oct.
Right on the shore, 3 steps leading to the crystal clear sea-water, in front of the hotel. Big terrace, bar, lounge, library, T.V., video, folklore evenings and many posibilities of an active holiday through sports.
rm 60/**b** 116

*** B´ DANAE HOTEL**
Egina Town **Tel.** 0297/22424-5
180 10 EGINA **Open:** Jan. - Dec.
rm 52/**b** 100

*** B´ MOONDY BAY HOTEL**
Perdika **Tel.** 0297/22605, 25146-7
180 10 EGINA **Open:** Apr. - Oct.
Bugalow-style hotel nestling between trees and set in a delightfull garden overlooking a picturesque bay near the fishing village of Perdika. The restaurant, practically on the beach, offers Greek and international delicacies and occasional buffet and barbeques. Greek and international music is played in the bar and disco.
rm 72/**b** 144

*** B´ NAFSICA HOTEL**
Egina Town **Tel.** 0297/22333
180 10 EGINA **Open:** Apr. - Oct.
rm 34/**b** 66

*** C´ AEGLI**
Aghia Marina **Tel** 0297/32221
180 10 EGINA **Open:** Apr. - Oct
rm 7/**b** 14

*** C´ AKTI HOTEL**
Aghia Marina **Tel.** 0297/32249, 32288
180 10 EGINA **Open:** Apr. - Oct.
rm 22/**b** 44

*** C´ AMMOUDIA HOTEL**
Aghia Marina **Tel.** 0297/32313, 32204
180 10 EGINA **Open:** Mar. - Oct.
rm 14/**b** 26

*** C´ APHAEA HOTEL**
Aghia Marina **Tel.** 0297/32227
180 10 EGINA **Open:** Apr. - Oct.
rm 18/**b** 32

C´ ARETI HOTEL
2, N.Kazantzaki Str. **Tel.** 0297/239-7, 23968
180 10 EGINA **Open:** Jan. - Dec.
The hotel is in the town-centre near the bus terminals and all the shops. Just a few steps to the beach.
rm 21/**b** 39

C´ AVRA HOTEL
4, N.Kazantzaki Str. **Tel.** 0297/22303, 23968
180 10 EGINA **Open:** Jan. - Dec.
Family run hotel, scrupulously clean, with an excellent restaurant, in the town centre near the bus terminals and shops. The sandy beach is just 20 m. from the hotel entrance.
rm 33/**b** 57

C´ BROWN HOTEL
4, Toti Hadzi Str. **Tel.** 0297/22271, 24485
180 10 EGINA **Open:** Mar. - Oct.
Near the centre of the town, very close to the beach. Central heating, breakfast room, bar, T.V. lounge, beach facilities.
rm 25/**b** 48
C.C.: American Express

C´ BLUE HORIZON HOTEL
Aghia Marina **Tel.** 0297/32303, 01/5612715
180 10 EGINA **Open:** Apr. - Oct.
An ideal C´ class hotel just ten min. from the beach. Modernly furnished rooms with balconies offering a panoramic view of the town and the sea. Prices reduced up to 15% during low season (Apr.-June and Sept.-Oct).
rm 12/**b** 28

*** C´ FAROS HOTEL**
Egina Town **Tel.** 0297/22218, 24294
180 10 EGINA **Open:** Jan. - Dec.
rm 44/**b** 72

*** C´ GALINI HOTEL**
Aghia Marina **Tel.** 0297/32203
180 10 EGINA **Open:** Apr. - Oct.
rm 35/**b** 67

*** C´ ISIDORA HOTEL**
Aghia Marina **Tel.** 0297/32414
180 10 EGINA **Open:** Apr. - Oct.
rm 17/**b** 33

C´ KARRAS HOTEL
Aghia Marina **Tel.** 0297/32464, 32557

180 10 EGINA Open: Apr. - Oct.
rm 28/b 52

*** C´ KARYATIDES HOTEL**
Aghia Marina Tel. 0297/32331
180 10 EGINA Open: Apr. - Nov.
rm 30/b 56 P

C´ KIRIAKAKIS HOTEL
Aghia Marina Tel. 0297/32588
180 10 EGINA Open: Apr. - Oct.
rm 30/b 57 P

*** C´ KLONOS HOTEL**
Egina Town Tel. 0297/22670, 22577
180 10 EGINA Open: Apr. - Oct.
rm 46/b 84 P

*** C´ LIBERTY HOTEL**
Aghia Marina Tel. 0297/32353
180 10 EGINA Open: Apr. - Oct.
rm 20/b 40 P

*** C´ MAGDA HOTEL**
Aghia Marina Tel. 0297/32325
180 10 EGINA Open: Apr. - Oct.
rm 21/b 40 P

C´ MARINA HOTEL
Aghia Marina Tel. 0297/32301, 32543
180 10 EGINA Open: Mar. 15th - Oct.
Modern, clean, friendly hotel nicely situated, a pleasant walk to the sandy beach. All rooms have private W.C.-shower, telephone and balcony with a sea view. An additional attraction is the ancient temple of Aphea, just 1,5 km away.
rm 29/b 55 S P

*** C´ OASIS HOTEL**
Aghia Marina Tel. 0297/32312, 32204
180 10 EGINA Open: Mar. - Oct.
rm 19/b 37 P

*** C´ PANORAMA HOTEL**
Aghia Marina Tel. 0297/32202
180 10 EGINA Open: Apr. - Oct.
rm 25/b 49 P

*** C´ PANDELAROS HOTEL**
Aghia Marina Tel. 0297/32431-2
180 10 EGINA Open: Apr. - Oct.
rm 55/b 106 P

*** C´ POSIDON HOTEL**
Aghia Marina Tel. 0297/32392
180 10 EGINA Open: Apr. - Oct.
rm 24/b 48 P

Hydra

A´ MIRAMARE HOTEL BUNGALOWS
Mandraki Bay Tel. 0298/52300-1
180 40 HYDRA Open: Apr. - Oct.
Built in the traditional Hydra style, a patio with a large pergola shadowing each room, the bungalows are in front of the only sandy beach of the island, 2 km off the town, which they are linked with by sea and road. The attractive ever-serene bay before the hotel is ideal for marine sports and also a place eminently suited to cultural and artistic pursuits.
bung 28/b 55

*** A´ MIRANDA (Pension)**
180 40 HYDRA Tel. 0298/52230
Open: Jan. - Dec.
rm 14/b 26

*** B´ HYDROUSSA HOTEL**
180 40 HYDRA Tel. 0298/52217, 52400
Tlx. 219338 ANCHO GR.
Open: Apr. - Oct.
rm 36/b 72

*** C´ LETO HOTEL**
180 40 HYDRA Tel. 0298/52280
Open: Jan. - Dec.
rm 39/b 74

Poros

*** B´ EPTA ADELFIA HOTEL**
1, Tombazi Str. Tel. 0298/23412, 24139
180 20 POROS Open: Apr. - Oct.
rm 16/b 30 P

*** B´ LATSI HOTEL**
74, Padopoulou Str. Tel. 0298/22392, 22543
180 20 POROS Open: Jan. - Dec.
rm 39/b 54 P

*** B´ NEON AEGLI HOTEL**
Askeli Tel. 0298/22372, 23200
180 20 POROS Open: Apr. - Oct.
rm 72/b 132 P

*** B´ PAVLOU HOTEL**
Neorion Tel. 0298/22734, 22736
180 20 POROS Open: Mar. - Oct.
rm 36/b 66 P

*** B´ POROS HOTEL**
180 20 POROS Tel. 0298/22216-8
Tlx. 216457
Open: Apr. - Oct.
rm 91/b 173 P

*** B´ SARON HOTEL**
Paralia Tel. 0298/22279, 23670
180 20 POROS Open: Apr. - Oct.
rm 24/b 46

*** B´ SIRENE HOTEL**
Monastiri Tel. 0298/22741-5
180 20 POROS Open: Jan. - Dec.
rm 122/b 228 P

B´ THEANO HOTEL (Hostel)
21, Lambraki Str. Tel. 0298/22567
180 20 POROS Open: Apr. 15 - Oct.
Family-run hostel, by the sea, not 2 km from the port-town.
rm 24/b 49 S

*** C´ AKTAEON HOTEL**
6, Heroon Sq. Tel. 0298/22281
180 20 POROS Open: Jan. - Dec.
rm 20/b 38

∗ C´ ANGYRA HOTEL
Neorion Tel. 0298/22432, 22368
180 20 POROS Open: Apr. - Nov.
rm 53/**b** 87

∗ C´ CHRYSSI AVGI HOTEL
Askeli Tel. 0298/22277
180 20 POROS Open: Jan. - Dec.
rm 77/**b** 145

∗ C´ MANESSI HOTEL
Paralia Tel. 0298/22273
180 20 POROS Open: Jan. - Dec.
rm 16/**b** 25

Spetses

∗ A´ AKROYALI HOTEL
Aghii Anargiri Tel. 0298/73695
180 50 SPETSES
rm 17/**b** 30

A´ KASTELI HOTEL
B.P. 16 Tel. 0298/72311-3, 72161, 72935
SPETSES Tlx. 214531

This hotel and bungalows, formerly known as XENIA OF SPETSES lies on a hill-side among 18 actes of pine trees, at the most beautiful location of the island. Having its own private beach and a wonderful sea view the place is the perfect spot for a quiet, restfull holiday.

rm 38/**b** 68 **bung** 41/**b** 123

C.C.: American Express, Diners

∗ A´ POSEIDONION HOTEL
180 50 SPETSES Tel. 0298.72208, 72308
Open: Apr. - Oct.
rm 55/**b** 83

∗ A´ SPETSES HOTEL
180 50 SPETSES Tel. 0298/72602-4
Tlx. 210902 SPEL GR.
Open: Jan. - Dec.
rm 77/**b** 143

∗ B´ ROUMANIS HOTEL
180 50 SPETSES Tel. 0298/72244, 72344
Open: Mar. - Aug.
rm 35/**b** 65

∗ B´ VILLA MARTHA HOTEL
180 50 SPETSES Tel. 0298/72147
Open: Apr. - Sep.
rm 23/**b** 43

∗ C´ FAROS HOTEL
Dapia Sq. Tel. 0298/72613-4
180 50 SPETSES Open: Apr. - Oct.
rm 47/**b** 84

∗ C´ ILIOS HOTEL
180 50 SPETSES Tel. 0298/72488 72268
Open: Apr. - Oct.
rm 27/**b** 51

∗ C´ MYRTOON HOTEL
180 50 SPETSES Tel. 0298/72555-6, 72215
Open: Jan. - Dec.
rm 39/**b** 74

∗ C´ STAR HOTEL
Dapia Sq. Tel. 0298/72214, 72462
180 50 SPETSES Open: Apr. - Oct.
rm 37/**b** 68

CAMPING SITES

CAMPING ATHENS
198, Athinon Ave. Tel: 01/5814113-4
PERISTERI Open: Apr.-Oct.

7 km out of Athens, in the beginning of the National Road to Korinthos, it's the nearest campsite to Athens and Piraeus. Located in green and clean surroundings it offers all modern comforts from parking facilities for clients on holidays in the islands to post office and first aid station. The pitches in this inland campsite are on earth and grass shaded by trees.

Sq. m 14,000/**c** 72

CAMPING COCOCAMP
2, Olimpiados Str. Tel: 0294/23775-28480
RAFINA Open: Jan.-Dec.

26 km east of Athens, turn right towards Rafina at Rafina-Marathon junction. From Rafina Square turn right towards Loutsa and drive on for 1 km. The campsite develops along a slight slope from the road down to the sea. The beach is sandy with pebbles. The pitches are on sand or grass shaded by pine trees. Paths are laid with concrete. Caravans to let.

Sq. m 12,000/**c** 100

CAMPING DAFNI
DAFNI Tel: 01/6811563
Open: Apr-Oct.

9 km from Athens, on the National Road to Korinthos, in Dafni location. The campsite develops in levels along a slope. The pitches in this inland campsite are on earth shaded by big pine trees. Just beside the grove where Dafni wine festival is organized every summer.

Sq. m 34,000/**c** 3120

CAMPING DIONISIOTIS
NEA KIFISSIA Tel: 01/8071494
Open: Jan.-Dec.

18 km from Athens on the National Road to Thessaloniki, to the left of the bridge at Kifissia traffic lights. This inland campsite extends on a flat ground with gravel laid paths and pitches on earth and grass shaded by pine and olive trees.

Sq. m 25,160/**c** 150

CAMPING VAKHOS

SOUNION Tel: 0292/39262-3
Open: 10 June-20 Sept.

6 km after Sounion on the road to Lavrion, this campsite extends on a partially sloped ground, 300 m from a sandy beach. It has pitches on earth or laid with concrete for caravans, shaded by pinetrees.

Sq. m 11,000/**c** 35

HELLENIC CAMPING VARKIZA BEACH

27th km Athens-Sounion Ave.
166 02 VARKIZA Tel: 01/8970012, 8972942, 3211039
Open: Jan.-21 Dec.

Camping VARKIZA BEACH, is situated in a unique position by the sea, 4 km after Vouliagmeni and 1 km before Varkiza on the coastal road to Sounion. A nice combination of nature, clear sea and modern facilities, will make your vacation a nice experience. It extends in levels between the road and the sea with pitches on soil shaded by poplars and eucalyptus. There are many small bays with sand or pebbles.

Sq. m 40,000/**c** 100

CAMPING NEA KIFISSIA

Potamou & Dimitsanas Str. Tel: 01/8016435,
NEA KIFISSIA 8075544, 8075579
Open: Jan.-Dec.

16 km from Athens, on the National Road to Thessaloniki, turn left at Nea Kifissia traffic lights, take the road that runs parallel to the National Road, direction Thessaloniki. After about 150m turn left and drive on for 300m. This inland campsite develops along a slight slope. The paths are laid with gravel and the pitches are on earth shaded by trees and reed mats.

Sq. m 22,000/**c** 67

CAMPING NEA MAKRI

190 05 NEA MAKRI Tel: 0294/92719
Open: June-Sept.

33 km from Athens on the East Coast, just outside Nea Makri village. The campsite is situated on an even ground very near a sandy beach, with pitches on earth and grass shaded by trees and reed mats.

Sq. m 15,000/**c** 78

CAMPING POLYCAMP

Skalopati Tel: 0294/23808, 24996
190 09 RAFINA Open: Jan.-Dec.

26 km from Athens, turn right towards Rafina at the Rafina-Marathon junction. 2 km after Rafina square on the road to Loutsa, the campsite develops on an even ground very near the sea. There is one sandy and one pebble beach. Pitches are on earth and grass shaded by pine trees.

Sq. m 73,000/**c** 109

CAMPING RAFINA

Marathonos Ave. Tel: 0294/23118, 28436-7
190 09 RAFINA Open: Apr.-Oct.

This inland campsite is located in Marathonas lake, 2,5 km from Rafina, 24 km from Athens. It develops in levels along a hill slope with a pine wood. The paths are laid with gravel and the pitches are on earth and grass shaded by pine trees.

Sq. m 30,000/**c** 860-960

CAMPING VOULA

2, Alkionidon Str. Tel: 01/8953249, 8951641, 8952712
166 73 VOULA
Open: Jan.-Dec.

This campsite is situated in Voula on the coastal road to Vouliagmeni. It lies on even ground between the road and the sea. It has tarmac roads and pitches on earth or grass shaded by poplars and mulberry trees and screened by bushes. The beach is sandy.

Sq. m 40,000/**c** 99

CAMPING MARATHON

190 07 MARATHONAS Tel: 0294/55757, 55587
Open: Jan.-Dec.,

34 km east of Athens, on Marthon Ave., 1 km after Nea Makri turn right at the junction for Marathon Coast "Aghios Pandeleimon". The campsite lies on the right, after about 1,5 km. Extending on a flat ground between the road and the sea the campsite has gravel laid paths and pitches on sand and lawn shaded by trees and reed mats.

Sq. m 13,000/**c** 100

CAMPING KOKINO LIMANAKI

190 09 RAFINA Tel: 0294/26601-5, 31603-4

26 km east of Athens, turn right towards Rafina at the Rafina-Marathon junction. 1 km after this junction turn left and drive on for 2km. The campsite extends along a slope down to the sandy beach. Paths are tarmac, pitches are on earth shaded by reed mats and pine trees.

Sq. m 12,300/**c** 65

CAMPING ACROPOLIS

NEA KIFISSIA Tel: 01/8083104, 8014615
Open: May-Sept.

16 km from Athens, turn left at Nea Kifissia traffic lights and you see the campsite. Paths are laid with gravel and pitches are on earth shaded by pines, poplars or reed mats. The ground is partly even and partly slightly sloped.

Sq. m 20,000/**c** 100

CAMPING RAMNOUS

190 07 MARATHONAS Tel: 0294/55855
Open: Apr.-Nov.

39 km east of Athens, 6 km after Nea Makri, on Marathon Avenue, turn right towards Schinias. When you see the pinewood turn right at the small bridge and drive on for 1 km. The campsite lies between the road and the sandy beach on an even ground. Paths are laid with gravel and pitches are on sand shaded by poplars or reed mats.

Sq. m 11,500/**c** 71

PRACTICAL INFORMATION

A-Z Summary

Advance Planning

The Greek National Tourist Organization has offices in many countries to assist you with plans and itinerary. (see page 191)

What to bring

Documents: Passport; insurance cards; green card for car insurance if necessary; credit cards; drivers' license; student card. (Check to see if still valid!)

Americans: US Customs will require records of overseas purchases.

Clothing: Greece is not a dress-up country. Unless you are a diplomat, you won't even need a tie or high heels.

High season: About April 15-Oct 15: Bring few clothes. You may need a sweater or jacket for cool evenings (island winds are high). It is unlikely to rain. It is likely to BE HOT from June to August, 85´-100´ F., 30´-38´ C. Greek women rarely wear shorts in the city. Shorts and uncovered tops not permitted in churches - men or women. The beach is altogether different. Women will be glad to have a pure cotton half-slip (man-made fibers are sticky in the heat) to wear under lovely see-through floaty Greek dresses.

(You'll want sunglasses. Kiosks sell them.)

Low Season: October to April: It isn't really winter until late November. The coldest it gets is freezing 0´ C., 32´ F., maybe once or twice. You'll want a winter coat from November to March.

> **INFOTIP** Shoes: Athens is often vertical - stairs, steep slopes, and slippery marble pavements. Archeological sites are full of broken columns and rubble. Wear non-skid footwear. If you buy Greek sandals, get them with rubber soles, not slippery slithery leather.

Odds and Ends: These small items are available in Athens, but you may not want to spend time looking for them. Towel, for beach or hair. Hotel towels are sometimes skimpy. (European hotels rarely provide face cloths.) Hangers, if you use a lot. (Bring fewer clothes!) Small plastic bags for wet items in suitcases. Travelling clothesline and pins. Flat round universal drain stopper, for closing shower basin to launder in, or replace missing washbasin stoppers. If you have any special needs, remember to bring extras such as glasses, contact lenses, medicines, prescriptions, sunscreen.An air cushion could be handy for stone amphitheatres.

Medical Tips: Check with your insurance company to see if you are covered while travelling. EUROPASSISTANCE offers travel insurance from many countries (Athens representative, 363-5855).

Make a note of generic name of prescription drugs; in case of loss, ask a pharmacist for advice - he may stock it. Pharmacists are mostly highly trained and helpful. Many speak English, especially in the town centre.

Aspirin; Paracetamol (Panadol, Panasorb, Depon); Dramamine; Kaopectate; Alka Seltzer; are easily available. So are antibiotics like Ampicillin or Pentrexyl, without prescription.

If on a sugar-free diet, note that you can now obtain aspartame (Nutrasweet, Equal) at pharmacies under the name "Canderel", as well as diet soft drinks; fructose, sorbitol and honey, but not saccharin or calcium cyclamate. Batteries for hearing-aids are available - kiosks again.

Athens, as you may have heard, often has an air-pollution problem. If you have breathing difficulties, bring your medication.

SUNSCREEN: If you need a screen with a strength above 14, it may be hard to find. The sun is STRONG!

DO NOT BRING NARCOTICS. PENALTIES ARE SEVERE!!

> **INFOTIP** If you suffer from jet lag, we are assured that the regime outlined in OVERCOMING JET LAG, by Ehret and Scanlon and published by Berkley books is effective and makes long plane trips much easier.

Entry regulations

American, E.E.C., Canadian, Australian and New Zealand valid passports get automatic visas for three months. South African citizens have visas for two months.

Customs

There will be a lane marked in red for "Something to Declare" where all baggage is inspected, and a green one for "Nothing to Declare". (You may be stopped while passing through the green lane for a spot check).

Duty free imports: Personal belongings, ONE each of the following: Camera; cine-camera; projector; binoculars; musical instrument; record player; radio; typewriter; tape recorder; bicycle and sports gear, and:

	EEC passports	Other passports
Cigarettes	300	200
Cigarillos	150	100
Cigars	175	----
Tobacco	400 gram	250 gram
Spirits	1.5 litres	1 litre
Wines (under 22%)	4 litres	2 litres
Perfumes	75 gram·	50 gram
Cologne	3/8 litre	1/4 litre

Works of Art may be imported free. (Antiquities may not be exported).

Private Cars entering Greece:

Easier with a "carnet de passage en douanes" from the Automobile Association of your home country. Without this document, the car will be entered on passport for temporary stay, and must be taken out in 6 months (unless you are granted an extension. Inquire at ELPA or your consulate). International or EEC Driving Licence, (plus Austrian or Swiss). If you arrive without one, an international license can be issued against your own for a small fee by ELPA (see page 171) You will have to present:

Your passport or ID card, your valid current license and one photograph.

Car registration papers

Nationality plate or sticker

Green Card - an extension to your regular insurance policy that makes it valid for foreign countries. Third party insurance is mandatory.

For more on cars see MOTORING, page 171)

Boats - Pleasure craft: Sailboats, motorboats may circulate freely for 4 months when registered in owner's passport at an entry/exit port. In Attica: Vouliagmeni, Lavrion, Zea (Piraeus).

Currency: Cash in excess of $500 should be declared on entry, so you may take it out again. Maximum drachmas in any form allowed in or out, 3000. Checks and letters of credit and title deeds in foreign currencies (issued to the order of the traveller and not endorsed) and travellers checks are not restricted.

Pets: No quarantine, do require health certificates. Ask your travel agent, Greek National Tourist Organization (page 191) or Greek consulate for details if you must bring your pet.

ANTIQUITIES see , page 192

Getting to Athens

By Air: Most major airlines offer services to Athens. There are direct flights from major cities of Europe and from North America as well as Asia, Africa, and Australia. As fares change rapidly, consult your local travel agent for special offers and charter flights.

By Rail: Trains operate from Europe: Unless you can afford a sleeper (not couchette) it's a long, exhausting trip with scrappy food service, too many people, and, er, overextended toilet facilities.Yugoslavia is a very long country. You can also choose to go to Italy by train and take the ferry from Brindisi or Ancona to Patras, or Venice to

Piraeus. This is more fun, though more expensive.
By Bus: There are buses that scramble from London to Athens in (theoretically) 2-3 days, if you are very young and strong and have a few days to recover at each end. It is cheap but wearing. If you want to join one of these buses en route, forget it, as overbooking means your reserved seat may have been taken.
By Sea: From Mediterranean ports. By private yacht. Good luck.
By Car: Major routes to Greece from England: Belgium-Cologne-Munich, Graz (Austria) to Belgrade (Yugoslavia) and south. Yugoslavia is a long long long country, and border formalities can take hours, especially in high season. The Yugoslavia coastal road is not much longer and far more scenic. Or, via Reims (France), Lausanne, Milan and Trieste - then either through Yugoslavia (still a very long country), or through Italy to ferries at Brindisi, Ancona (daily), Venice (every 10 days), Genoa, Otranto in high season. Ferries land in Patras (with major road to Athens), with a call at Igoumenitsa. The Venice ferries sail direct to Piraeus.

AIR LINES, Air travel see GETTING AROUND , page 163
ART GALLERIES, see ENTERTAINMENT, page 158
(also MUSEUMS, p. 107)
BANKING, see BUSINESS GUIDE
BUSINESS GUIDE, page 195
CARS see Motoring , page 171
CAMPING see page 153
DOCTORS see HELP, page 169

Electricity

Greek Current is 220 v., 50 cycles. Multiple adaptor plugs are a must if you have American electric equipment.

Entertainment

Art Galleries and Exhibitions

(see also Museums, page 107)

Athens is as cosmopolitan in art as any capital city. Galleries exhibiting both Greek and foreign modern artists are gathered, many, in the Kolonaki area. Opening and closing times vary, so phone in advance (Season usually Sept - June). A partial listing follows:

ANEMOS: 36, Kiriazi St. KIFISSIA Tel: 8082344
BERNIE: 51, Marasli St. Kolonaki Tel: 7235657
KREONIDIS: 7, Iperidou & Nikis St. Plaka Tel: 3224261
DIOGENIS: 33, Nikis St. Plaka Tel: 3231978
DRACOS ART CENTER: 2, Irodotou St. Kolonaki Tel: 7217103
EVMAROS: 26, Fokidos St. Ambelokipi Tel: 7776485
GALLERY 3: 3, Fokilidou St. Kolonaki Tel: 3628230
IAKINTHOS: 27, Zirini St. KIFISSIA Tel: 8011730
MEDOUSA: 7, Xenokratous St. Kolonaki Tel: 7244552
NEES MORFES: 9, Valaoritou St. Kolonaki Tel: 3616165
ORA: 7, Xenofondos St. Syntagma Sq. Tel: 3230698
SILLOGI: 4, Vas. Sofias St. Syntagma Sq. Tel: 7245136
TRITO MATI: 33, Xenokratous St. Kolonaki Tel: 7229733
ZIGOS: 33, Iofondos St. near HILTON HOTEL. Tel: 7229272
IOLAS-ZOUMBOULAKI: 20, Kolonaki Sq. Tel: 3608278

Athens Festival

The Athens Festival and Summer Theatre.
Every summer from June through September the Greek National Tourist Organization arranges performances at the Herod Atticus Theatre and at the Ancient Theatre of Epidaurus in the Peloponnese. The Bolshoi, the Royal Shakespeare, and the State Opera of Vienna are among the many international groups who have performed here,

as well as the Greek National Theatre and other local companies. This is an opportunity to see productions of a very high standard at a cost you will not believe... about $2.50 (students) to $15.00 (tops).

The Festival office and box office is in the arcade of 4, Stadiou St. near Syntagma. Tickets go on sale ten days in advance of performances. Tel. 322-1459

(For Epidauros, book special coaches separately. It is not possible to return the same day by public transport.

An open air theatre on Likavitos has a summer festival too, organized by the Greek National Tourist Organization, and consisting of plays, jazz or popular music.

Children's Entertainment

Children's library (with English books and games), a small zoo and a large playgound in the National Gardens.

Playgrounds *(Pediki Hara)* are plentiful, we list a few: Philopappou; Arakinthou; near Dora Stratou Theatre; Thission (small playground, entrance opposite bus terminals);
Fokionos Negri St., off Patission;
Pikioni Filothei, off El. Venizelou Ave. in Poulaki Park
Plaka, at Stratonos and at Vironos;
Koundourioti Sq. 1/4 mile from Olympic terminal Syngrou near Hotel Ilissos;
Peace and Friendship Stadium, Faliron

Luna Parks (Amusement Parks)

Faliron, by Metro station
Alimos, on sea road.
Psychico, Kifissias Avenue
Maroussi, Kifissias Avenue

Mini golf, Glyfada, sea road

Children's Theatre

Sat. matinees: see THE ATHENIAN magazine or daily newspaper
Karagiozis puppet theatres in Plaka, facing the Monument of Lysikrates, and N. Smyrni.

This is a traditional shadow-puppet theatre, starring the clownish *"Karagiozis"*, a character whose antics are adventurous, absurd, satirical. He originated in the East and came to Greece by way of Turkey, though he is now very Greek.

Planetarium, sea end of Syngrou Avenue (Sept-June).
Scouting, Boy and Girl: inquire at your consulate.
Babysitting: ask your chambermaid, or Pronias Agency (see Athens News).
Bookshops , see page 173
Libraries , see page 170

Cinema

Athens is plentifully supplied with cinemas. The films may be Greek, but we also get American, British, Australian, German, French, Polish - an internat onal selection. Mostly they are shown in their original language with Greek subtitles, not dubbed.

It summer, only a few indoor movie houses remain open in the centre - air conditioned, of course. Summer cinema is usually in the open air, and starts at 9:00 p.m.

> **INFOTIP:** In late June and early July it isn't yet dark, so you won't see the first few minutes too clearly. Then, at the second show at 11.00 p.m, the sound will be way down so as not to disturb all the neighbours with their open windows. Sit as close to the speakers as you can if you want to hear the sound track.

New films are released between October and June. Summer showings are therefore reruns - of all ages, from Charlie Chaplin to James Bond (Connery) to James Bond (Moore) to the spring releases of this year.

In addition to the regular cinemas, there are film clubs: Teniothiki, 1, Kanari St. Kolonaki (361-2046, 361-7440: winter); Amaryllis, Aghia Paraskevi (only summer), open air with snack tables.

The British Council (363-3211); the Hellenic-American Union (362-9886); and the Goethe Insitute (360-8111), also hold regular screenings of national classics.

Dance

Ballet Athens Ballet, (723-3370)
Dance Theatre of Nafsika, (363-3840)
Lyriki Skini, (361-2461)

Folk

Dora Stratou, National Folk Dance Troupe - Performances nightly throughout the summer on Philopappou Hill. The performers are accompanied by the violin and other instruments, including lute, santouri, clarinet and drum. Their programme book is beautifully illustrated not only with photographs of groups of dancers national costume but also with reproductions of vase paintings and sculptures depicting similar dances. These latter date back through the centuries and provide an authentic connecting link through unnumbered generations. Box-office 921-4650

Modern and Jazz

Small Dance Theatre of Lia Metelopoulou (she taught at La Mama) (671-7779, 801-3781).
Experimental Ballet of Athens (822-7284)
Hellenic Chorodrama of Ralou Manou (modern dance) 2, Ilissou at Vas. Olgas Ave. (923-2956)

Exhibitions

There is always something on, all year round. if it's not a Book Fair, it's a Homes or Boat Show, or a Computer Exhibit. In summer Athens is packed with special exhibits on history, art, architecture, costume, social studies. The local horticultural society hold a flower show in Kifissia in May. See Athenian, Athens News.

TRADE FAIRS see Business Guide , page 195

FESTIVALS see Athens Festival"

MUSEUMS see part B, pages 107 to 120.

Music

Summer: see Athens Festival

Winter: The Cultural Organizations often sponsor visiting performers. Many orchestras, soloists and choral groups give concerts throughout the year, local and visiting.

Opera: Summer, see Athens Festival

Winter: Athens State Opera, Lyriki Skini, 59, Akadimias St., 361-2461

NIGHT LIFE see RESTAURANTS and NIGHT LIFE , page 176

Planetarium

Eugenidis Institute, Syngrou Ave., near the Race Course, Faliron. 941-1181, Sept. to June

Radio/Television

Radio: English news broadcasts:
U.S. Armed Services (AFRS) 1584 AM; 1485 FM; daily
Radio 1: 729 AM; 91.6 FM; 6:30 am, weather; 7.40 am, weather and news.
Radio 2: 891 AM; 2:20 pm, and 9.20 pm.
BBC World Service: 12.095, 9.410, 6.180 KHz and on 1323 KHz (or 24.80, 31.88, 48.54 meters, and 227 MW)
TV. There are two channels at present, ERT 1 and 2. They show many programmes in English with Greek subtitles.

Seminars

There are workshops and seminars continually, on subjects ranging from archeology to heart transplants to scientology to yoga. These are hard to find unless you see them in the appropriate professional journals which may be found in the libraries, (see page 170) or catch the announcement in the daily English press.

SIGHTSEEING see all of PART B; and TOURS

Sound and Light Show

From June to October. Nightly in English, French or German, on the Pnyx Hill, near Acropolis. April 1 to October 31 unless there is a full moon. English 9:00 p.m. Book at Athens Festival Office, or at entrance. Phone 322-1459, 322-3111/240. Dramatization of the attack on the Acropolis during the Persian War, complete with the burning of the temples.

Theatre

See also "Athens Festival"

Other summer theatres, some of which are pocket sized, offer anything from Soviet rock opera to Oriental dance recitals to experimental children's theatre to chamber music: the ATHENIAN monthly magazine gives excellent performance details.

Performances may be offered in the Roman Agora; The Eleftherias Park Theatre near the American Embassy; the Panathenaic Stadium East of Zappion; The Lofos Strefi; Petra Theatre (try and find it!), way off at the end of the area called "Petroupolis"; Tenta Theatre, 103, Syngrou Ave. The Nea Smyrni Woods Park (Alsos); Argyroupolis Municipal theatre; Glyfada Theatre, Glyfada Marinas; Averoff Theatre; Duchess of Plakentia (Plaisance) Mansion, Pal. Pendeli; The Veakeio, in Piraeus.

The winter season of theatre offers many visiting and local productions, including translations into Greek of familiar works of Ibsen, Shaw, Shakespeare, Ayckbourn, Beckett and other moderns. If you know the play it can be fascinating to see what adjustments the Greek producers have made. Idiom, humour, allusions will vary and yet the play will be entirely recognizable.

(The Delphinario, Faliron, is a theatre, not a delphinarium).

TOURS AND CRUISES see page 192

Wine Festival, Dafni

From the end of June to the end of September, there is a nightly revel in the woodsy area near the Dafni Monastery. At intervals in the park, there is an array of barrels containing various Greek wines, with a water fountain nearby for rinsing glasses or a change of beverage. Admission covers free sampling, as much as you wish, and you can buy carafes and glasses at a kiosk or bring your own. There are tavernas on the grounds, and there's dancing and singing. If you have a vivid imagination, this is where the satyrs hang out: they don't demand nectar or ambrosia, just a rowdy good time.

How to get there: Bus 353, 862 from Koumoundourou (Eleftherias) Square, Pireos Street. Get off at terminal: Wine Festival is between the Monastery and the Camping site.

Feasts and National Holidays

Some holidays are ancient, many are religious or historical. The celebrations can be great fun for the visitor, with fairs, dancing, and *"kefi"* - that happy mood. Many people leave the cities and the traffic for several days is likely to be heavy. Shops and banks will be closed.

Tavernas will be open and celebrating EXCEPT on Easter weekend, and Christmas Day, when it's hard to find an open restaurant except in the large hotels. Even the saucepans have gone home to The Village!

New Year's Day, St. Basil's Day — **January 1**

(This saint looks a lot like Santa Claus)

May start with a brass band playing the *"Kalanda"* on the street under your window. Children play triangles and sing to collect money or sweets. the New Year Cake *(Vassilopita)* is a Byzantine custom, and is sliced to celebrate - some lucky person gets the coin baked inside.

Epiphany **January 6**

The 12th and last day of Christmas. Gifts still exchanged. The Churchmen immerse the cross in order to bless the water, a big event in Piraeus.

Trion Ierarchon (Three Wise Men) **3 weeks before Lent**

and the first day of Carnival (Mardi Gras), varies in accordance with Easter: three weeks of parties, costumes on the kids, and a fancy-dress parade through Athens on the last Sunday, starting at Omonia and ending at Zappion.

Shrove Monday **Last Monday before Lent**

Kathará Deftéra, Clean Monday: A day for kite-flying and picnics on the hills. A fast day, with special food - shellfish, salad, squid, octopus, unleavened bread - and wine.

Independence Holiday **March 25**

A parade celebrating the outbreak of the war of independence from the Turkish occupation, 1821.

Good Friday **See Easter**

At night, the *Epitafios,* a model of the bier of Christ, is carried from the church through the streets, followed by the congregation with lighted candles. Often, the processions from other churches cross in the street and mingle. (DON'T try to drive through Athens at this time: join a throng instead!)

Easter Sunday (and Monday) Date varies

Orthodox Easter coincides with Western Christian churches only once every four years.

Easter is the major holiday in Greece, when gifts are exchanged (now the kids try for both Christmas and Easter), and families return to the village for an annual reunion.

Easter services are held on Saturday night. Before midnight all lights and candles are extinguished. On the stroke of midnight, the bells ring out and the church is fully lit with the joyful news of the resurrection - *Christós Anésti.* People light candles from the church and pass the flame on from candle to candle to others waiting outside, and the lit candles are carefully carried home. A cross to bless the house is marked over the doorway with the smoke, and a household candle is lit from that flame. Then the fast of Lent is broken with a traditional soup called *magirítsa,* made from the heart and lungs of the lamb which will be the main dish of the Easter dinner. The lamb really must be roasted on a spit; the newfangled oven is not the right thing. Easter Sunday brings *tsouréki,* a traditional sweet break (like challah) which is baked with a red egg in the top: and a contest to see whose red-dyed boiled egg will last longest through a tapping battle which ensues around the table. Red eggs are distributed at church.

INFOTIP: A word of warning. All this joy is accompanied by fireworks and guns fired in the air. These are sold everywhere to the kids and naturally, they can't wait for Easter to make a big bang, so the pre-Easter period tends to be noisy.

May Day **May 1**

A parade, workers' holiday, and garlands of flowers.

Assumption of the Virgin **15th August**

Another time when everyone is at the Village, and Athens is empty. Falls at peak of vacation season for all of Europe.

OHI Day, National Holiday **October 28**

When the Greeks said NO to Mussolini, 1940. Military and school parades.

Christmas **December 25-26**

The Panigiri Saints Days

A local churches holiday, at many with a parade of the Icon complete with brass band and candles on the appropriate saint's day, when the church has a service for 24 hours and street merchants set up stalls nearby.

INFOTIP: Name Days: Greeks may not celebrate birthdays, but do receive visitors and gifts on the day of the saint for whom they are named.

Getting Around in Athens

Public Transport

Public vehicles in Athens are plentiful and cheap. All city transport is free before 8 am.

There is minimal seating and maximum standing room - which is used to the full. Although buses become entangled with the traffic, like everything else on four wheels, they almost never refuse a passenger so waiting time is cut to the minimum.

Town services include blue (or green) buses, yellow trolley buses and the electric train which runs between Piraeus and the northern suburb of Kifissia.

Bus or Trolley Bus. Riding the bus

Have the fare ready, because buses without conductors don't give change. Entrance is at the front of the bus. Centre and rear doors are for exit only. (Some very modern articulated buses have entrances in the second section instead of the first).

Just to keep you on your toes, there are a few old buses in operation, which still have a conductor, and the traffic flow within the bus is the other way - back to front (entrance in rear, exit centre and front).

Look hard for these on the doors: ENTRANCE: ΕΙΣΟΔΟΣ EXIT: ΕΞΟΔΟΣ

Destinations are shown in Greek only and it may be necessary to ask for help in finding the right bus. Make sure you are headed the right way, because the signs indicate both termini, such as ΑΘ. ΔΑΦΝΙ (Athens-Dafni) and it could be going either way. Bus stop signs, where they exist, use the same principle. Ask as you get on.

INFOTIP: If you are a back-packer, do not get into a trolley and put your pack down between the seats near the front of the bus. Within two stops that nearly empty trolley will fill up and a hundred people will fall or climb over your luggage as they are pushed by the new boarders. The best fun will start when you try to extricate your pack and lift it over your head and off the bus. The best place to travel when you have anything to carry is at the back, either standing in the area provided or sitting on the back seats with your luggage beside you.

On the bus there will almost certainly be some passengers who speak English and who will help you to find the right stop to get off. The biggest problem you are likely to have is getting out of a crowded bus. Push, shouting "Stásis, Parakaló!"

The exit doors are controlled by the driver and you must press the button marked ΣΤΑΣΗ to signal him to open that exit. Some doors have the button overhead, some a red switch on the standing pole at eye level. If you become flustered, shout "STASIS!" loudly and someone will help.

Routes: Although the blue buses are the town service, they cover a very wide area, including Piraeus in the south, Dafni in the west, Glyfada and Voula beyond the airport on the south-east coast, Kifissia and Kastri to the north, and even to destinations outside of the city, such as Loutsa on the north east coast of Attica, and Mount Parnes, 20 km north of Athens - all for the same low fare.

Most buses run until midnight, trolleys a little later.

Most of the bus lines radiate outwards from the city from central termini.

Local services likely to be of special interest:

040 (Green bus) from Filellinon St , Syntagma Square, to Piraeus every 20 mins., Every hour after 1:00 am.

049 from Athinas St , (Omonia) to Piraeus. Every 15 minutes, every hour after 1:00 am.

Buses from:	Direction:	
Zappion	South	*Glyfada, Voula, Vouliagmeni, Varkiza - The Beaches*
Eleftherias (Koumoundourou) Sq., Pireos St.	West	*Dafni and Elefsina (Eleusis)*
Kaningos Square, Nr. Omonia	North	*Halandri, Maroussi, Psychico, Kifissia, etc.*
Acharnon Street	North	*Mount Parnes (Parnitha)*
Thission Electrico Station	East	*Loutsa, Spata, Paiania, Koropi, Eastern Attica. (No descent till Agia Paraskevi) (can be boarded opp. Zappion).*

The useful 230 bus from GOUDI runs along Alexandras, down Ippokratous to Akadimias, stops Syntagma, Acropolis (and Herod Atticus Theatre) (terminal Thission). Going the other way from Thission, stops Acropolis, National Gardens near Syntagma, Panepistimiou and Amerikis Street, Har. Trikoupi and Solonos (near Acadimias), Alexandras Avenue, Ambelokipi (Athens Tower area), Goudi.

Electrico Train, (Metro)

The electric train runs from 6:00 am. till about 12.15 a.m.

Stations: PIRAEUS, FALIRON, MOSCHATO, KALITHEA, PETRALONA, THISSION, MONASTIRAKI, OMONIA, VICTORIA, ATIKI, AGIOS NIKOLAOS, KATO PATISSIA, AGIOS ELEFTHERIOS, ANO PATISSIA, PERISSOS, PEFKAKIA, NEA IONIA, IRAKLION, IRINI, MAROUSSI, KIFISSIA. Trains run continuously throughout the day.

Taxis

Taxis in Athens are yellow, metered and cheap. Always check the meter when getting into a taxi.

Coming and going from the airport, the driver will expect a tip. When in town, however, Athens taxi drivers don't expect it for a straightforward short journey, though extra luggage, door-to-door service and extra care merit some acknowledgement.

If you don't travel far from your hotel the minimum charge will get you home. Getting a taxi can be a problem at busy times when all the taxis appear to be taken. Do not despair, the driver will often take you even if he already has a fare - but only if you are travelling in the same direction. If you flag down an occupied taxi and give the name of your hotel, the driver will either open the door for you or will lift up his head and eyes and drive on, usually without looking at the road first. This is not a silent prayer to heaven to save him from tourists but the Greek gesture for 'no'. It takes a little getting used to.

So does having to repeat the name three or four times while the driver and the other passengers kindly try to guess what it was you said. Remember, it is important to get the accent on the right syllable in Greek or you will be unintelligible. You may find you have to stop several taxis before you find one going your way. Taxi drivers do not always know every hotel or street: carry your hotel's card with the address in Greek.

> **INFOTIP:** Write the name of your hotel on a large piece of paper and carry it with you rolled or folded. When you want to go home hold it up where passing taxi drivers can see it. One of us has used this system regularly to get home easily with loads of shopping at a time when taxis are busy and streets crowded.

Radio Taxis can come within a short time, but you may have to pay the fare from wherever they received your message or a surcharge. If you call well in advance, they can accommodate you on their route and then you pay only from the pickup point. Radio Taxis are metered. Some Radio Taxi numbers: 321-4058, 512-0180, 490-6914

Chauffeured limousines wait for clients on Voukourestiou street, behind the Grande Bretagne Hotel or may be telephoned at 323-3957

BY CAR see MOTORING , page 171

Getting Outside of Athens

By Rail (OSE)

There are two rail systems in Greece, one serving the Peloponnese and the other the northern mainland including Larissa, Thessaloniki and through Europe. The two lines run parallel through Athens and the two stations are situated close to each other, north-west of Omonia Square.

Larissa Station has exchange facilities and a telephone/telegraph office. The Tourist Police are right there on the station and will help with accommodation and information. The station is served by the No 1 trolley bus from Syntagma and Omonia Squares and by the 405 bus from Alexandras Ave. Phones for Trains, 520-0646.

Peloponnisos Station, which can be reached from there by footbridge, is also served by the 847 from Menandrou St. near Omonia Sq. (It's only two stops away. If you are not starting from nearby to Omonia, take a taxi). Phones for Trains, 513-1601.

Both stations have refreshments, clean toilets and left luggage offices. Luggage can be left at reasonable daily rates and the offices are open from 6.30 am - 9 pm. No luggage will be accepted while any train is at the station or for 20 minutes before its arrival, so be there in good time if you want to leave bags before going on a train trip - or leave it the day before.

INFOTIP: There is a notice board at Peloponnisos station and it seems to be available for use by anyone with a message to leave for a friend. A boon if you are trying to meet someone in an unspecified place at a previously unspecified time, which is a thing travellers seem to make a habit of in Greece! Another notice board: Magic Bus office, 20, Filellinon St.

Long Distance Buses and Coaches

OSE also run long distance bus services in more or less the same areas as those served by the trains. In many cases they are quicker and cheaper. The buses start from the respective train station and tickets can be booked at the station or at one of the OSE booking offices between 8 am - 5.30 p.m.

OSE Booking offices:

1, Karolou St. near Omonia Square (trains)	522-2491
(buses to Germany)	524-0519
6, Sina St. (trains and buses)	362-4402
17, Filellinon Str. (international travel only)	323-6747
(trains and buses)	323-6273
Larissa Station	823-1514
Peloponissos Station	513-1636
(to France and Turkey)	513-5768

Bus Stations:

100, Kifissou Ave. for Epidaurus, Mycenae, (513-4588); Loutraki, Corinth, (513-4588) and other parts of the Peloponnese.

Bus no 051 from Menandrou St., near Omonia serves this bus station (terminus), every 10 minutes. The 420 which runs between Piraeus and Aghia Paraskevi passes bus station.

260, Liossion St., for long-distance buses to Central and Northern Greece, inluding Delphi and Halkida 831-7153 (Greek only)

Bus no 024 from Amalias St., by National Gardens, passes bus station. In spite of the address, this bus station is one block off the main road and is easy to miss (the only sign is in Greek). Ask someone to tell you where to get off.

Mavromatéon/Egyptou Sq. for buses to:

Sounion, Port Rafti, Rafina, Skala Oropos (for Amfiaraion). Egypto Square is on Patission near to Pedion Areos park and to Victoria Station on the electric train line. Take trolleys No. 2, 4, or 9.

By Sea

The main port of embarkation to the islands is Piraeus. (See page 98) Regular services also sail from Rafina to Andros, Tinos, Mykonos. From Lavrion to the tiny islands of Kea and Kithnos.

Boats come in all shapes and sizes and are run by different companies. If you ask for information at a shipping office you will only receive information about that company's boats.

A ferry carries cars. If it doesn't take cars it isn't a ferryboat, it's a *Karavi.*

> **INFOTIP:** GNTO issues regular lists of all sailings during the ensuing few days, (GNTO desk, Nat. Bank of Greece, Syntagma Square). As the weather and other factors can affect sailing times these lists also include telephone numbers for last minute checks. Unless you are a serendipitous traveller, you would be wise to check.

Piraeus Port Authority	451-1311
Rafina Port Authority	0294-23300

Hydrofoils

Flying Dolphins leave from Piraeus harbour for Egina , and from Zea Marina (the other side of the Piraeus peninsula) for other Saronic Gulf islands, and Monemvasia and Neapolis in the Peloponnese. (see page 98)

Check with the Hydrofoil company, if possible, rather than with the harbour authorities.

Telephone nos for hydrofoil booking and enquiries:

Egina:	459-1423
All other destinations:	452-7107

> **INFOTIP:** Around Greek Easter (Orthodox church date) and 15th August all ferries, buses, trains and planes are full of Greeks returning to their villages and islands for the festival and all transport is booked out a month in advance. This is your opportunity to enjoy a virtually traffic-free Athens. Don't miss it!

By Air

Athens Airport is situated at Ellinikon, near Glyfada, on the south east coast of Attica. There are two terminals, East for international airlines other than Olympic, West for Olympic Airways only. Occasionally an Olympic international flight may leave from the East Terminal, so check when you confirm your reservation.

All internal flights are via Olympic, and will leave from the West terminal. Domestic flights are cheaper between 11 pm and 5 am.

To East Terminal - (international airlines).

From Athens: Yellow bus from 18, Amalias Avenue (in front of Amalia Hotel) Every 20 mins, non-stop. from 06.00 to midnight.

Bus 121 from Vassilissis Olgas Ave. (Zappion).

From Piraeus: Bus 19 from Karaiskaki Sq. Approximately half-hourly summer, hourly winter - 07.30 to 23.10.

Bus 101 from Klissovis st, via Poseidonos Ave, passing Faliron train station. Every 20 min.

To West Terminal - (Olympic Airlines, all internal flights)

From Athens: Non-stop bus from Olympic Airways Central Booking Office at Syntagma every 30 min, 06.00 to 20.00; and later to connect with flights.

Bus 133 from Othonos St. (Syntagma) every 15 min., 06.00 to midnight

Bus 122 from Vas. Olgas Ave. (Zappion), every 20 min.

From Piraeus: Bus 107 or 109 from Klissovis Street. Via Poseidonos Ave. passing Faliron electric train station.

Air terminal interconnecting service: Approximately every half-hour in summer.

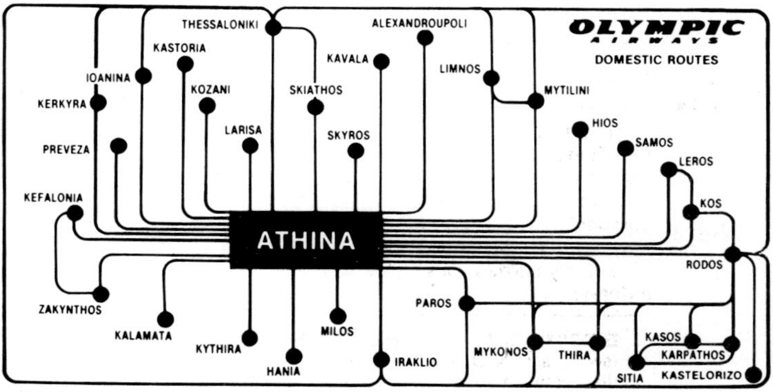

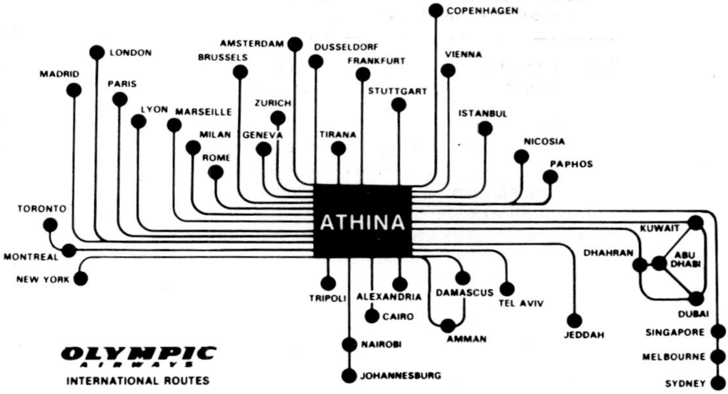

Major Airlines with Offices in Athens

All of these are located near Syntagma Square unless otherwise indicated. Usual hours: Monday to Friday 9:00-5.00. Sales agents usually open also on Saturday from 9:00 to 2:00.

Aeroflot, 14, Xenofondos St., 105 57 Athens, 322-0986, 322-1022, Telex: 21-4475
Air Canada, 10, Othonos St., 105 57 Athens, 323-5143, 322-3206
Air France, 4, Karageorgi Servias St., 105 62 Athens, 323-0501-6
Alitalia, 10, Nikis St., 105 63 Athens, 322-9417-9
Austrian Airlines, 4, Filellinon St., 105 57 Athens, 323-0844-6
British Airways, 10, Othonos St., 105 57 Athens, 322-2521
British Caledonian Airways, 6, Psila and Filellinon St., 105 57 Athens, 324-7511
Canadian Pacific, 4, Karageorgi Servias St., 105 62 Athens, 323-3044-7
Cyprus Airways, 10, Filellinon St., 105 57 Athens, 324-6965-7
Eastern Airlines, c/o GOLDAIR Ltd., 15, Panepistimiou St., (El. Venizelou) 105 64 Athens, 324-1116, 325-5061, 322-4228
Egyptair, 10, Othonos St., 105 57 Athens, 323-3575-7 Res 323-8907
El-Al Israel Airlines, 8, Othonos St., 105 57 Athens,323-0116-8
Finnair, 16, Nikis St., 105 57 Athens, 325-5234-5, 325.4831
JAL, Japan Airlines, 4, Amalias St., 105 57 Athens, 324-8211-5
KLM, Royal Dutch Airlines, 22, Voulis St., 105 63 Athens, 324-2991-3, 3226011-3, 322-2207-9
Lufthansa, 4, Karageorgi Servias St., 105 62 Athens, 329-41, 329-4235
Luxair, 6, Kriezotou St., 106 71 Athens, 360-3134, 363-2572, 363-2443
MEA, Middle East Airlines, 10, Filellinon St., 105 57 Athens, 322-6911-5, 323-5683-6
OLYMPIC AIRWAYS, ticket office: 6, Othonos St., 105 57 Athens, 929-2555, Reservations: 961-6161, Telex: 21-5134, 21-6017
Terminal and Main office, 96, Syngrou St., (south of temple of Olympian Zeus) 117 41 Athens, 929-2111, 929-2251:
Additional Office: Athens Hilton Lobby, 929-2445
Flight Information: 981-1201-4, Telex: 21-5824, 21-5307

Pan American Airlines, 4, Othonos St., 323-5242, 322-1721
Qantas Airways, Corner of Nikis and Filellinon, 105 57 Athens, 323-2792
Sabena, Belgian Airlines, 8, Othonos St., 105 57 Athens, 323-6821
SAS Scandinavian Airlines, 6, Sina and Vissarionos St., 106 72, 363-444-9
Saudia Airlines, 17, Filellinon St., 105 57 Athens, 324-4671-5
Singapore Airlines, 22, Filellinon St., 105 57 Athens, 323-9111-8
Swissair, 4, Othonos St., 105 57 Athens, 323-1871-5
TWA - Trans World Airlines, 8, Xenofondos St., 105 57 Athens, 323-6831

Help!

Tourist Police offer help with translations on the telephone; the offer aid in finding accommodation; they answer questions to th best of their ability in foreign languages either in person or on phon no. 171 (any time, from any place in Greece). These police are a uni que resource for the foreigner in Greece. They are not there to polic the tourist, but to assist the tourist. If you have any serious problem or complaints, start with the Tourist Police. If you need informatior ask them for it - radio taxi numbers, open pharmacies, a doctor where to ask for an airline schedule.

Tourist Police Offices in Attica:

Larissa railway Station,	821-357
Ellinikon Airport	981-0454, 981-409

Consulates

Consular activities are listed below. These services exist by agreement with the host countries and are bound by certain local regulations, as well as by orders from their home countries.

Questions regarding:
Visas and passports
Citizenship, dual nationality, national status
Military service status of dual-nationality persons
Difficulties with local regulations (Customs, the law, etc.)
Assistance with absentee voting in home country
Notarization or witnessing of documents
Assistance in case of death
Assistance with repatriation problems

Consulates are supposed to be notified in case of hospitalization of a foreigner, if the nationality of the patient is known.

In case of arrest, your consulate should be notified. In this situation, they can do very little for you. Both Greeks and foreigners are subject to the same laws in Greece. They may inform you of your rights, notify your family, register complaints and/or try to contact one of the organizations that visits prisons.

Australia 15, Messogion Ave., 775-7651
Austria 43a, 3rd September St., 884-3714
Belgium 3, Sekeri St., Kolonaki, 361-7886
Canada 4, Ioann. Gennadiou St., 723-9511
Denmark 15, Kolonaki Sq., 724-9315
Egypt 1, Zalokosta St., 361-2954
Finland 1, Eratosthenous St., Pangrati, 701-1775
France 2, Akadimias St., 361-1663-5
West Germany 3, Loukianou St., 369-4111
Great Britain 1, Ploutarchou St., Kolonaki, 723-6211
Ireland 7, Vas.Konstandinou Ave., 723-2771
Israel 1, Marathonodromon St., Pal. Psyhiko, 671-9530-1
Italy 19, Menadrou St., Ilissia, 723-9045, 724-9117
Japan 64, Vas. Sofias Ave., 723-3732
Netherlands 7, Vas. Konstandinou Ave., 723-9701
New Zealand 15-17, Tsocha St., 641-0311-5
Norway 7, Vas. Konstandinou Ave., 724-6173-4
Sweden 7, Vas. Konstandinou Ave., 722-4504
Switzerland 2, Iassiou Str., 724-9208, 723-0364
U.S.A. 91, Vas. Sofias Ave., 721-2951
Yugoslavia 25, Evrou Str., Ambelokipi, 777-4344, 777-4334
E.E.C. Press and Information: 2, Vas. Sofias Ave., 724-3982-4

Medical Emergency Telephones Athens/Piraeus

NOTE: in case of difficulty in communicating with police or any public service, call 171 (Tourist Police) 24 hours daily, for translation help.
Red Cross First Aid Station: 20, 3rd September St. (Omonia)

Ambulances

Public First Aid, Athens/Piraeus to hospitals on duty	166
Red Cross First Aid (to hospitals booked by patient)	150
U.S. Citizens contact assistance	721-2951
Accident Hospitals Always Open:	
KAT Accident Hospital, 2, Nikis St., Kifissia,	801-4411/20
Voula Hospital Asklepion, 1, Vas. Pavlou Ave.,	895-8301-5
Children: 24 hours	
Pediatric Centre of Athens	
5, Kifissias and Distomou St., Maroussi	682-0140/54
Aghia Sofia Children's Hospital	
Thivas & Mikras Asias St., Goudi	777-1611/2
Kyriakou Children's Hospital	
Thivas & Levadias St., Goudi	778-5214

If you must be admitted to hospital, your consulate can give advice on how to handle payment. Nobody will be refused treatment. "Class" in the hospital refers to the room or ward, not to the medical care, which is good, though public ward nursing and personal care is rather sketchy.

Poison control	779-3777
Blood Transfusion	821-9391
Daily Duty Rosters (In Greek)	
Doctors Sundays and Holidays, 2:00 p.m. to 7:00 a.m.	105
Hospitals	106
Pharmacies open 24 hours	107

INFOTIP: Pharmacies are usually closed weekends, but there's one open in every area. Check with your hotel, the newspapers, telephone No. 104, or the Tourist Police at phone 171 (who can translate). Every pharmacy shows a list of names and adresses of the day's roster (in Greek).

In the unlikely event of being bitten by a doubtful animal call

Rabies Centre 84, Iera Odos	346-2263, 346-2724
Or Animal Welfare Society,12, Pasteur St.,	643-5391, 644-4473
ELPA (Automobile Association)	104

International Social Services: Social workers assist with cross-national problems: 1, Sofokleous St., 9:00-2:30, 321-7758, 321-7749.

Police Emergencies

Crime

Random theft is a foreign importation, like picking pockets or 'joy-riding' in someone else's automobile. Unfortunately, a few young motor cyclists have now taken up bag snatching in the busier shopping areas but crimes of violence are usually matters of family honour and the stranger is rarely molested. Athens is one of the safest cities in the world in which to walk about at any time of the day or night. If you think someone is going to bother you, go up to them and ask for help - the tradition of hospitality towards strangers is very strong, and is usually more important than immediate gain.

EMERGENCY PHONES
(Dial 171, Tourist Police, for translation assistance if needed)
EMERGENCY NUMBER, anywhere 100

Only this central number has cars available at all hours. Local stations do not.

Fire 199 or 100	Traffic Police:	Athens	523-0111
Coast Guard 108		Piraeus	411-3832

Death

The death of a foreign citizen requires instant consultation with his/her Consulate by friends, relatives, hospital or police authorities.

Lost Property

The following may help you replace your lost or stolen property.

Report loss or theft immediately. Even if your property cannot be recovered, the record will be needed to replace documents, tickets, travellers' checks, or to claim insurance. You will need a police translation of your statement to the police into English, or the language used by the issuer of the documents.

Loss or theft of ID - Passports,etc., should be reported to the Aliens Service Bureau, 173, Alexandras Ave., 10th floor, Tel. 770-5711, Ext. 230.

Other thefts: Go in person to the local police station. Obtain a copy of your report, making sure it has a reference number. At least, get the reference number. Make sure that you have clarified whether you have suffered a loss *(apólia)* or theft *(klopi)*. Say as little as possible, since misunderstandings are easy.

It is suggested that you report the incident to your Consulate, as documents without resale value are often turned in; money, jewellery and valuables rarely are.

Leave valuables in safe place - hotel safe if appropriate. Don't carry passports in obvious places such as handbags or outside pockets.

Greeks are honest, but there are exceptions - and foreigners! Do not leave anything in an unguarded car at night, nor in an unlocked car. Don't set down belongings in a shop when you look at or try on something.

Replacement of Certain Items

Airline tickets: Report the loss/theft to the airline and request replacement. Copy of police report should be presented to the airline. Replacements can usually be issued only after the complete ticket information has been provided, and verification of your lost ticket obtained from the issuing office. Youth fare tickets: you probably will have to buy a new ticket and obtain refund at issuing office.

Credit Cards: Report loss immediately to credit card company.
AMERICAN EXPRESS, 2, Ermou St., 323-4781/9
VISA: Commercial Bank of Greece, 11, Sofokleous St., 321-0911
MASTER CHARGE/ACCESS:
National Bank of Greece, 132, El. Venizelou St., 958-9701, 952-2255
DINERS CLUB: 5, Merlin St., Athens 364-0830/9

Driving License:
U.S. citizens must obtain duplicate from issuing state before driving. Others consult your Consulate for advice.

Railway Tickets: OSE (Railway organization of Greece - may be able to issue replacement IF the number of the lost pass can be confirmed with the issuing office.

Passports: Report immediately to your Consulate, best in office hour.

Student Cards: See the International Youth Travel Service 11, Nikis St., Athens (Near Syntagma) 323-3767. You must have a valid university or college ID card.

Travellers' Checks: Issuing firms normally replace these. Depending on what proof (serial numbers, receipt from purchase, etc). you can offer, the time of replacement varies. American Express 2, Ermou St., 323-4781/9

Libraries with books in English

Most libraries are open from 9-1:30 p.m. Some are closed in August. Temporary visitors are not usually permitted to take books away.

American Hellenic Chamber of Commerce, 17, Valaoritou St., 361-8385

American Library, Hellenic-American Union 22, Massalias St.
Books, periodicals, Microfilm/fiche reader; video films, slides, records 363-7740

Benaki Museum Library (permit required) 1, Koumbari St., Reference, Greek arts and history 362-6462
British Council, Kolonaki Square: Books, periodicals, records, Reference/lending 363-3211
Children's Library, National Gardens
Evgenidou Foundation, Syngrou Avenue 941-1181
Technical and scientific books in several languages.
American School of Classical Studies 61, Souidias Str., Greece, ancient/modern: Rare books/manuscripts, works of art. 721-0536
Multi-National Women's Liberation Group 69, Mavromichali St., off Akadimias. Feminism, women's issues, health, fiction. See THE ATHENIAN for contact telephone.
National Centre of Social Research, 1, Sofokleous St., 5th Floor: Books/journals on social studies 321-2611
National Research Centre, 48, Vas. Konstandinou Ave. Scientific journals, reference only, photocopies available 722-9811
YWCA (XEN): 11, Amerikis St., Books in English/Creek 362-4291 (Cafeteria on first floor)
Polytechnion (College), Patission Street: Architecture, Engineering reference 361-1859
United Nations Information Centre 36, Amalias Ave. UN-related subjects, films, bulletins, press releases 323-4208
National Library, Panepistimiou St. Reference, manuscripts, books, periodicals, all subjects 361-4413
National Historical Ethnological Museum, Benakis Annex, Stadiou St., (Kolokotronis Sq). 322-7148
KEPE, Centre of Economics and Planning Research, 22, Ippokratous St., 362-7321-5

Motoring

ELPA: The Automobile Association

This is the Greek equivalent of the AA, RAC, AAA. The main office is at 2-4, Messogion St., Athens Tower B 779-1615
and 6, Amerikis St. near Syntagma 363-8632

The offices can give you driving maps, advice and issue international driving licenses, if you bring your own license and two photos. (see Entry Regulations, page 157) Members of Automobile Associations at home are granted the same free road help as if they were members of ELPA. Non-members can ask for the same assistance, but must join ELPA on the spot, paying a registration fee (includes a year's membership).

Road Assistance and petrol stations open (24 hours) 104

Yellow ELPA service vehicles patrol the roads during busy season, doing their best to be available. Roads, Routes, hotels reservations, free legal advice 8:00 am-3:00 pm 779-740/ 5
Tourist Information 174
Car hire, insurance, camping and road patrols 8:00 am - 3:00 pm 779-1615/9
Road Maps: ELPA at National Tourist Office 2, Amerikis St. 322-3111

There are also permanent trailer offices as follows in the Athens area:

Ano Patissia: near Elektriko Station, Patission St., 202-0667
Glyfada: Agios Konstandinos Square
Ilioupolis: Main Square, opp. Town hall 993-1840
Kesariani: Gr. Theologou St., nr. Ag. Nikolaos church
Nea Smyrni: Main Square 932-4555
Neo Faliron: Opposite Elektriko Station
Nikea: Davaki Square, Petrou Ralli St.
Paradissos: Opposite Olympic Stadium, Kifissias Ave.
Piraeus: Karaiskaki Square
Peristeri: Vas. Georgiou Ave., nr. Church of Ag. Antonios, 574-4575
Chalandri: Kennedy Square, 681-5017
Cholargos: Kiprou and Messogion Ave., behind Ministry of Communications

Traffic Laws

Drive on the right side of the road, not left.

Cars on the right have right of way in all circumstances unless otherwise indicated by signs or policeman.

Flashing lights from another car mean STAY WHERE YOU ARE, not GO AHEAD!

Fire extinguishers and red accident triangle warning are required in all cars.

Move to right for emergency vehicles - even private cars or taxis signalling emergency.

Use the "flash" - directional signals before turning.

Horns are forbidden in built-up areas. It says here.

Drive with headlights, not parking lights, at night.

Car must have safety belts. Everybody must wear safety belts in front seat.

ELPA can provide a chart of International Road Signs.

Speed Limits

Built up areas: 50 km/h   Expressways: 100 km/h
Country: 80 km/h

City Traffic restrictions

In an effort to control air pollution levels, cars may circulate in central Athens on alternate days, according to the license plate numbers, between the hours of 6:30 am and 4:00 pm on weekdays, or on days when special conditions apply (includes rental cars). Cars with foreign plates may circulate freely for the first 40 days and thereafter are subject to the same rules. Permitted license numbers are announced daily.

Parking

Extremely hard to find in central Athens. There is an underground car park in Klafthmonos Square (Stadiou street) open carparks and garages, some lots which act as carparks, a few multistories, and anywhere you can find. Parking is prohibited in streets with yellow lines, where signs indicate and on pedestrian walks (which are increasing in central Athens). Illegal parking penalties are fines, removal of license plates (20 days) and possible towing.

(To retrieve license plates: Traffic Police 38, Agiou Konstandinou St., 523-0111. Bring drivers' license, passport and money).

Fuel and Petrol *(Venzíni)* may be difficult to obtain at night or in some country areas. Safest to keep topped up. If in difficulties, call ELPA 104 for directions to the nearest open station.

In case of accident

Stop. Move only if necessary.

Emergency police number	100
Tourist Police, translation and help, any hour	171

Call policeman (and ambulance if required). Exchange names and addresses, and get those of witnesses. Make sure you get license number of other car(s), and insurance company. Report as soon as possible to your insurance company. Parties to accidents are sometimes held at police stations. Contact your consulate for advice. Say as little as possible: you may not be understood correctly.

> **INFOTIP:** Drive very carefully in rain, as the dust on Greek roads makes a dangerous slick surface. Not all railway crossings are guarded. Use extreme caution.

If car is damaged:

1. Call ELPA	104
2. Express Service	952-4950

3. Prefer representatives or authorized dealers for repairs.

Alfa Romeo 27, Lagoumidzi St., Koukaki	922-3082

Audi 570, Vouliagmenis Ave., Argiroupoli	992-2810
Autobianchi 99, Falirou St., Koukaki,	923-8635
BMW Irous St., Terma Kolokinthou,	513-0601/3
Citroen 51, Plateon St., Metaxourgio,	346-3193
Fiat 14, Lagoumidzi St., Koukaki,	325-4037-4050
Ford 108, Athinon St.,	513-5011
Lancia 99, Falirou St ., Koukaki,	923-8635
Mercedes 40, Athinon Ave.,	571-2912
Opel 276, Messogion Ave.,	653-1910
50, Kifissias Ave., Maroussi,	682-9380
Porsche 101, Tatoiou Ave.,	281-0958
Renault 30-32, Tsaldari Ave., Polygono	646-8811
Toyota 168, Kifissou & Kavalas Ave.,	590-4222/8
Volkswagen 570, Vouliagmenis Ave., Alimos	922-2810

Rental cars

There are numerous car hire firms in Athens. Most of them have offices in central Athens, Syngrou Avenue, and at the airport. Below is a partial listing:

AJAX 160, G. Lambraki St., 4118319, 4174077 Piraeus
AMBASSADOR 12, Syngrou Ave. 9238822, 9223760
ANSA INTERNATIONAL 31-33, Syngrou Ave. 9220713
APOLLO 44, Pireos St., 5247515/19, 9227584/6
ARMIKAR 119, Kallirois St., 9236703, 9220813
AUTORENT 94, Syngrou Ave., 9232514, 9238438
AVIS (Athens Office) 48, Amalias Ave. 3224951/5
East Airport terminal
Incoming Passengers Bldg 3224951/5
West Airport terminal
Incoming Passengers Bldg 3224951/5
Piraeus 71, Akti Miaouli 4520639, 4526184
BUDGET RENT A CAR 8, Syngrou Ave. 9224444, 9219555
East Airport Terminal 9613634
CONCORD RENT A CAR 40-42, Syngrou Ave. 9215267
CORFU 20, Syngrou Ave. 9230808, 9222606/7
HELLASCARS 7, Stadiou St. 9235353/9
HERTZ (Athens office) 12, Syngrou Ave. 9220102/4
East airport terminal 9613625
West airport terminal 9813701
INTERRENT/BATEK S.A. 4, Syngrou Ave. 9233452
JUST RENT A CAR 43, Syngrou Ave. 9239104, 9233389
MAP 13, Syngrou Ave. 9021647, 9223461
MINI 81, Akti Miaouli Piraeus 4523777, 4133896
PAPPAS 44, Amalias Ave. 3220087, 3226472
RETCA 20, Kallisperi St. 9224998
SPEEDO 74, Kyprou St. Glyfada 8941852
THRIFTY 24, Syngrou Ave. 9221211/3, 9216000
TOUR RENT A CAR 29, Syngrou Ave., 9229672, 9230548
VISA RENT A CAR 20, Dousmani & Metaxa St., Glyfada, 8947572

INFOTIP: Note that petrol (gas) tanks will probably NOT be filled when you take your car, or even motorcycle, so check your tank before starting off. Remember oil and windshield water as well. If you're used to automatic shift, we remind you about the choke when starting!

Major companies offer cars in mint condition, quick delivery and replacement of car in case of damage.Small companies offer good cars and better prices.

Publications in English and English Booksellers

Pamphlets are obtainable free from the Offices of the Greek National Tourist Organization. Enquiry office at National Bank of Greece, Syntagma (7 days a week).

Road maps are also available at the same place, as well as current boat schedules, and many other current information sheets.

Maps We Like:

VELLIOS map, Athens centre, Piraeus, Suburbs, Attica and Greece with street guide.

PLAKA AND THE ACROPOLIS, Poster Map, also called "Action Map and Adventure Guide" for artists and travellers.

English Language Publications

General Interest:

Athens News (daily newspaper, except Monday)	323-1384
The Athenian (monthly) General magazine: good at events	322-2802
Daily Bulletin, Athens News Agency, 20, Akadimias St.,	363-9816:
News summary, Athens Press review, shares/exchange	363-1858

Travel

Greek Travel Pages (monthly) Dimotikou Stadiou St., Kallithea 958-2612

If you think of staying on

Source Books with further information (If you don't find these books in a bookshop or kiosk, don't hesitate to ask the publisher indicated).

FOREIGN WOMEN IN GREECE, Multi-National Woman's Liberation Group.

THE NETWORK DIRECTORY FOR GREECE

A compendium of practical detailed information for foreign residents, League of Volunteers (Omilos Ethelonton) 34, Omirou St.,

SURVIVAL HANDBOOK for ATHENS

P. Efstathiadis Sons, S.A., 14, Valtetsiou St., 361-5011

Bookshops

Compendium, 28, Nikis St.,	322-6931
Book Nest (Kakoulidis) 39, Panepistimiou St., Mezzanine,	322-9560
Bookstall, Akadimias, Stoa Atrium	
Efstathiadis, 84, Akadimias St.,	363-7439
Eleftheroudakis, 4, Nikis St.,	322-9388
Kauffmann, 28, Stadiou St.,	322-2160
Kostarakis, 2, Ippokratous St., (Scientific books),	361-5926
Lexis Bookshop, Emm. Benaki 82 & Akadimias St.,	364-5823
The Newsstand, 36, Kiriazi St., Kifissia	
Pantelidis, 11, Amerikis St.,	362-3673
5, Mavrokordatou St., (Akadimias),	362-3564
Rombos, 6, Kapsali St., Kolonaki,	724-2082
Samouchos, 24, Amerikis St.,	362-4151

also at Hilton, Royal Olympic, President Hotels; Astir Beach, Glyfada; American Newsstand, Voula Beach A and B, Astir beach and Vouliagmeni beaches, Vouliagmeni; Varkiza Beach; Saronic Gate Hotel.

English books and magazines can be found at kiosks in areas frequented by foreigners - Syntagma, Glyfada, Kolonaki, Psychiko, Kifissia.

There are many shops for second-hand books, and most of them will buy them back.

Compendium (see above)
Don Sebastian, 5, Iperidou St., 322-1838
Pantelides, 11, Amerikis St., in arcade
121, Ermou St., entrance in back on Astingos
Monastiraki: Ifestou St., Normanou St ., (upstairs)

PETROL see Motoring, page 171
PHARMACIES see Help, page 168

Post Office

Post offices are open from 7.30 am to 3.00 pm, Mondays through Fridays. Post Offices at Syntagma, 100, Eolou St., (Omonia), and 60, Mitropoleos St., are open on Saturdays, also Sundays from 9 am to 1.30 pm. Stamps may sometimes be bought from hotels or kiosks.

Surface Air Lifted Parcels (10 kg.) combining long-distance air travel with short distance surface travel give a quick delivery (2-6 days) at a price which is little above the surface mail cost.

Posting boxes are yellow and black, with a hunting horn design.

Parcels: You want to mail things home. If possible get the shop to do it. Failing that, these are the alternatives:

In Athens, 4, Stadiou St., and 29, Koumoundourou St., have facilities for mailing large parcels (more than 1 kilo, 2.2. lbs) abroad.

DO NOT WRAP PARCELS! This is very important, because the contents must be checked by a Customs Inspector before the package is closed. For a fee, these post offices will wrap for you and provide boxes, paper and the etceteras. Otherwise you must bring string, wrapping paper, something to cut with and labels or your felt-tipped pen to the post office.

Small packages can be sent from local post offices, but again they will want to peek. Do not seal them. You'll be required to re-open them.

Tourist items (only) can be posted from the Customs office at 33, Nikis St., from Monday to Friday, till 1.30. They have wrapping materials.

Forwarding Agents: Freightway Express, 2, Ermou St., Syntagma. 323-6936

Post Restante: Letters can be sent Post Restante to any Post Office.

> **INFOTIP** Ask your correspondents to write surnames in capital letters.

Transalpino Tourist Agency at 28, Nikis St., also hold letters Post Restante, even for non-clients and in spite of being very busy are always pleasant and helpful.

Incoming Parcels

Parcels are not delivered, even if directed to your own address. The postman leaves a note asking you to collect. Take your passport when collecting, for identification purposes. Small packets received by letter post are subject to double duty.

Philately: Main P.O., 100, Aiolou St., or 1, Apellou St., near Omonia, 324-3211, Ext. 435

RADIO AND TELEVISION. See ENTERTAINMENT page 160

Religious Services in English

St. Andrew's Protestant Church, 66, Sina St., Rev. Calvin Gardner 652-2209

St. Paul's Anglican/Episcopal Church, Father Jeremy Peake. 323-4790, Filellinon St., opp. National Park. 721-4906, or c/o British Embassy 723-6211

St. Peter's Anglican Church at St. Catherine's British Embassy School, Kifissia, 808-3239

Roman Catholic Archbishopric of Athens, Tourist Office, 9, Omirou St., 362-6186

Church of Christ, 40, Laodikias St., Glyfada. 895-6530, 961-6813, 895-3835, English services Sunday 5:30-6:30

First Greek Evangelical Presbyterian Church, 50, Amalias St., 323-1079

Hellenic International Christian Church (Interdenominational, Charismatic) 77, Nividou St., Kifissia 692-7373

Crossroads International Christian Centre 30, Kesarias St., Ambelokipi, 770-5829, 801-7062

Trinity Church (Southern Baptist) 58, Vouliagmenis Ave., Ano Ellinikon 895-3629

Grace Baptist Church, Pastor J. Hinson, Kifissia/N.Erythrea 807-1133

Protestant Adventists Church of the Seventh Day 18, Keramikou St., 522-0896

St. Denis (Ag. Dionysiou Areopagitou) 24, Panepistimiou St., 362-3603

St. Paul Roman Catholic Church, 4, Kokkinaki St., Kifissia 801-2526
Russian Orthodox - St. Nikodimos, 21, Filellinon St., 323-1090
Mormon Church of Jesus Christ of the Latter Day Saints 15, Meandrou St., Ilissia. (Nr. Holiday Inn) 723-7183, 724-2680
Jewish (Orthodox) Beth Shalom Synagogue, 6, Melidoni St., 325-2823 (Ladino, Hebrew, Français, Greek)
First Church of Christ Scientist, 7a, Vessarianou St., 721-1520
Buddhist Society of Northern Greece, 2, Petaloudes St., Ekali 813-1200
Mosque, Roof of Caravel Hotel, Vas. Alexandrou St., 729-0731

Restaurants and Night Life

The Greek Menu

Eating Times are rather different from the West, because of the siesta hours between 2:30 and 5:00 p.m. A morning's work ends at 2:00 which is time for the midday meal. After the siesta, work continues till 8:00 or 8:30, and dinner time goes from then till very late. If attending a performance of the theatre which ends after 11:00, it is still easy to find a place to dine.

Greek food can be exquistite when properly cooked, using spices and herbs in different proportions to those of our foreign kitchens, with olive oil as the main cooking fat. Large juicy fresh fruit and vegetables are plentiful in their season, and sold loose, so they don't absorb the taste of plastic wrappings. Fresh fish, shellfish and meat are easily available and of course, Greece produces her own varieties of wines, with and without the resin taste.

Breakfast consists of bread, butter, jam *(Marmeláda)*, coffee. Occasionally someone indulges in yogurt. Greeks fend off starvation by having coffee, a cheese pie or a pastry in mid-morning. Your hotel or a nearby coffee bar may advertise a real breakfast. A few have something called *"saganáki"* - a fried mixture of eggs, sausage and cheese.

Kafé: turkish coffee served in tiny cup. *Nes:* Nescafe
In a shop where real coffee is obtainable the menu will be in English and offer American coffee, Espresso, Cappucino, etc.

Tsái: Tea
Záchari: Sugar
Gála: Milk
Avgá: Eggs
Psomí: Bread. *Psomáki*, bread rolls.
Tost: Not toast, but a toasted sandwich of cheese or ham.
Yoghurt: *Ya-oúrti*
Butter: *Voútiro:*
Sokoláta: hot cocoa (if talking about drinks).

Lunch and Dinner

Restaurants, *estiatória* in greek, usually are open for lunch and probably dinner, starting at about 11:00 a.m. These have casserole dishes - baked macaroni, baked fish, stews, roast chicken or meat, salads. They are likely to serve wine in bottles.

Tavernas, spelled *Tavérna* in greek, are often indistinguishable from restaurants in tourist districts. They move outdoors in summer time, either under trees on the square, to the sea front, or sometimes into a courtyard in the back. Here you are welcome to go to the kitchen and look at the foods prepared, and point to what you want. They may specialize in sea food or offer dozens of small plates of different delicacies, served as *Appetisers (Orektiká)*

PRONUNCIATION

Dolmádes: Those stuffed vine leaves you've heard about
Gígantes: (large beans in tomato sauce),
Dzadzíki: (yoghurt with chopped cucumber and garlic),
Melidzánes: (aubergines/Eggplants)
Kolokíthia: (courgettes/zucchini)
Kalamaráki: (fried baby squid)
Patátes: (guess!)
Taramosaláta: (a pink dip made of cod roe and potato)
Melidzanosaláta: (eggplant/aubergine chopped in dressing).

Nothing is likely be hot. See also Salads below.
Psistaría: is a place which specialize in grilled meats or meat roasted on a spit. These days they may double as pizzerias. Of course, fast foods are available as sandwiches, *"tost"* (a toasted cheese or ham sandwich), hamburgers, and similar familiar dishes, into which traditional Greek fast foods sort of infiltrate so that there seems to be a pita bread with souvlaki also available. Greek snacks include *"Tirópita"*, cheese pie, *"spanakópita"*, spinach pie, *"kreatópita"*, meat pie - a tender pastry wrapped around a filing. *"Bougátsa"* is a sweet version with custard in.

Speaking of sweets, meals are usually concluded with fruit. In some restaurants which cater to foreigners, desserts and coffee are available, but it's not Greek. Elaborate sweet pastries are dearly loved, and are eaten separately from meals, with cold water, and obtained from *"Zaharoplastía"*. Coffee, thick and sweet ,is another separate undertaking.

Most menus are written in Greek, a sort of English, and sometimes a sort of French or German as well. Fish are translated when possible, but some fish are uniquely mediterranean and have no names in English, and other are European and not familiar to Americans. Lobsters have no big claw, for instance but they are lobsters nevertheless.

Soups: *Soúpes*
Usually quite thick and filling:
Avgolémono: (chicken stock thickened with egg and lemon)
Fasoláda: (bean soup)
Psarósoupa: (fish soup)

Meats: *(Kréas)*
Lamb: *Arni´*
Lamb chops: *Payidákia*
Beef: *Moschári*
Pork: *Hirinó*
Brizóla means steak or chop: *filétto* is the filet.
Souvláki means "small skewer", and can be pork, beef, fish, lamb grilled on sticks.
Loukánika: Sausages
Keftédes: Meat Balls
Biftéki: Meat patty
Kokorétsi: grilled lamb livers, kidneys, etc., wrapped, and spiced
Sikóti: liver
Soutsoukákia: meat balls in tomato sauce

Poultry: *(Pouleriká)*
Kotópoulo: Chicken
Galopoúla: Turkey (Winter holidays only)
Pápia: Duck
Peristéri: Pigeon

Fish: *(Psári)*
Astakós: Lobster - not your economy special
Bakaliáros: cod
Barboúni: Red Mullet, expensive
Garídes: big Shrimps
Glóssa: Sole
Fagrí, Sinagri da: Sea bream
Kéfalos: grey mullet
Marídes: whitebait
Chtapódi: octopus
Kalamaráki: baby squid
Lithrínia: bass
Soupiés: cuttlefish

Casseroles:
Giuvétsi: baked meat in sauce
Stifádo: stew, often beef and onions
Moussaká: casserole of aubergine (eggplant), chopped meat, tomatoes with an egg and cheese topping
Pastítsio: baked macaroni with meat
Piláfi: boiled rice

Salads: Vegetables, cooked or raw, are listed as *"Saláta"*.

ROASTED (in oven): *Psitó*	
BARBECUED (on spit): *Sti Soúvla*	GRILLED: *Skáras*
FRIED: *Tiganitó*	BOILED: *Vrastó*
BAKED: *Stó Foúrno*	SMOKED: *Kapnistó*

"Greek salad" *(Horiátiki saláta)* consists of tomatoes, cucumbers, feta cheese, black olives. Some places may add onions, green peppers, whatever. It is often cheaper to order a tomato and cucumber salad, which will probably have some added olives, and feta separately. You also get more cheese that way.

"Hórta" is cooked greens. Some are bitter and some are sweet.

Spinach *(spanáki)* is one. *Vlita* is a delicious one. They are served with oil and lemon.

Tomato, tomato and onion, tomato and cucumber are also standard in summer. In cooler months we have:

Láchano: shredded cabbage
Maroúli: lettuce
Domáta: tomato
Arakás: peas
Fasolákia: beans
Kolokíthia: zucchini, courgettes
Kremídi: onion
Angoúri: cucumber
Anginári̇es: artichokes
Melidzánes: eggplant, aubergine
Róssiki salata is cold potato salad made with a lot of mayonnaise.

Fruits: *(Froúta)*
Mílo: apple
Achládi: pear
Ananás: pineapple
Portokáli: orange
Mandarìni, Clementína: mandarin, tangerine
Rodákino: peach
Veríkoka: apricots
Damáskina: plums
Pepóni: melon
Karpoúzi: watermelon
Stafília: grapes
Síka: figs
Lemóni: lemon

Drinks: *(Potá)*
Neró: water
Sóda: soda water
7-up, coca, pepsi
Portokaláda: orangeade
Lemonáda: sweet bottled lemonade
Vissináda: black cherry drink

Boxed and bottled fruit drinks and juice are available in shops, not often in restaurants. Low-calorie drinks are water, soda water, mineral water, low-calorie soft drinks and fruit juice.

Alcoholic Drinks: Imported drinks are expensive: locally produced wines and liquors are astonishingly inexpensive.

Bíra: Beer (lager)

Liquors: Oúzo is the Greek drink aperitif, a clear white spirit that turns cloudy when mixed with water. It tastes of anise, is not sweet, but quite strong. For this reason, when drunk in an *ouzerí* it is usually served with a large glass of ice water and accompanying mezedes, small mixed snacks which may include a bit of sausage, a small squid, toasted cheese, pickled onions, a red pepper, on a tiny plate. Imported drinks - vermouths, campari, or spirits - are available, but very expensive. Some local or off-brands are acceptable - Melrose Gin, House of Stuart or Fraser MacDonald whisky, Potts rum. Liquors are pronounced more or less same as English.

Wines: Greeks under the supervision of the god Dionysos have been making wines since prehistory. Greek wines were always stored in pine barrels sealed with resin, which gives the flavour to *Retsína.* It is sometimes put up now in bottles, but the only real way to drink retsina is from the *varéli* (barrel) and decanted into carafes for the table in 1/4, *(tétarto),* 1/2 *(misó),* or whole kilo quantities. Retsina comes in red and white, although one taverna may not have both on hand. It should not show a white cloudiness when it's settled from pouring. The taste of retsina is complementary to olive oil.

Classical references inform us that the ancients watered their wine. You may see diners doing so still: try it. Taverna wine cut with soda water is very pleasant, especially in hot weather.

There are plenty of excellent bottled non-resinated wines available as well. These are well-known labels:

White: *(áspro)* Cellar, Boutari, Amalia, Cambas Hymettus, Santa Helena, Elissar, Tsantali

Rose: *(kokkinélli)* King Minos, Cambas, Cellar, Apelia, Cimarosa, Roditis,

Red: *(kókkino)* Boutari Demestiha, Naoussa, Chevalier de Rhodes, Castel Danielis, Tsantali

Sweet: *(glikó)* Mavrodaphne, Samos

Rhodes produces a champagne better than New York's.

There are hundreds of small vineyards and types of wine that can only be found by trial and error. Cavas - wine and liquor shops - have shelves full of mysteries, many of which are treasures. As wines can still be obtained for less than $1 U.S., experiment. Cognac is produced in Greece and the well-known brands are Metaxas, Cambas and Botrys, which come in qualities from 3-star up to elaborately packaged 12-star.

Sweets: the *"Galaktopolío"* offers milk, yoghurt, custards and puddings, coffee, and pastries, and may be where to look for breakfast.

Pasta is not spaghetti, but wicked sticky sweet things, sold in a *"Zaharoplastíon"*. Many of these have tables and offer drinks, coffee and pastries, and often ice cream. You may find the tables across the street. Of course, they sell their cream cakes and *"pástes"* in boxes to take out as well.

Pásta - choose by pointing: may be chocolate covered layers, custard filled, or any variation fo this type.

Galaktoboúreko: a semolina-stiffened milk custard in pastry
Baklavá: Pastry rolled around a mixture of nuts and honey
Kataífi: looks like shredded wheat, rolled around nuts and honey
Ravaní: A plain cake, soaked in lemon and honey with a tart quince topping, a little less sweet than the others Seasonally: Easter and Christmas; *Tsouréki,* a sweet bread just like Challah.

Christmas: *Melomakárona,* a spice cookie, soaked in sweetness *Kourambiédes,* almond cookie, dusted in powdered sugar.Summer: *Pa-go-tó* , Ice Cream: *Vaníllia, Sokoláta, Frá-oula* (strawberry), *Fistiki* (pistachio), *Parfait* (extra rich ice cream).

INFOTIP Greeks dance. In tavernas too, and often invite customers to join in a circle dance. Accept! it's fun. Everybody is used to visitors not knowing the steps, which are not difficult.

Greek and International Guisine

Apokalipsis (Astir Palace Hotel): Syntagma Sq. Tel. 3643112. Elegant surroundings. Poseidon steak, veal mignonettes, live dinner music.

Blue Pine: 37, Tsaldari St. KIFISSIA Tel. 8012969. Country club atmosphere. Baked crab, spagetti diabolo. Closed Sunday.

Dionysos: 43, Rovertou Gali St. ACROPOLIS Tel. 9233182. Restaurant, pastry shop. "Lois" fillet of sole, "Vine Grower" baby lamb.

Dioskouri: 16, Dimitriou Vasiliou St. NEO PSYCHICO Tel. 6713997. Beef stamnas, wine lover's meze. Closed Sunday.

Four Seasons (Chandris Hotel): 385, Syngrou Ave. Tel. 9414825. Menu a la carte, drinks live music.

G.B. Corner (Grande Bretagne Hotel): Syntagma sq. Tel. 3230251-61. Steak, sea food and Greek specialities.

Gerofinikas: 10, Pindarou St. KOLONAKI Tel. 3622719. Greek and Oriental cuisine, cosmopolitan atmosphere. Lamb aubergine, lamb fricasse.

Grand Balcon (St. George Lykabettus Hotel): 2, Kleomenous St. KOLONAKI Tel.7290712. Shrimp caprice du chef. Orchestra.

Ideal: 46, Panepistimiou St. Tel. 3614604. Stereo music, open for lunch.

Je Reviens: 49, Xenokratous St. Tel. 7211174. Turnedos, Coq au vin.

La Taverna (Athenaeum Inter-Continental Hotel): 89-93 Syngrou Ave. Tel. 9023666. Greek-Cypriot hors d'oeuvres, guitar, bouzouki.

Magemenos Avlos: 4, Kalevkou & Aminda St. PANGRATI Tel. 7223195. Snacks, full meals, sweets and ice creams. Open all day.

Milton's: 91, Adrianou St. PLAKA Tel. 3249129. Charming island atmosphere. Sea food and steaks.

Mostrou: 22, Mnisikleous St. PLAKA Tel. 3225337. Greek cuisine, orchestra. Closed Sunday.

Myrtia: 35, M. Mousourou St. Tel. 7012276. Lamb in lemon sauce. Garden. Closed Sunday.

Paezano: 16, F. Negri St. Tel. 8224324. Kofta (Arabic meat balls), mixed grill, poutaneska. Open up all night.

Ta Nissia (Hilton Hotel): 46, Vas. Sofias Ave. Tel. 7220201-11. International cuisine.

Vladimiros: 12, Aristodimou St. Tel. 7217407. Hounkiar beyendi, borch, russian cuisine. Piano and songs. Bar. Garden.

Vrachos: 101, Adrianou St. PLAKA Tel. 3247252. Greek cuisine. Orchestra. Terrace.

Ziller's: 1, Akti Kountouriotou KASTELLA PIRAEUS Tel. 4132636. Tastefully decorated with nice cuisine. Shrimp caprice du chef. Overlooks the sea. Verandah.

ARABIC CUISINE

Ali Baba: 13, Poseidonos Ave. GLYFADA Tel. 9830435 Arabic and Lebanese cuisine. Floor show.

CHINESE CUISINE

Golden Dragon: 132, Syngrou Ave. Tel. 9232315. Rice crackers with shrimp.

Pagoda: 3, Alexandras Ave. & 2, Bousgou St. PEDION AREOS Tel. 6431990. Chicken with almonds and bamboo shoots.

Red Dragon: 12, Zirini St. KIFISSIA Tel. 8017034. Whole shrimps with Malesian sauce.

FRENCH CUISINE

Bagatelle: 9, Ventiri St. Tel. 7218893. Lobster, fillet of sole. Closed Sunday.

L'Abrevoire: 51, Xenokratous St. KOLONAKI Tel. 7229061. Coq au vin, cafe de Paris.

La Brasserie des Arts (N.J.V. Meridien Hotel): Syntagma Sq. ATHENS Tel. 3255301. Staffed quail, fillet of sole.

La Rotisserie (Athenaeum Inter-Continetal Hotel): 89-93 Syngrou Ave. ATHENS Tel. 9023666. Shell-fish and shrimp marinated in oil and lemon. Closed Sunday.

GERMAN CUISINE

Alt Berlin: 35, Kolokotroni St. KIFISSIA Tel. 8010436. Saddle of beef, cafe Grossenwahn.

INDIAN CUISINE

Taj Mahal: 5, Syngrou Ave. Tel. 9222278. "Moghul", tandouri. Closed Sunday.

ITALIAN CUISINE

Al Tartufo: 65, Poseidonos Ave. P. FALIRO Tel. 9826560. Rigatoni al Tartufo, scallopine Venetziana.

Da Walter: 7, Evzonon St. KOLONAKI Tel. 7248726. Rigatoni four cheese, fillet piedmontaise.

L'Arcobaleno: 14, Nap. Zerva St. GLYFADA Tel. 8942564 Rigatoni L'Arcobaleno.

La Bussola: 26, Adrianou St. KIFISSIA Tel. 8083912. Large selection of specialities.

JAPANESE CUISINE

Kyoto: 5, Garivaldi St. PHILOPAPOU Tel. 9232047. Tempura, seshimi. Closed Sunday.

Michiko: 27, Kidathineon St. PLAKA Tel. 3220980. Sukiyaki, tempura. Closed Sunday.

POLYNESIAN CUISINE

Kona Kaï (Ledra Marriot Hotel): 113-115, Syngrou Ave. Tel. 9225211. Polynesian, Chinese and Japanese specialities. Closed Sunday.

FISH AND SEA FOOD RESTAURANTS

Aglamair: 52-54, Akti Koumoundourou PIRAEUS Tel. 4115511. Kakavia (fish soup).

Antonopoulos: 1, Friderikis St. GLYFADA Tel. 8945636 Old and comfortable restaurant, extensive sea-food menu.

Ahilio: 134, Akti Themistokleous Piraïki PIRAEUS Tel. 4516346. Fish, shrimp saganaki.

I Psarofili: Lemos VOULIAGMENI Tel. 8961887. Red mullet, gopes, maridaki (smelt).

Kaplanis: Mikrolimano PIRAEUS Tel. 4111623. Fish baked in pepper, lobster thermidor.

Psaropoulos: 2, Kalamon St. GLYFADA COAST Tel. 8945677. One of the oldest sea food restaurants, on the marina. Fresh fish, squid.

TAVERNAS AND KOUTOUKIA

Anatolitiko Saloni: 158, Marathonos Ave. GERAKAS Tel. 6610068. Ox-tail soup, Anatolian beef patties. Garden

Apostolis: 11, Gortinias St. KIFISSIA Tel. 8011989. Wine mezes, sweetbread pies. Garden.

Bakaliarakia: 41, Kidathineon St. PLAKA Tel. 3225084. Bakaliaros, souvlaki.

Epistrofi: 276, Akti Themistokleous PIRAEUS Tel. 4182524. Fricasse, dolmades. Garden. Glosed Sunday.

Ipokambos: 23, Kekropos St. GLYFADA Tel. 8943664. Spinach crepes, cheese pie sfoliata. Garden. Closed Sunday.

Greek House: 7, Garivaldi St. ACROPOLIS Tel. 9515256. Moussaka, baked tiropitta (cheese pie). Garden.

Kaliva: 60, Vas. Pavlou St. Kastela PIRAEUS Tel. 4122593. Kokoretsi, Kid on the spit. Verandah.

Klimataria: 5, Klepsidras St. PLAKA Tel. 3241809. Roast beef. Guitar trio. Garden. Closed Monday.

Lambros: Opposite lake VOULIAGMENIS Tel. 8960144. Grilled meat, shrimp salad.

Palia Taverna Kritikou: 24, Mnisikleous St. PLAKA Tel. 3222809. Beef stamnas, "wine lover's" mezes. Guitar. Terrace. Closed Wednesday.

Pini & Lini: Agnanton & Pramanton St. PHILOPAPPOU Tel. 9216247. Gigandes (beans), kokoretsi.

Socrates Prison: 20, Mitseon St. MAKRIGIANI Tel. 9223434. Baked lamb with mushrooms. Closed Sunday.

Strofi: 25, Rovertou Gali & Propyleon St. ACROPOLIS Tel. 9314130. Stifado, kid in oil and oregano. Terrace.

Ta Kanaria: 224, Ethn. Antistaseos St. KESARIANI Tel. 7219321. Crayfish, grilled octopus.

Theofilos: 1a, Vakhou St. PLAKA Tel. 3223901. Baked keftedes, "the drinker's flute". Guitar. Closed Sunday.

To Balkoni tou Imitou: 11, P. Mela St. KAREA TERMINAL Tel. 7640240-7655908

Xynos: 4, Angelou Geronda St. PLAKA Tel. 3221065. Old Plaka taverna. Barrel wine. Guitar. Closed Sunday.

TAVERNAS WITH VARIETY SHOW

Babis: 26, Othonos St. KIFISSIA Tel. 8013926. Closed T.esday.

Dionysos: 7, Lisiou St. PLAKA Tel. 3227589. Terrace.

OYZERIES

Apotsos: 10, Panepistimiou St. ATHENS Tel. 3637046. Probably the oldest ouzerie in Athens.

Dihti: 1, Thermopilon St. Agias Varvaras Sq. P. FALIRO Tel. 9813566. Shrimp saganaki, meat and fish charcoal grilled.

Salamandra: 3, Mantzarou St. KOLONAKI Tel. 3642990. Octopus with oregano, shrimp Mykonos style.

BISTROT

Ambassador: 29, Michalakopoulou St. ILISSIA Tel. 7239747. International cuisine.

Different: 10, Falirou St. MAKRIGIANI Tel. 3249660

Ploughman: 26, Iridanou St. ILISSIA Tel. 7212044. Dartboard. English cooking. Closed Sunday.

PIANO BARS

Byron Bar (Caravel Hotel): 2, Vas. Alexandrou Ave. Tel. 7290721.

Kava (Athenaeum Inter-Continental Hotel): 89-93 Syngrou Ave. Tel. 9023666.

Star Bar (Holiday Inn Hotel): 50, Michalakopoulou St. ILISSIA Tel. 7248322.

DANCING-DISCOES

Aerobic: 137, Syngrou Ave. Tel. 9739032 Disco music, New Wave.

Aftokinisi (Dilina): 5th bus stop ELLINIKON Tel. 8945444.

Barbarella: 253, Syngrou Ave. ATHENS Tel. 9425601. Disco music, New Wave.

Horis Onoma: Rodeo KALAMAKI Tel. 9823838. Disco music, New Wave.

Prison 1: Beach GNTO VOULA Tel. 8952403.

35th Music Force (Stork-Make Up): AGIOS KOSMAS Tel. 9829865.

MUSIC HALLS

Neraida: 2, Vas Georgiou St. KALAMAKI Tel. 9812004.

Fantasia: ELLINIKO Tel. 9820300.

BOITES

Apanemia: 4, Tholou St. PLAKA Tel. 3225482.

Esperides: 6, Tholou St. PLAKA Tel. 3248580. Closed August.

CABARETS

Maxim: 6, Othonos St. SYNTAGMA Sq. Tel. 3234831. «Show» dancing, stript tease. Closed Sunday.

Roxy: 118, Syngrou Ave. Tel. 9218174. Modern floor show, famous ballets and sexy girls.

BOUZOUKIA

Athena: 165, Syngrou Ave. Tel. 9343485. Closed Sunday.

Ifigenia: 201, Syngrou Ave. Tel. 9349444. Closed Wednesday.

La Cite: DZIDZIFIES Tel. 9423028.

CREPERIES

Domi Et Silaude: 4, Panopis St. GLYFADA Tel. 8943190. Sweet and salty crepes, salads. Garden. Closed Monday.

Rive Gauche: 252, Kifissias Ave. KIFISSIA Tel. 8012871. Chocolate, banana flame.

DRUGSTORES

Drugstore: Korai Arcade, Klafthmonos Sq. ATHENS Tel. 3226464 - 3221890.

Solonos and Massalias: Opposite Law school of ATHENS Tel. 3641794.

VEGETARIAN RESTAURANTS

Eden: 3, Flessa St. PLAKA Tel. 3248858.

ICE CREAM PARLOURS

Alaska: Kefalari Sq. KIFISSIA Tel. 8011485. Baked Alaska, Hawaian pineapple ice-cream.

Edelweiss: Kolokotroni & Filadelfias St. KIFISSIA Tel. 8015031. Ice-cream in tropical flavors, tropicana tart.

Floca: 118, Kifissias Ave, GIROKOMIO Tel. 6914001. Kilimantzaro ice-cream, tarts.

Papagalo: 73, Poseidonos Ave. EDEM Tel. 9833728. Ice-cream Martinique, ice-cream Felicita.

COFFEE SHOPS - TEA ROOMS

Aithrion Coffee Corner: Atrium Shopping Center, Harilaou Trikoupi St. (between Acadimias and Panepistimiou St.).

Filomousa: 1, Filomousou Eterias Sq. PLAKA Tel. 3222293. Cold plate, tea.

Koperti: 46, Sina & Skoufa St. KOLONAKI Tel. 3637194. Natural juices, ice-cream.

Lotos: 14, Glafkou St. NEO PSYCHICO Tel. 6717461. Dinner and sweet crepes, chinese tea.

Orea Ellada: 36, Pandrosou St. MONASTIRAKI.

CAFES WITH FLOOR SHOW

Aigli: Alsos ZAPPION Tel. 3238950.

Alsos: PEDION AREOS Tel. 8212271.

Shopping

When shopping for souvenirs or for presents you will find yourself spoiled - there is so much to choose from and the quality is high. Remember that you can buy much here that is unique to Greece, or that is of exceptionally high quality, and look especially for these. The following descriptions may help you with your shopping.

Antiquities/Antiques

Naturally enough it is no longer possible to pack up a four thousand years old statue and walk off with it, even for cash. As for the smaller items, if every tourist who falls in love with Greece were permitted to walk off with even a tiny fragment as a memento there would soon be nothing left. But those who appreciate beauty of form can choose from a storehouse of reproductions from every era.

For the most part they are handcrafted with care and are a joy to own, but shop around for the best quality and prices. The National Museum has carefully detailed copies of the museum originals at very reasonable prices. If you prefer to buy from the tourist shops in Plaka and elsewhere you will enjoy shopping around and can even make substantial savings with a little bargaining.

In Plaka also are little shops selling a variety of memorabilia from the less distant past - old post cards, books, maps, boxes, art deco, gramophone records, a pair of co-respondent's shoes... Another happy hunting ground for this type of bygone is the Sunday morning flea market - but you may have to inspect an awful lot of junk to find a treasure!

Permission must be obtained for the export of any kind of antique. Apply to the Antique Dealers and Private Collections section of the Archeological Service at 13 Polygnotou Street.

If posting, remember all parcels must be able to be opened for inspection.

INFOTIP: Antiques, reproductions and any other tourist items, even flokati rugs, can be posted from the Customs Office at 33 Nikis St. (mornings only). This is a little known office, and it is often possible to get served very quickly. Wrapping materials are on sale.

Ceramics

Among the city's earliest known exports were ceramics, the most popular being the beautiful black glazed ware, which became so famous that it was extensively occupied even in ancient times. The examples to be found in the Museums are reproduced in modern factories today, and the decorative style is used on pottery ware of more humble and familiar shapes. As well as exact replicas of ancient vases and jugs, it is possible to buy boxed sets of cups and saucers with coffee or tea-pot, cream jug and sugar bowl. But if you prefer to gaze every day at a style which was in use when the Athenians were marvelling at Perikles' newly-built Parthenon, ask for the museum copies. If you are offered an ashtray - try another shop!

There are also copies of unglazed stoneware, hand-painted with scenes of heroic deeds or with pictures of the everyday lives of the Gods and heroes. Often painted on the premises, the same pictures are to be found everywhere; but the quality of the reproductions varies enormously, some painted freehand and some stamped with the design and painted over. Prices do not always reflect the quality. Shop around.

INFOTIP These brown clay plates are not dishwasher proof, the colours are not baked on and will run, even with hand washing. Use for decorative purposes only, dusting lightly from time to time.

Clothing

Greek dresses and skirts are always a popular buy for holiday wear and again there is a wide choice, along with shirts, jackets and knitwear. Plaka has plenty of shops catering for both men and women, the latter being concentrated in the Monastiraki area. Be careful about sizes, the numbers are not the ones you are familiar with and a numbered garment from one manufacturer will not necessarily be the same size as that from another.

> **INFOTIP:** If buying fabric, allow about 15% for shrinkage, and wash before making up. Be especially careful when washing colours.

Costumes

Recently opened in the centre of Plaka is the studio of two brothers who carry on the family trade of costume makers - as demand in the village has declined they have turned their skills to the costuming of Evzone solders and ethnic dance groups. If, like Lord Byron, you fancy yourself in the exotic dress of a handsome Palikari (swashbuckling hero) you will find a studio in a Regency house in Filomousou Square.

Costume Dolls

Dolls dressed in the colourful and elaborate Greek costumes are deservedly popular. The traditional Evzone kilt; the wide baggy blue trousers, black boots, waistcoast and fringed headcovering of the Cretan, and the magnificent heavy wool cape of the shepherd make handsome adornments for the male figures - and the female ones are just as varied and colourful. They are made in different workshops so shop around for your own favourites.

Fabrics

Some of the most sought after items of Greek craftsmanship are the woven fabrics which, like the costumes, vary from village to village and from island to island in their traditional colours and designs. Mykonos, Arahova (near Delphi), and Olympia are among the most famous centres for weaving. In Plaka you can buy woven covers, rugs and bags which originate from all these places.

Flokati

Simple, plain, unadorned - luxury!

Traditional flokati rugs from Trikala, with their long fluffy strands of pure wool are beautiful enough to adorn the most exclusive home (as many do), not at all expensive and surprisingly easy to clean. Of pure natural colour wool - off - white, brown or grey, or dyed sunshine bright, traditional patterns involve the subtle use of three colours together, the best rugs have long strands, closely laid.

There are a number of shops in Athens which specialise in flokati and who can be relied upon for quality and value and who will be pleased to give you a written guarantee of quality.

"It is not always true that one can get a better buy in Trikala simply because flokati are made there...", says "The Complete Handbook of Flokati and Carpet Making" by Don Sebastian. A book for the would-be purchaser or the proud owner who wishes to keep a flokati in mint condition with the least possible effort, it contains hilarious cartoons and fascinating information on the making of flokates, from the sheep's back to the bottom of the swirling waterfalls of northern Greece where the rugs are" ...tossed and twirled until they are transformed from masses of coarse beige string into luxurious carpets thick as the fur of a polar bear, shaggy as a sheep dog, soft as a cloud, and beautiful as a baby's smile!

Furs

The fur trade is centuries old and began in northern Greece where the winters are much colder and warm clothing essential. Garments of all qualities are now made by expert furriers. High quality coats, capes, stoles and hats at very reasonable prices are always popular with fashion-conscious Athenians and tourists alike.

The skill of Greek furriers is such that pelts are now imported from many parts of the world, dressed, dyed, matched, cut and sewn here and re-exported. An export trade started after the war now exceeds an annual value of seventy-five million dollars.

Garments designed and commissioned by the top couturiers, and made from the very finest pelts, appear in international collections under exclusive labels - but of course high quality furs bought here in Athens cost much less!

Honey

Honey, famous since ancient times, comes from the mountains covered with herbs, including the wild thyme which gives its own distinct flavour. In fact thyme honey is some of the best one can buy - and consequently is usually a little more expensive.

Honey is used everywhere in Greece, eaten with the ever-popular yoghurt (made from ewes, goats or cows milk) and used lavishly in the production of confectionery.

Thyme *(thimari)*, flower *(anthomelo)*, and orange-blossom *(portocali)*, and sometimes heather (riki) honey direct from the apiarists is for sale at shops in Sofokleous by the main meat market.

Icons

The painting of icons - religious pictures of the saints - is still a flourishing art.

Many reproductions are made from printed paper, glued to wood panels and treated to look antique. These are very cleverly made and make a beautiful and inexpensive wall-hanging.

Church-supply firms near the Mitropoleos have much to offer. Naturally enough the export of antique icons is no longer permitted.

Jewellery , Silver and Gold

From copies of jewellery made by the craftsmen of old to the most modern designs there is an infinite variety of exquisite trinkets from which to choose. To stroll from shop to shop in Pandrossou, Plaka, Perikleous, near Syntagma, or Voukourestiou in up-market Kolonaki is to be dazzled by the reflection of the sun in countless fine gold chains, rings, ear-rings and necklaces of the finest and most original workmanship. The elaborate silver filigree is well-known in Europe and the Middle East. Here in Greece the production of jewellery is still in the hands of families of proud craftsmen whose skilled fingers have wrought fine work to new themes and old for many generations. Designs based on Mycenean or Byzantine jewellery are very popular with customers who are looking for something uniquely Greek.

Top Greek jewellers now have branches in all the worlds major cities, but here is a chance to buy at prices not available elsewhere.

Chains are sold by weight according to the quality of the gold used in their manufacture.

Leather Items

Leather working is another ancient craft which is equally popular today. Most visitors buy a bag or purse and almost everyone buys a pair of sandals. There are soft dyed leathers too, made up into jackets, jerkins and skirts by leather craftsmen who usually sell what they make on the premises and who will be pleased to make clothes to your measure.

The leather soled, strapped sandals, of simple but strong construction have not changed in style throughout the eons though recently a rubber sole has been added to some models. Be quite sure when buying that you have a good snug fit. There can be few things more uncomfortable to wear than a sloppy sandal. The better shops will adjust the sandal to your foot. If you are not entirely happy ignore the shopkeepers assurance that the fit is perfect, that loose sandals are more comfortable, that it improves with wear - it won't. What will happen is that the leather will stretch a little and the loose sandal will become sloppy and uncomfortable. Try another pair or, if you are not satisfied, go to another shop.

Marble, Onyx, Alabaster

Marble quarried locally is readily available in Athens. Thousands of years have not exhausted the supply and it is used for staircases, wall panelling, paving and even kitchen sinks. It is of statues that we think first in relation to this durable stone and they are still made, but the labour that goes into even the smallest item makes it expensive. The fine art buyer knows the market and is prepared to pay the cost. For the tourist who seeks a small memento, the use of fine marble dust compressed into moulds makes it possible to produce cheap bookshelf-sized copies of famous statues which fit more easily into a suitcase than would the Venus de Milo.

Semi-translucent Onyx is also popular. Some pieces are made of powdered alabaster, a little cheaper but poor value. Look for the fine graining and shining surface of the real thing.

Metalware

Monastiraki is the centuries-old home of metalworkers. Iron, copper and tin hollow ware, bronze statues or coffee grinders are to be found here. Some of the most popular buys here are the enamelled wares. Spring clips and bottle openers are inexpensive, come in many designs and make attractive gifts.

Many of the shops are now only retailers but there are craftsmen here too - wander round during the week and you will hear the sound of hammers on metal in the many tiny workshops still surviving in between the trendy tourist shops. Toolshops sell rough locally made hammers along with the most sophisticated equipment. Across Ermou street in Psiri, the smiths carry on their trade beside brushmakers and other small tradespeople.

Olives, Nuts & Fruit

In the area round the fruit market in Athinas are tiny shops selling olives, almonds, pistachio, walnuts, sultanas, raisins, currants, dried apricots, dates and figs, rice, beans and grains "hima" (from the barrel). Take a stroll round, if only to see how local produce was probably sold in your own town a century ago...

Post Cards

In addition to the many views and vignettes available on ordinary post cards there are now two series which are a little different - one is a series of silhouettes of buildings such as the Parthenon or the Paraportiani church and windmills of Mykonos, with coloured envelopes as a background for the simple white outlines of churches and temples - the other is a series of cut-outs of model houses and tavernas. The houses are from various parts of Greece and the more elaborate ones have balconies, turrets and arches framed with flowers.

Wine

Hundreds of islands with a variety of different soils and rocks all produce relatively small quantities of wine, some of them superb. Some of the oldest pottery jars in existence were made for wine storage, and wine was transported in them to all parts of the Middle East. Special pottery containers were also made for mixing wine with water. Today people often order soda or even commercial mineral waters to add to their wine.

If this is a first visit you are in for some pleasant surprises. You may find one or two favourites to add to your shopping list.

Folk Art and Crafts

There are a number of organisations devoted to encouraging the preservation of traditional crafts.

The Benaki Museum, Vas. Sophias/Koumbari St., has its own shop with a wide choice of Greek handicrafts and art items.

The Centre of Hellenic Tradition, at 36 Pandrossou St., Plaka, has many traditional items, and a pleasant snack bar.

The Greek Women's Institution at 13 Voukourestiou St. offers silk embroideries on linen, embroidered cushions and woven bags.

The Lyceum of Greek Women at 17 Dimokritou St., (off Akadimias), has ceramics, jewellery, embroideries and fabrics from stock or to order. The National Welfare Organisation has shops at 24a Voukourestiou St., Kolonaki, and elsewhere.

The XAN (YWCA) shop in Amerikis, offers exquisite embroideries and a selection of greetings cards.

Where to shop

Many shopping areas are mentioned in the sightseeing section, but for a quick reference the following central areas are of special interest.

Plaka/Monastiraki

All the items mentioned above, and many more, can be bought there and, surprisingly, often at better prices than anywhere else in Athens - or even other parts of Greece. If you are making a stop in Athens before departing for the islands, window shop for your presents and souvenirs first and note the prices. You will almost certainly return here to buy.

Monastiraki

An extension of Plaka and with many similar shops, but best known for its Sunday Flea Market.

> **INFOTIP:** In Plaka and Monastiraki, try a little bergaining. It's good fun, quite acceptable and ~~a normal~~ part of the transaction in many shops.

Ermou Street

Ermou, from Syntagma to Monastiraki, is a shopping street where Athenians buy clothes, shoes and furs. Perikleous, running parallel, houses many tiny jewellers shops. Further down are shops selling underwear, wool, embroideries, buttons and buckles. This is also part of the old city and the streets of Evangelistrias and Agiou Markou have been paved for the convenience of shoppers. This is true of many areas as the city puts into effect extensive plans for brightening up the city, with lots of greenery around and plenty of seats for the footweary.

Shopping hours

Shopping hours in Athens are interrupted by the siesta, as most Athenians sleep during the hot afternoons. Shop hours vary from trade to trade but most open around 8 am. On Mondays, Wednesdays and Saturdays they close at 2.30 for the day while on Tuesdays, Thursdays and Fridays they close an hour earlier but open again at 5 (summer 5.30) till 8 o'clock or 8.30 in the evening.

Pharmacies are closed on Saturdays. (see HELP)

Shops catering to tourists are the exception and stay open all day, Sundays included, especially in Plaka and in the coastal resorts such as Glyfada.

In some shops it is necessary to obtain a bill for goods and pay for them at the cash desk, returning to the assistant or to a collection counter to exchange the receipted bill for the goods. This is slow and tedious, especially as there is often no proper system of priority except that of sharpest elbows, first served. Again, service in tourist shops in usually quick and helpful.

NOTE: If you decide to return something purchased, the shop will exchange it but will be unable to give a cash refund.

Sports and Athletics

General Secretariat for Athletics
Ministry of the Presidency 323-8025

For information about local sports clubs training facilities and sports events contact the following:

Air Sports
National Air Club of Greece 27, Akadimias St., 361-7242
Athens Aero Club 27a, Akadimias St., 361-6205
Piraeus Air Club, 8, Kaningos St., Piraeus, 411-0120

Athletics
Panellinios Athletic Association Evelpidon & Mavromataion St. 823-3720

Basketball
EOK Basketball Federation 30, Averof & Aharnon St. 822-4125, 822-4131

Bathing: see Water Sports

Bowling
Blanos Bowling 239, Vouliagmenis Ave., 971-4036

81, Vas. Georgiou, Glyfada, 893-2322
Bowling Center Kastella, Piraeus
Holiday Inn Bowling Alley 50, Michalakopoulou St., 724-8322-9
Bowling Center Shopping Land, Kifissia, 808-4662

Bridge
Federation of Bridge Clubs 6, Evripidou St., (4th floor) 321-0490

Camping: see Part III

Chess
National Chess Federation 38, Kapodistriou St., 522-4712, 522-2069

Cycling
Greek Cycling Federation 123, Liosion St., 883-1414

Diving: see Water Sports

Excursion: See Hiking, Mountainering

Fencing
Greek Fencing Organization 57, Akadimias St., (6th floor), 361-4197

Fishing
Piraeus, Akti Moutsopoulou, small craft are rented for fishing.
Amateur Anglers & Maritime Sports Club, Zea, Piraeus. 451-5731
Piraeus Central Harbormaster's Office for information. 451-1131
Boats and tackle can be rented in coastal villages

Golf
Glyfada golf Club, Nr. Eastern Airport 894-6820
Hellenic Golf Club, Varibombi, nr. Kifissia

Gymnastics
Association of Greek Gymnastics Clubs (SEGAS), 137, Syngrou Ave., 958-9415/7

Hiking
Greek Federation of Excursion Clubs 4, Dragatsaniou St., 323-4107
Ipethrios Zoi (Outdoor Life) 9, Vas. Sofias Ave., 361-5779

Hunting
Hunting Confederation, 2, Korai St., 323-2616 for information on rules and locations. Small game hunting is popular in Greece. Licenses from Department of Forestry of the Ministry of Agriculture. Aiolou 104 St. Athens. Written application and two photographs needed.

Ice Skating
Dance on Ice 127, Vouliagmenis & 34, Karpou St.
Athens Ice Skating 20, Sokratous St., Vari, 895-9356
"Skate", Samou & Karkavitsa St., Halandri, (ice and roller)

Jogging
Hash House Harriers, men and women Check listing in THE ATHENIAN magazine or inquire at U.S. Embassy Annex, ECLO office, 646-1211

Judo/Karate/Tae Kwon Do/etc.
Contact SEGAS, 137 Syngrou Ave., 935-9302, 925-9346

Mountaineering
Hellenic Mountaineering Federation 7, Karageorgi Servias St., 323-4555
Hellenic Alpine Club 52, Ermou St., 321-2429
Greek Touring Club 12, Polytechniou St., 524-8601
Federation of Excursion Clubs, 4, Dragatsaniou St., 323-4107

INFOTIP: Hiking and Mountaineering in dramatic scenery can be dangerous. Carry with you a method of signalling your location in case of accident. It is not sensible to wander through mountain gorges alone.

Horseback Riding
Hellenic Riding Club 18, Paradisou St., Maroussi, 681-2506 (call after 5 p.m.)
Athens Riding Club Gerakas, Agia Paraskevi, 661-1088
Tatoi Riding Club, Varibombi 801-4513
Attikos Riding Club, Ekali, 813-5576
Varibombi Riding Club Varibombi 801-9912
Kefallari Riding School, 53, Xenias St. Kifissia,

Racing
Faliron Race Course (Hippodrome) Sea end of Syngrou Ave. 941-7761 Mondays, Wednesdays and Saturdays, 2:30 p.m.
Roller-Skating
Athens Skating Club 20, Sokratous St., Vari, 895-9356
Blue Lake, 166, Karamanli Ave., towards Parnitha, 246-0106 (swimming pool, roller skating, playground)
Blanos Roller Skating and Bowling 81, Vas. Georgiou Ave., Glyfada, Square, 893-2322
Rodeo Amusement Park, Kalamaki (outdoor)
Skiing
Hellenic Skiing Federation 7, Karageorgi Servias St., 343-3455
Athens Ski Club 51, Sarantapihou St., 643-3368
Ski Centers:
Mt Parnassus: 27 km from Arahova and 17 km from Amfiklia. (Very complete establishment).
For Skiing accomodation prices, or instruction, EOT (Greek National Tourist Organization) Parnassos 0267-316-92, 0234-226-93-4
Soccer
Hellenic Soccer Federation 137, Syngrou Ave., 933-4922 (advance tickets for games: also sold at little yellow kiosks labeled ΔΗΜΟΣ ΑΘΗΝΩΝ.
Table Tennis
Greek Table Tennis Federation 12, Ag. Konstandinou St., 522-5879, 522-7103
Agios Kosmas Sports Centre Opp. Olympic Airways Airport, 9 81-5572
Peace and Friendship Stadium, Faliron, 412-4024
See also YMCA (XAN) 18, Akadimias St., 362-6970, YMCA (XAN) 1, Tatoiou Ave., Kifissia, 801-1610
Tennis
Greek Tennis Federation, 89, Patission St., 821-0478
Agios Kosmas Sports Center 981-1040, 981-5572
Milon Athletic Club, A. Korai/Vas. Megalou, Nea Smyrni, 933-1228
Panellinios Athletics Assn. 2, Evelpidon St., 823-3720
Glyfada Athletic Center, (opp. Glyfada Town Hall)
Hobby Center 14th km - Marathon H'way, 10, Imathias St., Geraka, 661-0406
Courts at public beaches (near Athens) Alipedou Voula A, 895-3248-9
Alipedou Voula B 895-9590, 895-9596
Vouliagmeni 896-0906-7
Varkiza 897-2102
Track and Field
National Athletic Club 6, Vas. Olgas Ave., (Zappion), 923-1039
Volleyball
Agios Kosmas Athletic Centre Opp. Olympic Airport 981-5579
Pan-Hellenic Athletic Association, 2, Evelpidon St., 823-3720
YMCA (XAN) 1, Tatoiou Ave., Kifissia, 801-1610
Astir Beach, Glyfada 894-6461
Voula B Beach 895-9590
Volleyball Federation 11, Lepesi St., Makrigiani, 922-2137
Water Sports
BOATS
Rowing:
Greek Rowing Federation 34, Voukourestiou St., 361-2109
Ereton Club, Passalimani, 542-1424
Naval Athletic Association Akti Koumoundourou, Piraeus, 417-4395
Sailing:
Hellenic Yachting Federation 15a, Xenofondos St., 323-6813
Open Sea Sailing Club Papadiamanti St., Mikrolimano, 412-3357
Yacht Club of Greece Mikrolimano, Piraeus, 417-9730
Piraeus Sailing Club Mikrolimano, Piraeus, 417-7636
Sailing School 34d Marina, Glyfada, 894-2115
Sea Shore Sailing School Glyfada Marina, 894-8503
Sailing Schools are housed in the Naval Club (Naftikos Omilos) in

Athens: Paleo Faliron Naval Club 981-4835, Vouliagmeni Naval Club 896-2416

Informative books on boating in Greece:

GREECE FOR THE YATCHTSMAN, Greek National Tourist Office

Marinas:

Vouliagmeni; Zea; Flisvos (Paleo Faliro); Alimos.

Swimming

Sea bathing in Greece has been deservedly popular for several thousand years. The Greek National Tourist Organization maintains and operates beaches all over Greece, many of which offer sports facilities as well as swimming. Some organized beaches charge a small entrance fee. Detailed lists of public beaches are available from their offices.

Swimming Federation of Greece 40, Zan Moreas St. Fix 921-8826, 921-6612

Glyfada National Athletics Centre, Metaxa and Pandoras St., Glyfada

Ilission Swimming Pool, Taxilou, Panepistimioupolis, Ilissia

Zeas Swimming Pool, Akti Themistokleous, Piraeus

Lessons: Swimming/Underwater Diving

Hellenic Federation of Underwater Activities

Agios Kosmas Ellinikon 981-9961

Vouliagmeni Life Savers and Divers School 34, Vouliagmenis Ave., 922-9685

Rhythmic Swimming Center, 8, Selefkou St ., 323-5842

P. Liami School, Akti Moutsopoulou, Zea Marina 451-0477

Argo Diving Cruises 9:30 a.m. daily April-October. 11, Nikis St., (Syntagma), 322-4321

Depressurization Chambers

Athens: Hellenic Federation of Underwater Activities, Agios Kosmas (small transport chamber only) 981-9961

Water Skiing

Water-Skiing Federation, 32, Stournara St., 523-1875

Wind-Surfing

Hellenic Wind-Surfing Association, 7, Filellinon St., (Syntagma), 323-0068, 323-0330

Winsurfing equipment can be hired at Greek National Tourist beaches and water-ski training centres.

WARNING If parts of a beach are closed, or do not permit bathing, there may be a good reason. It would be wise to inquire if it is safe. A few beaches have strong currents plus an almost-quicksand base under the water and even excellent swimmers get into serious trouble.

Unwelcome Companions in the Water

Jellyfish stings respond to ammonia. Sticks of prepared ammonia ("Folissima") can be bought at the pharmacy. If none is at hand, urine helps. (Small boy!) The stuff helps insect bites as well.

A species of poisonous stonefish called *"drakena"* is found in some areas on the sea floor. If stung, go to hospital immediately - very painful effects.

Those lovely sea-anemones are not flowers. They are carnivorous animals with stings. Don't step on them.

Weightlifting

Weightlifting Federation 43, Syngrou Ave., 923-1683, 923-1780

Telephone and Telegraph

Local calls: Telephone calls require 5 drachmas. Coin phones are usually red, and may be found in coffee shops, hotels, restaurants, kiosks. Grey phones with a meter controlled by the proprietor may be found on most kiosks: lift the receiver and attract attention, and the owner will switch on the line. After your call, you pay him.

A few telephone booths stand in the main squares. Blue trimming means local calls, orange is for long distance.

Long Distance and Overseas Calls: If you are not calling from your hotel, the orange booths may serve, but you probably need to go to

the OTE (Telephone Company) offices which will place such calls for you.
Main Offices
Airports (24 hours)
15, Stadiou St., 7:30 am to 11:30 pm Monday to Friday,
Omonia same hours
50, Athinas St., nr Klaoudatos Dept store (quieter, day hours)
38, Patission St., near Victoria Electrico Station, open 24 hours
53, Solonos St.
15, G. Olympiou St., Makrigiani
14, Ag. Konstandinou St., Glyfada
9, Giannopoulou St., Neo Faliron
191, Irakliou St ., Paleo Faliron
2, Afroditis St., Varkiza
Piraeus: Kallipolis 2, S. Dragoumi St & Skouloudi
19, Karaoli Dimitriou St.
Kifissia 8, Papadiamantis St., & 7, Kratinou St.

INFOTIP: The phrase *"Parakaló, periménete sto akoustikó sas"* means "please wait on the line": they will answer as soon as they can.

Service Numbers, English-Speaking
Long Distance 132
International Operator 161, 162
Recorded Instructions for International Calls in English, French, German 169
Telegrams: Inland 155
International: 165
National Tourist Office, Transport and Vacations in Greece 172
ELPA (Automobile Assn, Tourist Information) 174

International Dialing Codes From Athens

Austalia 0061	Italy 0039
Canada 001	Japan 0081
Denmark 0045	Netherlands 0031
Germany 0049	New Zealand 0064
Finland 00358	Norway 0047
Great Britain: 0044	Sweden 0046
Israel 00972	U.S.A. 001

Useful Phrases
Noúmero - numbers (see page 15)
Plirotéo apó ton paralípti - Reverse the Charges
Ti óra ineh ekí? What time is it there?
Dhén Pirázi - Never mind

Time

British Time + 2

This ratio is consistent whenever everybody is on the same timetable for Summer or Daylight Saving Time:

12:00 noon in Athens, 10:00 a.m. London, is
4:00 a.m. New York, 1 a.m. San Francisco

In Spring and Autumn there may be a couple of weeks when there's an hour's difference because of the change to summer or winter time.

Tipping

Restaurant: Service charges are included at restaurants and tavernas, but it is expected that a little something additional will be found on the table for the bus boy. Rounding up the figures is done in any case. The charge included will be 10-15%, depending on the kind of restaurant. You could give 5% more to the waiter if you wish.

Maid: In Europe it is correct to leave something for the chambermaid in your room when you leave the hotel: about 30-50 drs for each day.
Taxi: Very small tips are in order here - 10 or 20 drachmas. Greeks don't usually tip, but do round off fares.
Cinema: There is always a person with flimsy papers in Greek, which is a "programme" of the film plus Greek ads. You are supposed to give him or her 10 drachmas.
Theatre: If you buy a programme, ask the price. Tip for the front seats.
Women's Hairdressers 10%
Men's Barbers: 5%
Tour Guide: This varies: the group may pass the hat, or you may wish to give a private gift. But the equivalent of one US dollar or about 75 pence UK for a day tour is right.

Tourist Services

National Tourist Organization of Greece

Athens offers a number of special kinds of assistance for the tourist. The National Tourist Organization of Greece is a government service which can help you plan your itinerary, book rooms in and out of town, give you up to date information on ship departures, and provide a number of free brochures on all locations in Greece. These not only have pretty coloured pictures, but lists and phone numbers for accomodation, sports, transportation, camp grounds, beaches, and archeological sites for each area. The organization owns and operates a series of hotels, often called "Xenia", (1st to 3d class) as well as hostel houses. See also Camping, page 153.

In summer the same organization offers the Athens Festival (see page), the Likavitos Theatre, the Sound and Light shows, wine festivals, beaches with organized sports, water skiing, and even assistance in finding hydrotherapy spas.

Every year, this organization asks tourists for suggestions for improvements. If you have suggestions or problems, go and tell them.

In Athens, the office where all this information may be found is inside the National Bank of Greece on the corner of Syntagma (Constitution) Square, 322-2545: at 2, Amerikis St., 322-3111-9: at the East main Airport, 979-9500.

In Piraeus, the offices of the Director of Tourism for Mainland Greece and the islands is to be found at 105, Vassilissis Sofias Ave., 412-9492 and 412-1400.

Abroad, the GNTO maintains offices in many countries which can provide you with the latest information.

Australia and New Zealand
51-57 Pitt Street,
Sydney, N.S.W. 2000, Tel. 241-1663-4, Telex: AA5209
Canada
Greek National Tourist Organization
2 Bloor Street West,
Cumberland Terrace, Upper Level, Toronto, Ontario, M4W 3E2,
Canada, Tel. 001416-968-2220. Telex: 0021621/8684
1233 Rue de la Montagne,
Montreal H36 1Z2, Que. 871-1532 Telex: 002155-60021
France
Office National Hellénique du Tourisme
3, Avenue de l'Opéra, Paris 75001
Tel. 00331 4206-4955, 4260-6585, Telex: 42/680.345
German Federal Republic
Griechische Zentrale fur Fremdenverkehr
Neue Mainzerstr. 22, 6 Frankfurt/Main 1
Tel. 004969 236-562-2 Telex: 41/412 034
Griechische Zentrale fur Fremdenverkehr
Pacellistr. 2, 8000 Munchen 2
Tel. 004989 222-035-6 Telex: 41/528.126
Italy
Ente Nazionale Ellenicoper il Turismo

Via L Bissolati 78:80, 00187, Roma
Tel. 474-4249, 474-4301. Telex: 611:331
Ente Nazionale Ellenico per il Turismo
Piazza Diaz 1, Ang, Via Rastrolli, Milano
Tel. 00392 860-470, 860-477. Telex: 313.685

United Kingdom and Eire
195-197 Regent Street, London W1R 8DR 734-5997 Telex 51/21122

U.S.A.
645 Fifth Avenue, Olympic Tower, New York, N.Y. 10022,
Tel. 421-5777, Telex 23/66489
611 West 6th Street, Los Angeles, California 90017,
Tel. 626-6696 Telex 250/686441
168 N.Michigan Ave., Chicago Ill. 60601.
Tel. 782 1084 Telex 250/283 468

The Tourist Police

This is not a law-enforcement service as much as it is a unique service to foreign travellers in Greece. For 24 hours daily, a telephone line at 171 is maintained speaking any foreign language required, even if they have to wake up the one person on their list who speaks Provencal dialect. English, German and French are easier.

If you need translation over the phone to sort out a difficulty; advice about any current situation that might inconvenience you, such as weather delays or strikes; a radio taxi phone number; translation of the daily duty roster of doctors or pharmacies open; any kind of public information where language is a problem - call on the Tourist Police.

ELPA - The Automobile Association: see MOTORING.

Tours and Cruises

There are many tour operators who run year-round visits to various sites in Greece. Tours are by bus unless otherwise stated. The following is a list of tours you may find available:

One day	Athens Sightseeing, Athens by Night Cape Sounion Corinth-Mycenae-Epidaurus Delphi Three-islands (cruise) Epidaurus during the festival
2 days	Corinth-Mycenae-Epidaurus Delphi Myconos and Delos (Cruise)
3 days	Delphi and Meteora Crete (air) Rodos (air) Aegean (Cruise)
4 days	Classical Bus Tour: Evia (Euboea), Pelion, Thessalian Plain, Meteora, Parnassus, Delphi Rodos and Crete (air) Corfu (air)
5 days	Archeological Tour: Corinth, Mycenae, Epidaurus, Nauplia, Tripolis, Sparta, Mistra, Mt Taighetos, Kalamata, Kalo Nero, Olympia, Patras, Nafpaktos, Delphi, Ossios Loukas Classical Tour with Meteora: Corinth, Mycenae, Nauplia, Epidaurus. Tripolis, Megalopolis, Olympia, Patras, Delphi, Amfissa, Lamia, Trikala, Kalambaka, Meteora, Thermopylae, Kamena Vourla, Island of Crete (from Athens by sea or air)
6 days:	Grand tour of Peleponnese Northern Greece
7 days:	Egypt and Aegean Islands (Cruise) Tours to Egypt and Yugoslavia (Cruises)
9 days	Grand tour of Greece

Licensed Guides may be obtained from the Association of Guides, (Somation Xenagon), 31, Voulis St., 322-9705.

Tour Operators and Agencies

Alfa Tourist & Travel Agency S.A.: 12, Vas. Sofias Ave 106 74 Tel. 7228361-5, Tlx 2163-13 Cbl Alfatours Member of: IATA (code 27-2-7115), ASTA, FUANN, HATTA.

All Season Holidays: 24, Nikis St. 105 57 Tel. 3254341.

American Express International: 2, Ermou St. 105 63 Tel. 3244975, Tlx. 21-5392 Cbl Amexco Member of: IATA (code 27-2-1838).

Amphitryon Travel: 48, Amalias Ave 105 58 Tel. 3231968, 3234652, Tlx 21-9911.

Arvanitis Tourist & Travel Bureau: 36, Voulis St. 105 57 Tel. 3232375, 3231130, Tlx 21-5781 Cbl Dinar Member of: IATA (code 27-2-1841) ASTA, CMT, COTAL, EUROMIC, FIAV, FIYTO, FUAAV, HATTA, MPI, SITE, AFTA, ASATA, TAANZ.

Bellair Travel & Tourism Ltd.: 35, Voulis St. 105 57 Tel. 3237593, 3216136, Tlx 225538 Gr Member of: ASTA, HATTA.

Camper/Caravans S.A.: 4, Nikis St. 105 63 Tel. 3230552-5, Tlx 22-3450.

Carayanides Travel Service: 58, Stadiou St. 105 64 Tel. 3211381-3, Tlx 21-5527, Cbl Carigon-Athens Member of: IATA (code 27-2-1847), ASTA, DRV, HATTA, LETA, UFTAA.

C.H.A.T.: 4, Stadiou St. 105 64 Tel. 322 3137, 3222886, Tlx 21-5177, 21-5594 Cbl Chatours.

Diners World Travel Ltd: 5, Merlin St. 106 71 Tel. 3640110-3, Tlx: 21-9174, Cbl Dintrov Member of: IATA (code 27-2-9448), HATTA.

Fuji International Travel Agency: 18, Syngrou Ave. P.O. Box 17001 117 43 Tel. 9234919, 9234149. Tlx 22-2022. Cbl Fujiservic. Member of: HATTA.

Ghiolman Yachts & Travel: (Ghiolman Greek Holidays) 7, Filellinon St. 105 57 Tel. 3230330, 3233696, 3233696, Tlx 21-6043, Cbl Ghiolmans Member of: ASTA, FUAAV

G.O. (Greek Organised) Tours Ltd.: 31-33, Voulis St. 105 57 Tel. 3225951-5, Tlx. 21-8909 Member of: HATTA.

GRECORAMA: 20, Nikis St. 105 57 Tel. 3237201-8, Tlx. 21-8979 (2 Lines), Cbl Rama Member of: HATTA.

Griffin Travel: 42, Nikis St. 105 58 Tel. 3235864, 3228655, 3225715.

Groutas Tours: 14, Xenofontos & Nikis St. 105 57 Tel. 3246427, 3226867, Tlx 21-8169 Member Of: ACTA, ASTA, BITEJ, HATTA, UFTAA.

Gulf Tourism Ltd: 43, Nikis St. 105 58 Tel. 3223110, 3223020, Tlx 21-9371 MADJ GR Member of: HATTA.

Horizon Travel Tourist & Transport Co. Ltd.
14, Nikis St. 105 57 Tel. 3233144-8, Tlx 21-5359, Cbl Horizon. Member of: IATA (code 27-2-1859), AFTA, ASATA, COTAL, FUAAV, HATTA.

Key Tours Ltd.: 2, Ermou St. 105 63 Tel. 3232520, 3233756, Tlx 21-5392, Cbl Keytours.

Kiuressis Ltd. Travel & Tourism: 63 Panepistimiou Ave 105 64 Tel. 3245212-9, Tlx: 22-1971. Member of: IATA, UFTAA, ASTA.

Kriti Travel Bureau: 4, Amalias Ave. 105 57 Tel. 3234000, 3223090, Member of: IATA (code 27-2-5429), HATTA.

Magic Bus-International Pullman (Greece) Ltd.: 20, Filellinon St. 105 57 Tel. 3237471-4, 3249225, 3227049, Tlx 21-8567

Manos Travel System S.A.: 39, El. Venizelou Ave. 105 64 Tel. 3250711-21, Tlx 21-5145, Cbl Minosystem Member of: IATA (code 27-2-7401) ASTA, COTAL, HATTA, IFTO, PATA, UFTAA.

Mini Tours (Minion S.A Travel Dept.): 13, Patission St. 104 32 Tel. 5237231, 5225394, 5246803, Tlx 21-4409 Member of: IATA (code 27-2-7996).

Panos Travel Ltd.: 4, Filellinon St. 105 57 Tel. 3237550, 3230380-1, Tlx 21-9541, Cbl Travelpa. Member of: IATA (Code 27-2-6762), ASTA, HATTA.

Plotin Travel S.A.: 24, Lagoumitzi St. 175 71 KALLITHEA Tel. 9227894-8, Tlx. 21-6819, 21-5370, Cbl Plotin Member of: HATTA.

T.E.A. (Trans Euroamerican) Tours Ltd.: 2, Michalakopoulou St. 115 28 Tel. 7238053, 7237972, 7014684, Tlx 22-1143.

Transalpino Travel Organization Ltd.: 28, Nikis St. 105 57 Tel. 3220503, 3238177, 3222045, Tlx. 21-6633.

Travel Plan: 3-5, Chr. Lada St. 105 61 Tel. 3238801-4, 3222152, 3225758, Tlx. 22-3700 Member of: IATA (code 27-2-0083), ASTA, HATTA.

Triaena Tours Ltd: 24, Char.Trikoupi St. 106 79 Tel. 3609552, 3601897, 3627347, 3609511, Tlx 21-8256 Member of: ASTA, COTAL, UFTAA.

Varvias Tourist Enterprises S.A.: 4, Nikis St. 105 63 Tel. 3233561-4, 3233595, 3235086, Tlx 21-5778, Cbl Tragency Member of: IATA (code 27-2-7286) ASTA, COTAL, GOETO, HATTA, ICCA, JATA, PATA, UFTAA, WATA.

Wagons - Lits Tourisme Associated with Thomas Cook: 2, Kar. Servias St. 105 62 Tel. 3242281-7, Tlx. 21-5880 Cbl Walits-Athens Member of: IATA (code 27-2-1880).

Welcome Tours Greece Ltd.: 35, Voulis St. 105 57 Tel. 3226821-2, 3234886, 3234866, Tlx 21-6000 Member of: HATTA.

PIRAEUS

Aktina S.A. Worldwide Travel: 91, Filonos St. 185 35 Tel. 4118907, 4128502, 4114232, Tlx 21-1507 Member of: IATA (code 27-2-6768).

Das Travel Agency: 17, Akti Miaouli 185 35 Tel. 4178340, 4175409, 4176067, Tlx 21-2449, Cbl Das. Member of IATA (code 27-2-9229), PAT.

GLYFADA

Athens Handling Services: 13, Vouliagmeni Ave. 165 61 Tel. 9622363, Tlx 21-8726 AHSA
Glyfada Tourist Service Center Inc.: 20, Dousmani & Metaxa St. 166 75 Tel. 8947572, 8931391, 8940771, Tlx 21-8571 Member of: IATA (code 27-2-0012).

Cruises

Cruises aren't just travelling from island to island: cruises are a change of pace, a special kind of relaxation, a chance to revel in unashamed luxury. Excursions ashore by day, and varied activities on board at night - dancing, casino, music or parties or quiet moonlight meditation. Every Greek island is different, from the volcanic drama of Santorini to the dazzling white houses of Myconos, to lush Corfu and romantic Paros. Rodos, the island where the Crusaders' fortresses stant whole - and incidentally, a free port for shopping: fruitful Crete, with her history of the Minoan civilization, and the amazing Labyrinth at Knossos.

Modern cruise ships offer holidays of two to 21 days, sailing the crystal blue Aegean in luxurious floating hotels. Many go as far as Israel, Egypt and Turkey: the Pyramids, the Sphinx, the ancient and lovely marble city of Ephesus and Istanbul. Here you'll see the Topkapi Museum the Blue Mosque, the famous Church of Agia Sofia, and of course, many bustling bazaars. Throughout the cruise you'll visit museums, temples and sunny beaches, while sunbathing, dancing, and relaxing between ports of call. Duty free shopping also available.

Single, double or triple cabins. Most lines will pick you up at your hotel and take you by bus to the ship; most departures are at 8:00 a.m.

Many cruise operators also offer flotilla sailing, with or without crews and skippers, depending on clients' qualifications. Most of these sailboats accommodate up to 6.

Chandris Cruises: 95, Akti Miaouli St. 185 38 PIRAEUS Tel. 4120932-3, 4132903, Tlx. 21-2327, Cbl Chandrislines Piraeus
Cycladic Cruises Tourist S.A. 81, Patission Ave. & Heyden St. 104 34 ATHENS Tel. 8229468, 8833475, 8832113, Tlx 21-6663
Epirotiki Lines: 87, Akti Miaouli 185 35 PIRAEUS Tel. 4526641-9, 4526782, Tlx 21-2302, 21-2741, Cbl Apotamianos
HML-Hellenic Mediterranean Lines Co. Electric Railway Station Bldg. P.O. Box 80057 185 10 PIRAEUS Tel. 4174341, 4176685, 4115611-14, Tlx 21-2518, 21-3388, Cbl Elmes-Piraeus
"K" Lines Hellenic Cruises S.A. 33, Akti Miaouli 186 35 PIRAEUS Tel. 4522011-5, 4531131, Tlx 21-2356, Cbl Kavolines
Royal Cruise Line Ltd. 81, Akti Miaouli 185 38 PIRAEUS Tel. 4519553, Tlx 21-2904
Saronic Cruises S.A. 14, Xenofondos St. 105 57 ATHENS Tel. 3234292-4 Tlx 21-6661
Sun Line Cruises: 2, Karageorgi Servias St. 105 62 ATHENS Tel. 3228883-5, Tlx 21-5621, 21-4451

BUSINESS GUIDE

Contents

Business Briefing

Main industries: Motor vehicle assembly, textiles, chemicals, food processing, tourism.
Main agricultural products: Wheat, barley, sweetcorn, citrus and other fuits, tobacco, cotton.
Main imports: Practically all raw materials, luxury goods and industrial products.
Main exports: Fruit, vegetables, textile yarns and products, iron, steel, nickel, aluminium, petroleum products, ships, tobacco.
Principal trading partners: Japan, West Germany, Italy, France, UK, USA, Saudi Arabia, Netherlands.

Exchange Import and Export of Currency

This can be done at most banks during banking hours. The National Bank of Greece (Ethniki Trapeza) in Syntagma Square is open all day, and Saturday and Sunday mornings for foreign exchange. The Ethniki Trapeza at Mitropoleos is also open at weekends.

There are also banks for foreign exchange at the airport and Larissa station. Some Post Offices now have exchange facilities.

Drachmas - restricted to 3,000

Foreign cash should be declared on arrival if you wish to re-export over $500. This does not apply to travellers' cheques which are not subject to export restrictions.

Banks

Foreign Banks in Athens/Piraeus

American Express, 17, Panepistimiou St. Syntagma	323-4781/4
53, Omonia Sq.	324-2360
26, Akti Poseidonos, Piraeus	412-1665
Bank of America,	
39, Panepistimiou St.,	325-1901/19
II Merarchias & Kołokotroni, Piraeus	452-7251/60
Bank of Nova Scotia, 37, Panepistimiou St.,	324-3891/8
23, Miaouli St., Piraeus	411-8711/14
Barclays International, 15, Voukourestiou St.,	364-4311
Chase Manhattan Bank, 3, Korai St.,	323-7711, 324-2511/2
87, Akti Miaouli, Piraeus	452-9306
Citibank, 8, Othonos St., Syntagma	322-7471
2, Sq. Kolonaki	322-7471
47-49, Akti Miaouli, Piraeus	452-3511
First National Bank of Chicago 6, Syngrou Ave.	921-8904
Grindlays Bank, 7, Merlin St., Kolonaki	362-4601/5
Akti Miaouli, Piraeus	411-1753/4, 411-1759
Midland Bank, 1, Sekeri St.	364-7410/7
93, Akti Miaouli, Piraeus	413-6469
National Westminster Bank, PLC	452-9215/7

7, II Merarchias St., Piraeus 411-7415, 413-5602
Rothschild Banque, 18, Akadimias St. & Voukourestiou 363-8627
Williams & Clyn's Bank, 61, Akti Miaouli, Piraeus 452-7483/7

Greek Banks

Bank of Greece (currency control, etc.) 2, Panepistimiou St. 320-1111
National Bank of Greece, Central Branch 86, Aiolou St. 321-0411, 321-0501
Commercial Bank of Greece, 11, Sofokleous St. 321-1101, 321-0911
Agricultural Bank, 23, Panepistimiou St. 323-8231/7, 323-0521/7
Ionian and Popular Bank of Greece, 18, Pesmazoglou & Panepistimiou St. 322-5501
Credit Bank (Pisteos), 40, Stadiou St. 324-5111
Bank of Crete, 22, Valaoritou St. 360-6511/5
General Hellenic Bank, 1, Ermou St., Syntagma 324-1283/4
Ergo Bank, 36, Panepistimiou St. 360-1011
National Mortgage Bank, 118, Vas. Sofias Ave. Ambelokipi 779- 9011
ETBA (ETVA-Hellenic Industrial Development Bank) 18, Panepistimiou St. 323-7981, 323-7381
ETEBA (National Investment Bank for Industrial Development) 14, Amalias Ave. 324-2651
Piraeus Bank, 34, Stadiou St., Athens 323-0171
Navarinou & Aristidou, Piraeus 412-2648
Bank of Attica, 23, Omirou St. 364-6910

Credit Cards

American Express, 2, Ermou St. 934-3611
Master Charge/Access/Eurocard see National Bank of Greece
Diners Club, 5, Merlin St. 364-0830/9
Visa see Commercial Bank of Greece

Foreign Chambers of Commerce

American Hellenic Chamber of Commerce, 17, Valaoritou St. 363-6407
Arab-Greek Chamber of Commerce 180-182, Kifissias Ave. 647-2342
British Hellenic Chamber of Commerce, 4, Valaoritou St. 362-0168
French Chamber of Commerce, 4, Vas. Sofias Ave. 723-1136
German-Hellenic Chamber of Commerce, 10-12, Dorileou St. 644-4546
International Chamber of Commerce, 27, Kaningos St. 361-0879
Italian Chamber of Commerce, 10, Patroou St. 323-4551
Japan External Trade Organization, (JETRO) 4, Koumbari St. 363-0820

Greek Chambers

Chamber of Commerce and Industry of Athens, 7, Akadimias St. 360-2411, 360-4815/9
Chamber of Commerce and Industry of Piraeus 1, Loudovikou St. Roosvelt Sq. 417-7241/3
Handicrafts Chamber of Athens, 18, Akadimias St. 363-0253/5
Handicrafts Chamber of Piraeus, 111, Karaiskou St., Piraeus 411- 0443
Hellenic Chamber for Development and Economic Cooperation with the Arab Countries 180, Kifissias Ave., N. Psychiko 671- 0211, 672-6882
Hellenic Chamber of Hotels, 6, Aristidou St. 323-6641, 323-3501
Hellenic Chamber of Shipping, 85, Akti Miaouli, Piraeus 411-8811
Professional Chamber of Athens, 44, El. Venizelou St. 360-1651/3

Professional Chamber of Piraeus, 3, Ag. Konstandinou St., Piraeus 417-9065
Technical Chamber of Greece, 4, Kar. Servias St. 325-4591

Business/Social Associations

Athens Business and Professional Women's Club, 8, Ermou St. 324-2115
Athens-Cosmopolitan Lions Club 360-1311
Foreign Press Association, 23, Akadimias St. 363-7318
Propellor Club, 9, Patission St. 524-6324
Rotary Club, 3, Kriezotou St. 362-3150

Greek Associations

Athens Association of Commercial Agents, 15, Voulis St. 323-2622
Athens Stock Exchange, 10, Sofokleous St. 321-1301
Centre of Planning and Economic Research 362-7321
Greek Productivity Centre (EL-KE-PA), 28, Kapodistriou St. 360-0411/9
Hellenic Export Promotion Council, 24, Stadiou St. 322-6871/8
Hellenic Organization of Small and Medium Sized Industries and Handcrafts (EOMMEX) 771-5002
16, Xenias St., Ampelokipi 770-1751
Hellenic Shipowners Association 85, Akti Miaouli, Piraeus 411- 8011/8
Industries Association of Attica and Piraeus 1, Loudovikou Sq., Piraeus 417-4180
Municipality of Athens, 22, Liossion St. 524-2211
Municipality of Piraeus, 1, Dragatsi St. 412-6410/5
National Statistical Service of Greece 14-16, Lycourgou St. 324-8512/8
National Tobacco Board, 36, Kapodistriou St. 524-7311/8
Piraeus Association of Commercial Agents, Import-Export 1, Loudovikou St. 417-0392
Piraeus Port Authority (OLP) 11, II Merarchias St., Piraeus 452- 0910/9
National Hellenic Research Foundation 48, Vas. Konstandinou Ave. 722-9811/5
Thessaloniki International Fair (HELLEXPO) 154, Egnatias Ave., Thessaloniki 031-239221
Mitropoleos-Fillelinon, Athens 323-0959, 323-8051
United Nations Offices in Greece 36, Amalias Ave., (Information) 322-9624

Business Publications

Briefing Documents (binder) detailed updated guide about business Coronakis Press, 10, Fokidos St. 770-8260
Buying Greek (annual)
Greece's Weekly (Business and Finance), business and general.
Horizon Public Relations Organization Guides 50A, Nikis St. 322-2052, 322-4509
ICAP: Financial Publications (Business Directory, annual) 724-7884
Monthly Statistical Bulletin National Statistical Service of Greece, 14, Lykourgou St. 324-4746
Olympic Maritime (bimonthly) Springfield Shipping Co. Panama 85, Akti Miaouli, Piraeus
Shiping (monthly) 3, D. Areopagitou St. 923-6304
Shipping Mirror (monthly) Compass Hellas Press Ltd. Office: Piraeus, 19, Zoodochou Pigis St. 452-6016, 452-4178, 451-7062
Trade in Greece (quarterly) Athens Chamber of Commerce & Industry 7, Akadimias St. 360-2411, 360-4815

Business Services

Aces, 8, Dioharous St. (Hilton) 724-1354/5
Executive Services, Athens Tower B 778-3698, 770-1062
Freelance Unlimited, 50, Papadiamantopoulou St. 775-5523, 775-9059
Interpreters, translations, 778-0078
ICAP Hellas, S.A., 64, Vas. Sofias Ave. 724-7884
Directories, Credit Information, Market Research International Business Services, 29, Michalakopoulou St. 724-5541, 721-0774
Link International, 36, Voulis St. (5th floor) 322-2858
Personnel consultants, Secretarial, Accounting, Management.

Messenger Services

Skypack, 22, Smolenski St. 360-7754
DHL International Hellas 1, Marathonomachon St., Argyroupolis 994-0851/4
Ermis Courier, 23, Lekka St. 322-7259

Trade Fairs

Athens - Piraeus

"XENIA" Exhibition (Hotel and Restaurant equipment) January Peace and Friendship Stadium
Commercial Exhibition of souvenirs and folk art (jewellery - ceramics - icon copies-leatherwork weavings etc.) January Hilton Hotel 46, Vas. Sofias Ave. Tel: 7220201-11
"GREEK NAUTICAL SALON " (boat accesories and equipment - engines - batteries etc.) February Peace and Friendship Stadium Neo Faliro
"COMPUTERIZATION " (computers - office furniture and equipment - telephones etc.) March Peace and Friendship Stadium Neo Faliro
"GREEK JEWELLERY AND SILVERWARE EXHIBITION" March Hommeh exhibition room
"General Exhibition IDEAL HOUSE & GARDEN" (furniture - decorations - apliances) March Athens Exhibition Centre Kifissias Ave.
"General Exhibition Sport - Camping - Windsurfing - Caravanetes" July Athens Exhibition Centre Kifissias Ave.
"GRAPHIS" Special Exhibition of Graphic Arts (Printing - machinery - photo - typesetting - desing and printing items-book binding) May Athens Exhibition Centre Kifissias Ave.
"DEFENDORY" Defensive industry, air, land and sea equipment October. Piraeus Port, Aghios Nikolaos (O.L.P.)

Thessaloniki

All exhibitions listed below are organized by HELLEXPO (Official Organizer of International Fairs and exhibitions) in Thessaloniki International Fair 154, Egnatia St. Thessaloniki Tel: 031/239221
"AGROTIKA" (international exhibition of farming machinery-equipment) February
"FURNITEC" (international exhibition of furniture - decorations - lighting - apparatus - equipment - machinery) March
"INFACOMA" (international exhibition of construction materials - machinery - planning - environment - technical information - building equipment - solar systems) March
"Recreation - Holidays International Exhibition" (sports - caravanettes - boats etc.) April
"PHILOXENIA" International Tourism Exhibition April
"MARMIN" (international exhibition of marble - minerals - machinery - equipment) May
"TEXTILIA" (international exhibition of textiles - ready made garments - textile

equipment) June
"ORNAMENTS" (Greek Jewellery exhibition) April
"Thessaloniki International Trade Fair" September
"TEXTILIA" (international exhibition of textiles - clothing) November
"INTERKID" (International exhibition of clothing - education - entertainment - helth items for children and adolescents) November

Translators and Interpreters

Official Translations, 20, Amerikis St., 9:00 am - 12:30 pm 362-8365
Panhellenic Association of Conference Interpreters (English/français/Deutsch/Italiano/Dutch) 823-5258
Swedish and Finnish, Marja Georgakis, 921-5791
Simultaneous Translation equipment and audiovisual aids can be hired from: Panou Co. 642-1300
Philips Ext. 222, 921-5311

Conference Facilities

Evgenides Foundation, Syngrou Ave.	c. 770	941-1181
War Museum, Vas. Sofias Ave. & Rizari	c. 400	729-0543/4
National Research Institute (Ethniko Idryma Erevnon) 48, Vas. Konstandinou Ave.	c. 265	721-2729
Pandios School of Political Science, 136, Syngrou Ave.	c. 550	922-0100
Zappion Exhibition Hall	c. 3,300	322-3509
Peace and Friendship Stadium, conference and exhibition halls and theatre, Neo Faliron	c. 1,000	412-4024

In addition major hotels offer conference rooms of capacities from 25 to 1,800. See Hotel listings.

Key to symbols and abbreviations

rm rooms
bung bungalows
apt apartments
Central heating
Air-conditioning
Rooms with telephone
Rooms with music
Rooms with T.V.
Rooms with private shower and toilet
Rooms with private bath and toilet
Rooms with air-conditioning
Restaurant
Taverna
Bar
Cafeteria
S Daily room-servce
S24h 24 hour room-service
Cleaner's
Hairdresser's
Kindergarten
Pets not allowed
Discotheque
Swimming-pool
"Private" beach
Beach with water sports facilities
Tennis Court
Courts for other sports
Open Parking
Garage
Organized excursions/tours
(C.C.) Credit Cards

Camping

C capacity
Caravans
Tents
Bungalows/Cabins to let
Hot water
Chemical W.C. waste disposal
Shower
Current supply
Gas container supply
Food shop
Public phones
Washing Facilities
Ironing facilities
Children's Playground